# Drive Around

# Bavaria

## and the Austrian Tyrol

Titles in this series include:

- Andalucía and the Costa del Sol
- Bavaria and the Austrian Tyrol
- Brittany and Normandy
- Burgundy and the Rhône Valley
- California
- Catalonia and the Spanish Pyrenees
- Dordogne and Western France
- England and Wales
- Florida
- Ireland
- Italian Lakes and Mountains with Venice and Florence
- Languedoc and Southwest France
- Loire Valley
- Provence and the Côte d'Azur
- Scotland
- Tuscany and Umbria
- Vancouver and British Columbia
  and

- Selected Bed and Breakfast in France (annual edition)

For further information about these and other Thomas Cook publications, write to Thomas Cook Publishing, PO Box 227, The Thomas Cook Business Park, 15–16 Coningsby Road, Peterborough PE3 8SB, United Kingdom.

# Drive Around

# Bavaria

## and the Austrian Tyrol

The best of Bavaria's gilded baroque
churches and mountain-top castles,
plus the cities of Munich, Salzburg
and Innsbruck and the flower-filled
meadows and ski resorts of the Tyrol

Brent Gregston

## Thomas Cook
### Publishing

www.thomascookpublishing.com

Published by Thomas Cook Publishing,
a division of Thomas Cook Tour Operations Limited
PO Box 227,
The Thomas Cook Business Park
15–16 Coningsby Road
Peterborough PE3 8SB
United Kingdom

Telephone: +44 (0)1733 416477
Fax: +44 (0)1733 416688
E-mail: books@thomascook.com

For further information about
Thomas Cook Publishing, visit our website:
**www.thomascookpublishing.com**

ISBN 1-841574-49-X

Text: © 2005 Thomas Cook Publishing
Maps and diagrams:
Road maps supplied by Lovell Johns Ltd, OX8 8LH
Road maps generated from Collins Bartholomew Digital Database © Collins Bartholomew Ltd, 2000
City maps prepared by RJS Associates, © Thomas Cook Publishing

**Head of Thomas Cook Publishing**: Chris Young          **Written, researched and updated by**: Brett Gregston
**Series Editor**: Charlotte Christensen
**Production/DTP Editor**: Steven Collins
**Project Administrator**: Michelle Warrington

# About the author

After studying International Relations at Pomona College in California, Brent Gregston worked for a charity in the Middle East. In his spare time, he toured the hills and deserts of Israel, the West Bank and Sinai on a one-speed Dutch bicycle. He later read Modern European Languages at the Albert-Ludwig-Universität in Freiburg, Germany, with frequent interruptions to cycle, ski, hike and drive in the Alps. He has worked as a translator for the US State Department and as a travel editor in San Francisco. He now unpacks his bags in Paris.

**Author's acknowledgements:**
I would like to say *Danke tausendmal* to the following people: the Bavarian Tourist Office, Tyrol Info and local tourist offices all over Bavaria and Tyrol and in Salzburg, for generous advice and more brochures than I could read in a lifetime; Herr Grießer for his revelations about the Wittelsbach family tree and memories of being a shepherd before becoming director of the Schwangau Tourist Board; Richard Möller for ski lessons and tips on how to survive in an avalanche; Christopher Catling, *Signpost Guide* editor (first edition), for his patience and unceasing encouragement; Laurie for everything.

# Contents

# About Drive Around Guides

Thomas Cook's Drive Around Guides are designed to provide you with a comprehensive but flexible reference source to guide you as you tour a country or region by car. This guide divides Bavaria and the Austrian Tyrol into touring areas – one per chapter. Major cultural centres or cities form chapters in their own right. Each chapter contains enough attractions to provide at least a day's worth of activities – often more.

## Star ratings

To make it easier for you to plan your time and decide what to see, the main sights and attractions are given star ratings. A three-star rating indicates an outstanding sight or major attraction. Often these can be worth at least half a day of your time. A two-star attraction is worth an hour or so of your time, and a one-star attraction indicates a site that is good, but often of specialist interest. The stars are intended to help you set priorities, so that travellers with limited time can quickly find the most rewarding sights.

## Chapter contents

Every chapter has an introduction summing up the main attractions of the area, and a ratings box, which will highlight the area's strengths and weaknesses – some areas may be more attractive to families travelling with children, others to wine-lovers visiting vineyards, and others to people interested in finding castles, churches, nature reserves, or good beaches.

Each chapter is then divided into an alphabetical gazetteer, and a suggested tour. You can select whether you just want to visit a particular sight or attraction, choosing from those described in the gazetteer, or whether you want to tour the area comprehensively. If the latter, you can construct your own itinerary, or follow the author's suggested tour, which comes at the end of every area chapter.

## The gazetteer

The gazetteer section describes all the major attractions in the area – the villages, towns, historic sites, nature reserves, parks or museums that you are most likely to want to see. Maps of the area highlight all the places mentioned in the text. Using this comprehensive overview of the area, you may choose just to visit one or two sights.

One way to use the guide is simply to find individual sights that interest you, using the index, overview map or star ratings, and read what our authors have to say about them. This will help you decide

## Symbol Key

🛈 Tourist Information Centre

🔁 Advice on arriving or departing

🅿 Parking locations

🔄 Advice on getting around

➲ Directions

🛉 Sights and attractions

🄲 Accommodation

🍴 Eating

🛍 Shopping

🏅 Sport

🔺 Entertainment

## Practical information

The practical information in the page margins, or sidebar, will help you locate the services you need as an independent traveller – including the tourist information centre, car parks and public transport facilities. You will also find the opening times of sights, museums, churches and other attractions, as well as useful tips on shopping, market days, cultural events, entertainment, festivals and sports facilities.

whether to visit the sight. If you do, you will find plenty of practical information, such as the street address, the telephone number for enquiries and opening times.

Alternatively, you can choose a hotel, perhaps with the help of the accommodation recommendations contained in this guide. You can then turn to the overall map on page 10 to help you work out which chapters in the book describe those cities and regions that lie closest to your chosen touring base.

### Driving tours

The suggested tour is just that – a suggestion, with plenty of optional detours and one or two ideas for making your own discoveries, under the heading *Also worth exploring*. The routes are designed to link the attractions described in the gazetteer section, and to cover outstandingly scenic coastal, mountain and rural landscapes. The total distance is given for each tour, as is the time it will take you to drive the complete route, but bear in mind that this indication is just for the driving time: you will need to add on extra time for visiting attractions along the way.

Many of the routes are circular, so that you can join them at any point. Where the nature of the terrain dictates that the route has to be linear, the route can either be followed out and back, or you can use it as a link route, to get from one area in the book to another.

As you follow the route descriptions, you will find names picked out in bold capital letters – this means that the place is described fully in the gazetteer. Other names picked out in bold indicate additional villages or attractions worth a brief stop along the route.

### Accommodation and food

In every chapter you will find lodging and eating recommendations for individual towns, or for the area as a whole. These are designed to cover a range of price brackets and concentrate on more characterful small or individualistic hotels and restaurants. The price indications used in the guide have the following meanings:

€      budget level

€€     typical/average prices

€€€    de luxe

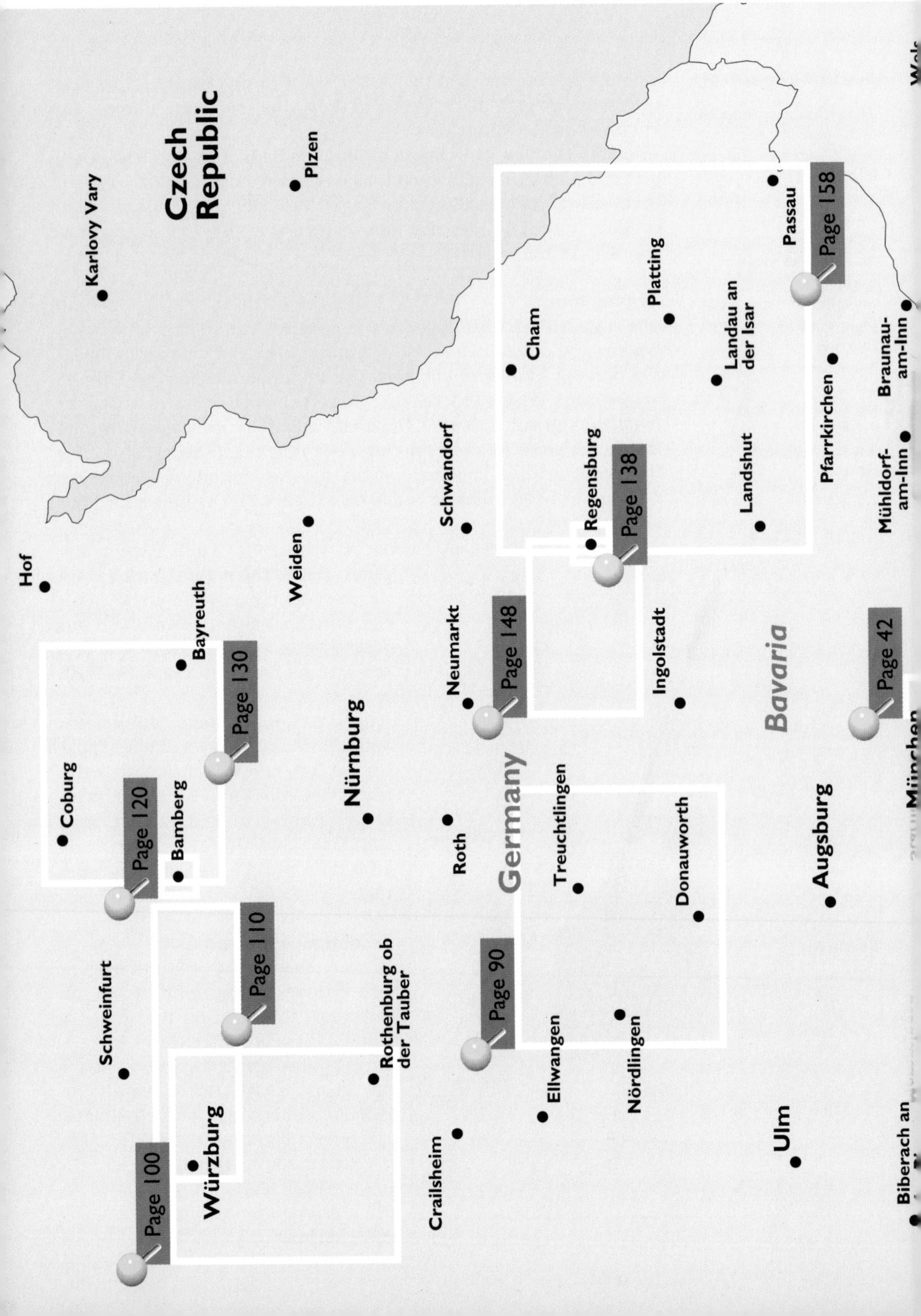

Czech Republic

Karlovy Vary

Plzen

Passau

**Page 158**

Platting

Landau an der Isar

Cham

Braunau-am-Inn

Pfarrkirchen

Regensburg

**Page 138**

Schwandorf

Landshut

Mühldorf-am-Inn

Hof

Weiden

Bayreuth

Neumarkt

**Page 148**

Ingolstadt

Bavaria

**Page 42**

**Page 130**

Coburg

**Page 120**

Bamberg

Nürnburg

München

Germany

Treuchtlingen

Augsburg

Roth

Donauworth

**Page 110**

Schweinfurt

Rothenburg ob der Tauber

**Page 90**

Würzburg

Ellwangen

Nördlingen

Ulm

**Page 100**

Crailsheim

Biberach an

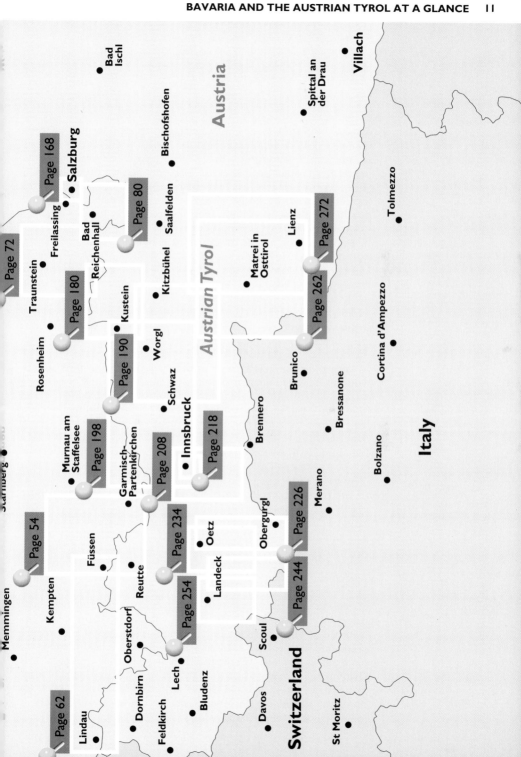

# Introduction

Bavaria, Tyrol and the city of Salzburg need no introduction. Between them, they have almost cornered the market for Alpine kitsch and travel posters. Never mind that Bavaria is as fiercely independent-minded as Scotland and that Salzburg only became Austrian in the 19th century. Ever since Walt Disney painted a Bavarian castle beneath Tinkerbell's magic wand and Hollywood made Salzburg the film set for *The Sound of Music*, they have become, in the eyes of many foreigners, 'Germany' and 'Austria'.

The reality behind the travel posters is more interesting. This is a part of Europe where great natural beauty and landmarks of European culture are strangely compressed. A blind turn can lead through a medieval gatehouse or into a Jurassic valley. No matter how often you look at the map, there will be unexpected encounters: a *Jugendstil* church in the Bavarian Forest; a mountain lake with 20°C water; a roadside chapel painted by a wandering Venetian 400 years ago. Spectacular high-altitude roads in the Alps cross the world's non-tropical vegetation and climate zones in the space of an afternoon.

There is an unusual willingness here to juggle serious high culture with all its variations and alternatives. Munich has one of Europe's greatest art collections, and its largest science museum, but also hosts the world's biggest beer bash, the *Oktoberfest*. For nightlife, there are chic yuppie bars, a major rave scene and folksy beerhalls. Salzburg may specialise in the music of native son Mozart and host Europe's top music festival – the *Salzburger Festspiele* – but there are musicians in the street as well as in the concert hall and the most popular opera performances are given by marionettes.

The region is deeply Roman Catholic and, at times, the calendar seems to be a succession of holidays and festivals. The most famous event is the all-day re-enactment of Christ's passion in Bavaria's Oberammergau and the Austrian villages of Erl and Thiersee. Depending on when and where you pull off the road, you can find yourself in the middle of a Franconian wine festival, the National-Day speech of a Tyrolean mayor to the village fire department, or listening to a priest pray over a loud speaker during a Corpus Christi procession.

The Bavarians and Tyroleans are hardy races of survivors. Their ingenuity and self-confidence have compensated for a lack (or exhaustion) of natural resources. They also have a sense of fun. Within Germanic Europe, they are seen – not without a touch of envy – as undignified hedonists. Certainly, there is more than enough of this Teutonic *joie de vivre* to go around. You will find that, for the most part, people take a live-and-let-live attitude: *Mir san mir* sums it up (roughly 'we are us'). In other words, no one objects if you try to drown out the oompah band as long as you sing in tune!

# Travel facts

## Accommodation

German and Austrian state authorities rate hotels and pensions based on rigorous criteria and regular inspections, but they are not very useful. The classifications do not determine a hotel's rates and, below the luxury level, the standards are remarkably uniform. Most hotel rooms are impeccably clean and comfortable and service is usually efficient and often welcoming. German and Austrian hotel rates include all charges and taxes and, with rare exceptions, breakfast. Prices are frequently quoted *pro person* ('per person', sometimes abbreviated as p.p.) so make sure to double that price if there are two people sharing a room. A *Gasthof* is the equivalent of an inn or pension. *Gasthöfe* are often family businesses, with the owner, his wife or children in attendance. Many have a *Gasthaus*, *Gaststätte* or *Weinstube* (*see Eating out, page 17*) where you can drink local beer or wine and eat local specialities.

Television sets and telephones are not standard equipment, but most *Gasthöfe* have bathrooms attached to the room like a hotel. Smaller pensions might not have a restaurant (but normally still serve breakfast) and the least expensive ones only have a sink in the room with shared facilities in the hall. Private homes and farmhouses offer the best value for money but you might have to brave a language barrier to find them. They are registered with the local tourist offices whose staff can usually make a reservation for you. The signs advertising the rooms will say *Fremdenzimmer* or *Zimmer frei* ('room to let'). Rooms are usually spotless and will most likely have private bathroom and toilet facilities.

In most places, a minimum stay of three nights is required so there might be a surcharge if you spend only one night. If you are willing to book for three nights, you can also take a 'farm holiday'. It is the best way to get to know local people and their way of life. The organisations listed below provide information.

### Entry formalities

Citizens of the EU, US, Australia, Canada and New Zealand do not require a visa to enter Germany and Austria. Non-EU citizens need a passport (valid for at least three months from the date of entry) and EU citizens must show an official identity card.

- **Urlaub auf dem Bauernhof in Bayern** *Kaiser-Ludwig-Platz 2, D-80336 München; tel: (089) 544 799950; fax: 089 544 799930; e-mail: info@farmholidays.de; www.uadby.de*

- **Urlaub am Bauernhof in Tirol** *Brixnerstrasse 1, A-6020 Innsbruck; tel: (0512) 561 882; fax: (0512) 567 367; e-mail: uab@Lk-tirol.at; www.tiscover.at/farmholidays*

## Time

Germany and Austria are one hour ahead of GMT. The difference is increased to two hours during 'daylight savings', which begins at the end of March, when clocks are set ahead an hour, and ends in the autumn when they are set back an hour.

## Thomas Cook Foreign Exchange Facilities

Thomas Cook Traveller's Cheques free you from the hazards of carrying large amounts of cash. The address of the Thomas Cook Foreign Exchange Bureau in Munich is given below. It provides full foreign exchange facilities and will change currency and traveller's cheques (free of commission in the case of Thomas Cook Traveller's Cheques). It can also provide emergency assistance in the event of loss or theft of Thomas Cook Traveller's Cheques.

## Thomas Cook Foreign Exchange Bureau

Thomas Cook Foreign Exchange
Petersplatz 10
Munich
Tel: (089) 235 0920
Fax: (089) 235 09214

## Airports

The Franz-Josef-Flughafen in Munich is the largest point of entry for travel to the region covered in this book. It is much closer to Salzburg and the Tyrol (only 1½ hours by car) than Austria's main international airport in Vienna. There are also scheduled and charter flights into the Salzburg and Innsbruck airports. Another alternative is Frankfurt, Germany's largest international airport and the destination of some of the cheapest flights. It is only one hour's drive from the Bavarian city of Würzburg, the beginning of the Romantische Strasse.

## Climate

Bavaria and the Tyrol are located in the Central European Temperate Zone. The presence of the Alps creates the widest range of climatic zones and the chance to hop between climates. You can ski on a glacier in spring, for example, then descend to one of the Bavarian lakes or the Bodensee for a swim. Winters and summers vary dramatically from year to year. Sometimes the lower resorts (including Kitzbühel) run out of snow early. A warm summer can make you think you are in Italy. One phenomenon that never fails is the *Föhn* – a hot, dry wind that blows in the spring and autumn, bringing with it clear weather and intense blue skies. It has a reputation for making people moody. Scientists have never established a definitive cause-and-effect relationship but it remains a socially acceptable excuse for being grumpy.

## Currency and credit cards

Both Germany and Austria are in the euro zone, and use the single European currency. Bank notes are available in seven denominations of different sizes and colours: 500, 200, 100, 50, 20, 10 and 5 euro notes. Eight denominations of coins include 1, 2, 5, 10, 20 and 50 cent, 1 and 2 euro. There are 100 cents to the euro (€) (for further information visit the website *europa.eu.int/euro/entry.html*). Indispensable are an ATM (cash-point) debit card and a Visa or MasterCard. ATM withdrawals abroad are the most convenient way of getting money at an excellent exchange rate. Call your bank before you leave and make sure that your PIN number will work in Europe. You can also get cash advances with a Visa or MasterCard at ATMs all over Germany – as long as you have a PIN number valid for Europe. Check with the credit card company to be sure (and ask about the fee). A few traveller's cheques are good insurance in case of emergency. You can pay by credit card at petrol stations, chain hotels, expensive restaurants and tourist shops; however, a lot of other places do not accept anything but cash, so check to avoid embarrassment. Some places also accept Eurocheques – ask beforehand to be sure.

## Wine

Bavaria's most important wine region is Franconia (see page 110). White wines greatly outnumber reds, reflecting its northern climate. There are no vineyards to speak of in the Tyrol but Tyroleans are amply supplied with wine from the Austrian province of Styria and the former Austrian province of Südtirol (now in Italy). The cheaper German and Austrian wines are labelled as *Tafelwein* or *Landwein*. *Qualitätswein* is the next step up, followed by *Prädikatswein* and *Qualitätswein Kabinett*. The classifications *Spätlese* and *Auslese* mean the grapes were harvested late in the year, the result being a wine that is naturally sweet and full of distinctive flavours. Traditional restaurants in wine regions usually serve *Offene Weine* (wines by the glass and carafe) from the region. People eating together are not necessarily expected to share a carafe of the same wine. They can order separately, by the 'glass', an *achtel* (125cm) or a *viertele* (almost a quarter of a litre served in a large glass or mini-carafe). Autumn is the season for drinking young, freshly fermenting wine (*Federweisser* or *Bremser* in Bavaria and *Sturm* in Austria) and, in summer, a *Schörle*, wine mixed with mineral water or soda.

## Customs regulations

There are no restrictions, taxes or duty on articles for personal use that you take into Germany and Austria (within reason). Germany and Austria allow EU citizens to import or export duty free: 800 cigarettes, 400 cigarillos, 200 cigars, or 1kg of tobacco, 10 litres of spirits or 90 litres of wine (not more than 60 can be sparkling wine) or 110 litres of beer. Goods carried by travellers coming from outside the EU and new EU countries may not exceed 200 cigarettes, 100 cigarillos or 250g of tobacco, 1 litre of spirits or 2 litres of wine, 50g of perfume and 250ml of toilet water with the total value not exceeding €175. All nationalities must declare, upon arrival or departure, sums of cash exceeding €12,500.

## Drinking

Coffee is the hot beverage of choice. Drinking it in a *Kaffeehaus* or *Café Konditorei* is a venerable tradition and an occasion for gossiping or reading a newspaper from the wooden rack. Tea is often served as a cup of hot water with a tea bag on the side. Although tap water (*Leitungswasser*) is perfectly safe to drink, most Germans and Austrians prefer bottled water. Bavaria's consumption of beer is legendary and it is a major pastime in the Tyrol. There are beer festivals all over Bavaria in spring and autumn, culminating in the mammoth Munich *Oktoberfest*. The spring *Gauderfest* in the Tyrol also pays homage to beer.

Pilsner is the single most popular beer, but there are many others, of various shades (*Hell* – amber, *Dunkel* – deep brown) and strengths. Beware of any beer with the suffix '*-ator*'. *Weizenbier* or *Weissbier* (wheat bier) is especially popular in summer; it is often served with a slice of lemon hanging from the lip of the glass. In Austria, a *Radler* is a refreshing mix of beer and lemonade.

## Eating out

Many hotels serve a breakfast that keeps you going all day long: coffee or tea, fruit juices, sliced baked ham, smoked ham, liverwurst, cheeses, hard-boiled eggs, yoghurt, jams, fruit and several kinds of bread. If that is not enough, ask for *Rühreier* (scrambled eggs, usually with bacon) which is normally served at no extra charge. Traditionally, lunch is the biggest meal of the day. A *Brotzeit* in Bavaria or *Jause* in Austria is a mid-morning or mid-afternoon snack. The evening meal at home, *Abendbrot*, is likely to be a modest affair of bread and cold cuts.

Bavaria and the Tyrol have more than their share of gourmet restaurants. They tend to combine local tradition with international culinary trends. Germany's *neue Küche*, for example, is the Teutonic answer to *nouvelle cuisine*. There is a distinct difference between restaurants and establishments with names such as *Gaststätte*, *Bräuhaus*

### Children

Children under the age of 13 are required by law in Germany and Austria to sit in the back seat of a vehicle if it has one. Safety seats for children under four are strongly recommended though not required by law. Consider bringing them with you; car hire companies impose an extra daily charge per safety seat.

Supermarkets in Germany and Austria carry a broad selection of infant formula, baby food and disposable nappies (see *Opening times, page 23*).

Adults are expected to make their kids behave themselves in public. Having said that, it is far easier for a family to find a place to eat and drink in Bavaria or Austria than in Britain or the United States. Children are welcome in pubs and cafés as long as adults accompany them. Furthermore, most hotels and pensions readily accommodate families.

Bavaria and the Tyrol are full of castles, museums and zoos that appeal to children.

and *Weinstube*. *Gaststätte* serve *gutbürgerliche Küche*, which roughly translates as 'hearty local fare' (*see Food below*) but they also function as a bar or café. You are not necessarily expected to eat, and it is fine to order just a beer or coffee. In a *Gaststätte*, it is customary for strangers to share tables when no other places are available, though it is polite to ask first. Foreigners often inadvertently break a taboo by sitting down at a table marked *Stammtisch*. The *Stammtisch* is for regulars and strictly off limits to anyone else. Cafés fall into two categories: trendy places with ultramodern décor; and the elegant, pre-War *Kaffeehaus* where Germans and Austrians ritually consume *Kaffee und Kuchen*. Some butcher shops and bakeries have a *Steh-café* ('standing-café') with high tables for eating a snack standing up. An *Imbiss* is another place for a quick snack either standing up or sitting in a plastic chair.

## Electricity

The supply in Germany and Austria is 220 volts, 50 cycles AC. Plugs are of the European type with two round prongs. All UK appliances will work with an adaptor. American appliances need a transformer.

## Food

The culinary traditions of Bavaria and the Austrian Tyrol have much in common. Above all, they share the *Knödel* – dumpling. It is made from potatoes, stale bread (*Semmelknödel*) or liver (*Leberknödel*). Dumplings often make their way into clear broth soups such as

## Tipping

Tipping in restaurants is not required. The service charge is included in the bill. If you want to show appreciation, round off the amount of the bill – pay €40 for a €39 tab, for example. Do not tip with a credit card.

*Markknödelsuppe*, made from bone marrow. *Spätzle* (*Nockern* in the Tyrol) are thin noodle-dumplings that come with almost everything in Bavarian Swabia. *Dampfnudeln* (Tyrolean *Germknödel*) is a steamed dumpling, smothered in a vanilla or sweet fruit sauce. *Tafelspitz* is beef, stewed until tender and usually served with horseradish. *Hirsch* and *Wildschwein* (venison and wild boar) are eaten with great relish in autumn and winter, accompanied by wild mushrooms or in a stew. For St Martin's Day (in November) and Christmas, a goose is rubbed with herbs, carefully roasted and served with apples and red cabbage. *Wiener Schnitzel* is a cutlet of *Kalb* (veal) or *Schwein* (pork) dredged in milk and egg, coated in breadcrumbs and sautéed. If the Tyrol has such a thing as a national dish, it is *Tiroler Gröstl* – a kind of farmer's fry-up of pork, veal and/or beef, onions, marjoram and potatoes. Portions are reminiscent of a medieval banquet. Think twice before ordering a *Tagesmenü*, which is a three-course meal (appetiser, entrée and dessert). Fish is a welcome exception to otherwise hearty cooking. You can often eat fresh trout, carp and pike-perch either blau (poached) or *Müllerin* (lightly breaded and sautéed). Sausages are the time-honoured fast food, served in stalls, beer halls and in taverns. They come in many variations: *Weisswurst* contains veal and is eaten with sweet mustard; *Blutwurst* is made with blood; *Bratwurst* is a pork sausage that is either grilled or fried and served with a bread roll and mild mustard. Admittedly, none of this is likely to appeal to a vegetarian, but fresh, enormous salads are often on offer (mention that you want it without any *Speck* – bacon), and there are excellent mountain cheeses put to good use in dishes such as *Käsespätzle* (noodles with melted cheese and caramelised onions). Bread is one of the joys of eating in Germany and Austria. Even an average corner bakery churns out around 20 different varieties of bread a day, from simple rolls to whole grain loaves, or combinations of three or six grains.

## Health

Standards of health care in this region are uniformly high. Tap water is safe everywhere; sadly, the same cannot be said of water in Alpine streams. Boil the water for ten minutes before drinking it, or use iodine tablets such as Potable Aqua.

The mountains pose many hazards. The higher you go, the faster you sunburn, particularly on snow. At higher altitudes, your body has to adapt to thinner air. The first symptoms of altitude sickness are headaches, nausea and dizziness. A serious case can lead to potentially fatal acute mountain sickness. Hypothermia is the technical word for the fall in the body's internal temperature. It sometimes kills hikers who neglect to carry extra layers of clothing or waterproof equipment.

Ticks can be a problem in some lower elevation forests. If you find one buried in your skin, do not pull it out. Coat it with oil or salt instead and it should dislodge itself.

The German word for pharmacy is *Apotheke*. They are not always open when you need one, but they take turns staying open for emergencies. The address and telephone number of the nearest open pharmacy is posted on the door of all the other *Apotheken*. Once you get to the one that is 'open', you still have to ring the doorbell.

## Insurance

No one should leave home without travel insurance. It can cover all sorts of emergencies (including the extra costs of private facilities), lost luggage, theft and cancelled tickets. Citizens of EU countries are entitled to free emergency medical care in a public hospital. Showing a passport might be enough but, ideally, you should carry a form E111, or a form E112 for those already undergoing treatment (available from post offices in the UK). Non-EU citizens are only covered if they have travel insurance. For further information for US citizens visit the *Bureau of Consular Affairs* website at *www.travel.state.gov/medical*. A home car insurance policy is not likely to help you abroad so you will probably have to purchase additional insurance. You should have: collision damage waiver for the car (American Express and some other credit card companies cover this if you rent a car with their card and turn down, in writing, the rental car's insurance policy); personal accident insurance for medical costs (this is included in travel insurance); and liability insurance, which protects you against legal claims (most rental car agencies charge extra for it).

## Maps

ADAC, the German Automobile Club, publishes some of the best road maps (in German). Falk, Michelin and Kümmerly und Frey also publish excellent maps. *Autobahnen* might be in blue or orange,

# Information

Bavaria and Austria have tourist offices in almost every town and in many villages. They are located at or near the main railway station and/or on the market square. The names vary – Verkehrsamt, Tourist Information, Tourismusverband, or, if it is a town with a spa, Kurverwaltung. They usually have city maps that show where parking is available and can help with finding a room (sometimes charging a small fee); they are particularly useful for finding accommodation in smaller pensions or private homes. You will be bombarded with brochures. Their usefulness varies: some have information about local events and guided tours; others are just full of glossy pictures.

The provinces of Bavaria and the Tyrol have their own tourist offices that handle written or telephone inquires:

Tirol Info: Maria-Theresien-Strasse 55, A-6010 Innsbruck; tel: +43 (0)512 7272; fax: +43 (0)512 72727; e-mail: info@tirol.at

Bayerischer Tourismusverband: Prinzregentenstrasse 18/IV D-80538 München; tel: +49 (0)89 2123 9730; fax: +49 (0)89 293582; e-mail: tourismus@bayern.btl.de; www.btl.de

## Tourist offices abroad

### Australia

Austrian National Tourist Office (ANTO): 1st Floor, 36 Carrington Street, Sydney NSW 2000; tel: (02) 9299 3621; fax: (02) 9299 3808; e-mail: info@antosyd.org.au; www.austria-tourism.at

German National Tourist Office (GNTB): GPO Box 1461, Sydney NSW 2001; tel: (02) 8296 0488; fax: (02) 8296 0487; e-mail: gnto@germany.org.au; www.germany-tourism.de

### Canada

ANTO: 2 Bloor Street East, Suite 3330, Toronto, Ontario M4W 1A8; tel: (416) 967 3381; fax: (416) 967 4101; e-mail: travel@austria.info

GNTB / Office National Allemand du Tourisme: 480 University Avenue, Suite 1410, Toronto, ON M5G 1V2; tel: (416) 968 1685; fax: (416) 968 0562; e-mail: info@gnto.ca; www.cometogermany.com

### UK and Ireland

ANTO: 14 Cork Street, London W1X 1PF; tel: 0845 101 1818; fax: 0845 101 1819; e-mail: info@anto.co.uk; www.austria.info/uk

GNTB: 18 Conduit Street, PO Box 2695, London W1A 3TN; tel: (020) 7317 0908; fax: (020) 7495 0917; e-mail: gntolon@d-z-t.com; www.germany-travel.co.uk

### USA

ANTO – New York: 500 Fifth Avenue, Suite 800, New York, NY 10110; tel: (212) 944 6880; fax: (212) 730 4568; e-mail: travel@austria.info

GNTB – New York: 122 East 42nd Street, Chanin Building, 52nd Floor, New York, NY 10168-0072; tel: (212) 661 7200; fax: (212) 661 7174; e-mail: gntonyc@d-z-t.com; www.cometogermany.com

### Online services

There is a vast array of websites related to travel and tourism for the places mentioned in this book. Some of the more useful ones are:

    Bavaria www.btl.de
    Tyrol www.tiscover.at
    Salzburg www.salzburginfo.at
    Munich www.munichfound.com

**Above**
Linderhof's Venus Grotto

**Internet**

E-mail can often be a less expensive and more versatile means of communication than the telephone (considering time differences). All that's required is setting up a web-access e-mail account before leaving home. Local Internet access is available at Internet cafés in larger towns.

depending on the map, with an 'A' in front of the number. International routes are usually in green with an 'E' before the number. *Schnellstrassen* (secondary roads) are called 'B' roads. Again depending on the map, they are displayed in red or dark yellow. The *Landstrassen* (country roads) are generally a paler shade of yellow.

## Museums

Bavaria, the Tyrol and Salzburg have world-class museums and art collections. Opening times are not standard but follow a similar pattern: most museums close on Monday; smaller museums outside the major cities close for lunch and have shorter (or non-existent) winter hours; and some of the larger city museums open one night a week (Tue, Wed or Thur) until 2000 or 2100. Admission prices are indicated by the € sign: €€€ for expensive, €€ for moderate and € for inexpensive.

## Reading

*The Dream King: Ludwig II of Bavaria* by Wilfrid Blunt.

*A Tramp Abroad* by Mark Twain.

*The Wine Atlas of Germany* by Hugh Johnson and Stuart Pigott.

*Autumn Sonata: Selected Poems of Georg Trakl.* Translated by Daniel Simko.

*Mozart and the Wolf Gang* by Anthony Burgess.

## Public Holidays

Neujahr – New Year, 1 Jan;

Heilige Drei Könige – Epiphany, 6 Jan;

Ostermontag – Easter Monday, changes annually;

Maifeiertag – Labour Day, 1 May;

Christi Himmelfahrt – Ascension Day, changes annually;

Pfingstmontag – Whit Monday, changes annually;

Fronleichnahm – Corpus Christi, changes annually;

Mariä Himmelfahrt – Feast of the Assumption, 15 Aug;

Nationalfeiertag – Austria National Day, 26 Oct.

Allerheiligen – All Saints' Day, 1 Nov;

Maria Empfängnis – Immaculate Conception in Austria, 8 Dec;

Erster Weihnachtstag – Christmas Day, 25 Dec;

Zweiter Weihnachtstag – Boxing Day, 26 Dec.

Tag der Deutschen Einheit – Day of German Unity, 3 Oct.

## Opening times

Opening times, set by a combination of law and tradition, are utterly confusing.

Larger shops in Germany open early and close at 2000 on weekdays and Saturday (previously 1600). They are only allowed to open for three hours on Sunday. Shops in Austria normally open weekdays 0800 to between 1800 and 1930 and Saturday until between 1300 and 1700. Smaller shops in Germany and Austria close at 1800 on weekdays and, outside the cities, for two hours at lunch as well; they are open on Saturday until 1300 and closed on Sunday. Austria has a *langer Samstag* ('long' Saturday) the first Saturday of the month when shops are open until 1700 and supermarkets until 1930.

Banks are generally open Mon–Fri 0800–1230 and 1330–1500 (until 1700 on Thursday).

Chemists are open Mon–Fri 0900–1800, Sat 0900–1200. All chemists give alternative addresses of services available outside the normal opening hours.

There are 350 officially recognised spas in Germany – many of them in Bavaria – providing therapeutic treatment and recreational facilities. A list of the spas and health resorts (and their treatments) can be ordered from the German National Tourist Office, or directly from Deutscher Heilbäderverband e.V. (German Spas Association), Schumannstrasse 111, 53113 Bonn *(tel: (228) 201 200; fax: (228) 201 2041; e-mail: info@dhv-bonn.de; www.deutscher-heilbaederverband.de).*

Tourist offices are open 0900–1800 and on Saturday until 1300 (in tourist destinations, they keep longer hours).

Petrol stations on the *Autobahn* are open 24 hours a day. Restaurants normally open at 1100 and close around 2300; many close in the afternoon. Traditional inns are more likely to serve food in the afternoon (being open through the day – *durchgehend*) or late at night.

## Packing

Warm clothes and waterproofs are essential for the mountains – regardless of the time of year. Germans and Austrians dress up a little more often than in English-speaking countries so you might want to bring something more formal. The following items are also recommended: adaptor plugs and/or transformers for electrical devices; English-language books (readily available but expensive); and Aspirin, which you can only buy in a pharmacy.

## Travellers with disabilities

Germany and Austria have done more than most countries to address the needs of the disabled. Many museums, theatres, cinemas and public buildings have access ramps for wheelchairs and, increasingly, trams are being equipped to handle them. Many German and Austrian cities publish local guides for people with disabilities and tourist offices will readily help disabled travellers find a hotel, public toilet, etc. Major hotel chains normally offer special facilities to disabled travellers. Parking is free for disabled persons in the blue zones of cities and towns if you have an international disabled sticker. In Britain, the Royal Society for Disability and Rehabilitation (RADAR) publishes a booklet called *European Holidays and Travel: A Guide for Disabled People* 12 City Forum, 250 City Road, London EC1V 8AF; tel: (020) 7250 3222; fax: (020) 7250 0212; www.radar.org.uk. In the US there is the Society for Accessible Travel and Hospitality (SATH), a non profit organisation representing travellers with disabilities (347 Fifth Avenue, Suite 610, New York, tel: 212 447 7284; www.sath.org). Tirol Info publishes a bilingual guide, Tirol ohne Handicap/ Tirol without handicap. See also the German National Tourist Office website (addresses on page 21).

# Postal services

Post offices are normally open Mon–Fri 0800–1800 and Sat 0800/0900–1200. In Germany, post offices located in airports and train stations may be open longer on weekdays. In Austria a few main post offices in large cities are open 24 hours. Outside the cities, some may close weekdays for lunch 1200–1400. They have many services so be sure to go to the right counter for *Briefmarken* (stamps) and *Pakete* (parcels). You can also change money. The larger post offices have public fax-phones that accept phonecards. For more information see the German post office website, *www.deutschepost.de* or the Austrian post office website *www.postaustria.at*

# Public transport

Germany and Austria have highly efficient public transport systems and it is normally possible to use the same ticket(s) for its different elements: trams, buses and subways. It is often easier to simply park your car (*see Parking, page 29*) and use public transport to explore the cities and larger towns. Munich, Innsbruck and Salzburg all have combination tickets that you can buy at the tourist office (good for one to three days) and use for unlimited access to the city's public transport and free or reduced admission to museums and other attractions.

# Safety and security

Bavaria and the Austrian Tyrol do not have a serious crime problem. Common sense will go a long way – locking the car, steering clear of dubious neighbourhoods, holding on to a wallet or handbag. If a robbery or break-in does occur, report it immediately to the police, particularly to back up insurance claims. By law, a person is always required to carry identification such as a passport. In Bavaria, dial 110 for the police, 112 for the fire department, 115 for an ambulance and 192 40 for poison control. In Austria, dial 133 for the police, 144 for an ambulance, 122 for the fire department and 141 for a medical emergency.

# Shopping

Popular souvenirs that you can buy in Bavaria and the Tyrol include woollens, leather goods and crystal. The local markets, held outdoors, offer local colour as well as handicrafts and the makings of a picnic. Flea markets are good places to visit on Saturdays to find some unusual and one-of-a-kind gifts. Advent/Christmas markets have a long tradition in Bavaria and Austria, and can be found in most cities. Christmas markets sell handmade ornaments. Other items to

## Stores

PennyMarkt, Aldi and Norma are among the cheaper German supermarket chains. Spar is common in Austria. There are Kaufhaus department stores in both countries.

## Telephones

Most public telephones in Germany and Austria use prepaid debit phonecards (*telefonkarten*) (buy them from tobacconists or post offices. Cafés will normally have a (coin-operated) phone for public use. Hotels are required by law to post their rates for room telephones – ranging from outrageous to exorbitant. Cheapest rates are between 2000 and 0600 and at weekends. Prepaid international calling cards are available in units of €10, €15, €35 and €50. Cellular phones – called 'handys' – can be rented at most international airports.

When telephoning Germany, the country code is 49. To direct dial from Germany, the prefix is 00, and its international operator is 0010. The country code for Austria is 43, the prefix to dial abroad is again 00, and its international operator is 09. Other useful international dialling codes include Australia (0061), Britain (0044), New Zealand (0064), and USA and Canada (001). For directory assistance call 11811 or check at www.gelbeseiten.at or www.teleauskunft.de. International directory assistance is 001188.

consider are: *Bergkäse* (mountain cheese); *Kerzen* (candles); *Schnitzfiguren* (carved wooden figures, usually religious in theme); *Schnaps* (often called *Obstbrand* in Austria); *Kristallglas* (crystal); *Schinkenspeck* (smoked ham); and jewellery from *Halbedelsteinen* (semi-precious stones).

*Trachten* (folk costumes) are not cheap and are never sold in souvenir shops. The items sold there are cheap copies made in China or Korea. If you want a real 'Bavarian' or 'Tyrolean' hat, *Schultertuch* (shawl), *Dirndl* (dress), or *Lederhosen* (leather pants), go to a local tailor or dressmaker (a couple are listed in individual chapters of this book).

Germany and Austria have a Value Added Tax (VAT) added to most goods and services. In theory, visitors from outside the European Union are entitled to a refund of this tax on purchases exceeding €155 from any one store. In practice, it is a hassle to obtain the refund. Look for the Tax-Free Shopping sign in the shop window and ask the clerk for the necessary paperwork. The papers must be stamped by a customs official before or upon leaving Germany or Austria. You then proceed to the tax-free cash point at the airport or border station to receive your refund (usually about 13 per cent of the purchase price). You will not receive a refund without the proper, stamped paperwork. You may be asked to show the goods you are exporting under this exemption.

## Sport

The Bavarian and Austrian Alps have hundreds of kilometres of well-marked trails. Extended hikes often involve staying overnight in mountain huts. The Austrian Tyrol is one of the most popular skiing regions in the Alps, and Bavaria has the best of German skiing. Most of the rivers and lakes are clean enough to swim in and almost every town of any importance has a *Freibad* (outdoor swimming pool) and a *Hallenbad* (indoor swimming pool). Cycling is very popular along the Danube and the Inn (from Landeck to Kufstein). There are spectacular routes for mountain bikers, too, on designated trails. The facilities for paragliding are top class. If wind conditions are right, an experienced paraglider can hop from peak to peak. Rafting takes two forms: shooting the mountain rapids in the Alps, and, in Bavaria, floating down the river on log rafts with barrels of beer and an oompah band.

## Toilets

On the *Autobahn* and in public toilets you are expected to pay a small fee to an attendant to use the restroom (*Herren* for men and *Damen* for women). Outside the tourist zones, it is usually acceptable to enter a café simply to use the bathroom.

# Driver's guide

## Accidents

**Automobile Clubs**

**ADAC** (Allgemeiner Deutscher Automobil Club); *Am Westpark 8, D-81373 Munich, Germany, tel: (0180) 510 1112; fax: (0180) 530 2928; www.adac.de.*

**ÖAMTC** (Österreichischer Automobil, Motorrad- und Touring Club);

*Andechsstrasse 81, A-6020 Innsbruck, tel: (0512) 33200; fax: (0512) 33 20 6400; www.oamtc.at*

If you have a serious accident in Germany, you are required by law to wait for the police to arrive (*tel: 112* in Germany, *133* in Austria). Make sure you take down the name, address, registration number and insurance details of any other party, preferably on the standard European Accident Statement form which your insurer should be able to provide. The advantage of this form is that it is identical in every language, so both parties understand that they are answering the same questions. Emergency services in both countries are highly efficient and will arrive quickly, by helicopter if need be. On the other hand, if it is a minor accident with no injuries, the police might not be willing to investigate at all. In that case, look for a witness and have them write down what they saw and sign it. Of course, you will also want to exchange insurance details with the other driver(s).

## Breakdowns

**Essentials**

Drivers should carry a warning triangle, a spare set of light bulbs and fuses and a spare tyre. Also advisable are a first-aid kit and a spare fanbelt. Drivers who wear glasses should carry a spare set. An appropriate country of origin sticker or number plate must be displayed on your vehicle.

The first thing to do if you have a breakdown is to pull over, off the road, if possible; then place a warning triangle 100 metres behind the vehicle. All drivers are required to carry a warning triangle and a first aid kit for emergencies; you will find them in the boots of rental cars. The next step is to call for help. If you are on an autobahn, look for an emergency telephone (located at 2km intervals; small arrows on the roadside reflectors point in the direction of the nearest phone). Lift the phone and wait for a dispatcher to respond. Some phones have a button; push it if there is one. Most dispatchers can understand English. He or she will ask for the location of the phone and your vehicle. You can also call ADAC (the German motoring club) directly from a regular telephone (*tel: 0180-222 22 22*) or a mobile phone (*tel: 222 222*).

In Austria, dial 120 for emergency assistance. A truck from the main Austrian motoring club, ÖAMTC (Österreichischer Automobil-, Motorrad- und Touring Club, see 'automobile clubs'), will come to your assistance. The driver might not speak English but he will come equipped with a multilingual auto parts manual. You will have to pay for towing and parts. However, if you are a member of an automobile club in your own country, you should be able to arrange for coverage. Both ADAC and ÖAMTC have reciprocal affiliations with motoring clubs in other countries. Enquire at your local automobile club about a Letter of Introduction or ETI booklet.

## Autobahn

There are no tolls for the German autobahn and only a couple of high mountain roads in the Alps (like the Rossfeld-Hohestrasse) charge a fee. Austria, by contrast, requires all drivers to pay a fee for use of the *Autobahnen*; by law, drivers are required to display an *Autobahn-Vignette* (toll sticker) on the windscreen of their vehicle. Failure to do so can result in a fine. The *Autobahn-Vignette* can be purchased for various periods, from a week to a full year. A rental car should normally come with an *Autobahn-Vignette*. Austrian post offices, the Austrian Automobile Club and most other European Automobile Clubs sell them. You can also buy them at stores and petrol stations near the *Autobahn* within Austria or in places near the border in neighbouring countries. Many of the high mountain roads in Austria – including the famous Grossglockner – charge a toll.

## Documents

In theory, Germany and Austria require an International Driving Permit but neither the police nor car hire agencies seem to bother about it. It is still worth getting it, just in case, from a local Automobile Association.

## Car hire

To rent a car in Europe, drivers must be over 19, 21 or 25 (depending on the car hire agency) and must have a driver's licence from their home country and a credit card. Car hire rates in Germany and Austria have become more competitive over the last few years. The major international rental companies are represented in Germany and Austria as are a range of European firms. Auto Europe (*www.autoeurope.com*) offers some of the most competitive rates. Toll-free numbers: *from Australia 0011 800 223 5555 5; from New Zealand, the UK, Austria and Germany 00 800 223 55555; from North America 1 800 223 5555*. It is important to shop around before you leave and pre-book.

Winter or all-weather tyres are sometimes considered an extra and have to be booked in advance. The question of insurance should be resolved ahead of time, too; rental should include both Collision Damage Waiver and Theft Protection for the vehicle. Many credit cards offer free supplemental car hire insurance, which might let you save on optional car insurance. Check with your credit card company. Furthermore, if you and your passengers already have travel insurance, you might not need personal accident insurance either. If you rent a car in a country outside of Austria, ask for an *Autobahn-Vignette* (toll sticker).

## Driving in Bavaria

The network of roads in Germany and Austria is among the best maintained in Europe - from the *Autobahn* to the *Schnellstrasse* to the *Landstrasse*. In winter, however, snowfall, ice, or avalanches can make alpine roads dangerous requiring winter tyres, and in extreme cases, snow chains (they can be hired at all major border crossings). Some mountain areas may be closed entirely for extended periods. When travelling during holiday periods (December-February, July-August) drivers should use extra caution. This also applies when driving through autobahn construction zones where lanes are often reduced to two-way traffic.

## Driving rules

The left lane of an autobahn is only for passing. Slower vehicles are required to keep to the right. If a driver approaching from behind in the same lane flashes his or her high beams, you are expected to move to the right immediately. Do not pass on the right. The following actions are illegal on the autobahn: stopping (except at *Raststätten*), U-turns, backing up (that includes hard shoulders and slip roads), running out of petrol and using the high beams (except to signal). You are also required to drive with the doors unlocked (to facilitate rescue

## Drinking and Driving

Germany and Austria, like most of Europe, have strict limits on the amount of alcohol a driver can have in his or her blood – 0.05%. A driver who exceeds this limit will have his or her licence taken away for up to a month. A driver involved in an accident with a blood-alcohol level of 0.03% or higher is automatically considered at fault.

## Fines

Germany's *Autobahnpolizei* (equivalent to the state highway patrol in the US) and *Schutzpolizei* deal with most traffic violations. Austria's police are called the Gendarmerie. Both are allowed to collect on-the-spot fines (*Verwarnungsgeld*) for traffic offences. Police cameras linked to radar are stationed above many high-traffic roadways and will simultaneously clock a car's speed and take incriminating photos (copies are no longer sent with the violation notice after several spouses discovered cases of infidelity when they opened the mail). The registered owner of the offending vehicle receives a ticket in the mail within a few weeks. If you're driving a rental car, the ticket will be sent to the rental agency who will forward it on to you after reporting you to the police as the driver.

**Opposite**
Regensburg

in an accident). In a major traffic jam (caused for example by an accident), motorists are expected to leave space for emergency vehicles between the left lane and the next lane (centre or right). Therefore, motorists in the left lane should squeeze as far as possible to the left and those in the next adjacent lane need to edge over as far as they can to the right.

Cars that are already on a roundabout have the right away. Trams complicate driving in the city. They ALWAYS have the right of way. In many places, they run along the centre of the road and its stops are on the pavement – i.e. passengers must cross the street to board a tram. You are not allowed to pass a tram when it stops to pick up passengers or to block its doors.

## Fuel

Rental cars usually require unleaded (*bleifrei*, pronounced BLY-FRY) petrol. However, some take diesel, which is available at most petrol stations.

## Information

**Deutscher Alpenverein** – German Alpine Club weather service *tel: (089) 14003-0; www.alpenverein.de.*
**Austrian weather advice;** *tel: (0900) 91156608.*
**Österreichischer Alpenverein** – Austrian Alpine Club weather service *tel: 0512 59547; www.alpenverein.at.*
**Lawinenwarndienste Tirol** – Avalanche warning service *tel: (0512) 1588; www.lawine.at*

## Parking

Most German and Austrian cities and villages are at least as old as the Middle Ages. The *Altstadt* (historic town centre) is often closed to motor traffic or surrounded by a labyrinth of one-way streets. In smaller towns, parking on the street is usually free but sometimes subject to a time limit (look for a blue P sign with a dial underneath). You are expected to place a cardboard clock on the dashboard indicating when you arrived (purchase one at a petrol station; rental cars should already have them). Street parking in larger cities is sometimes metered but a more common system uses a central machine (one per street). You put money into it and receive a printed ticket that you leave, clearly visible, inside the windscreen. Larger cities like Munich and Innsbruck have Park-and-Ride facilities on the periphery (indicated by a P+R) where parking is either cheap or even free. Signs saying *Parkhaus* (garage), *Parkplatz* (car park) or *Tiefgarage* (underground garage) indicate parking. Some have electronic signs that flash a green *Frei* if parking space is available and a red *Besetzt* if it

### Lights

In tunnels and in poor daytime visibility, dipped headlights must be used. Motorcycles are required to use dipped headlights during the day at all times. Before crossing the channel, drivers of right-hand drive vehicles must ensure that headlights dip in the right direction to avoid dazzle. This can be done with the use of stick-on optical beam adapters, masking tape (which reduces beam output) or changing your bulbs.

### Mobile phones

The use of mobile phones is prohibited while operating a vehicle (as soon as the engine is switched on) with the exception, though discouraged, of a hands-free phone.

### Seat belts

The driver and all passengers in the car, front and back, are legally required to wear seatbelts. Children under 12 years of age and less than 1.5 metres tall are not allowed in the front seat.

is full. Most are open until late at night (0600–2200 or -2300) or 24 hours. Generally, they have an automated payment system. You receive a time-stamped ticket when you enter the car park or garage. You are not required to leave the ticket in the car. Before leaving, step up to the *Parkenkasseautomat* (parking payment machine) and insert the ticket. After you pay the amount displayed (the machines give change), the ticket is marked as paid and returned. Retrieve your vehicle and drive to the exit. Insert the ticket to open the gate.

### Speed limits

There is no speed limit on open stretches of the German Autobahn. The 'recommended' speed limit is 130 kph. Is important to realise that the faster you go, the faster you will have to slow down at the next traffic jam. Lower speed limits are posted when the road is dangerous or passes through an urban area (usually 100 kph) or construction (usually 60kph) is underway – and you are required by law to slow down. The speed limit on the Autobahn in Austria is 130kph, but from 1000–1700 all motorways except the A1 (Salzburg-Vienna) and the A2 (Villach-Vienna) the speed limit is 110kph. On *Schnellstrassen* (secondary roads), or 'B' roads, the speed limits outside of urban areas vary between 80 and 100kph. In towns, the limit is 50kph. Some residential areas now post speed limits of 30kph. It can be truly dangerous to speed on the *Landstrassen* (country roads). Often, they have no hard shoulder and there is simply no margin of error if you drift even slightly off the road. They pass directly through towns and villages where a blind corner often comes between you, the driver, and pedestrians, including schoolchildren, who are crossing the road. In winter, the speed limit for vehicles with snow chains is 50kph.

The speed limit for cars towing a trailer is 80kph.

### Road signs

| | |
|---|---|
| ausser – except (on no-entry signs) | Geöffnet – open |
| Baustelle – road works | Geschlossen – closed |
| Campingplatz – campground | Notausgang – emergency exit |
| Einbahnstrasse – one-way street | Notruf – emergency telephone |
| Eingang verboten – no entry | Ölspur – oil slick |
| einordnen – get into lane, merge | Rastplatz – picnic area |
| Fussgängerzone – pedestrian zone | Ruhetag – closed ('rest day') |
| Gefahr – danger | |

## GERMAN ROAD SIGNS

### RESTRICTION SIGNS

Maximum speed
limit shown in km/h

Minimum speed limit
Limit shown in km/h

Road closed

One way street

### PRECEDENCE SIGNS

Give way

You have the
right of way

You must give way    You have right of way

Signs attached to traffic lights are used
only when lights are OFF or yellow light is flashing

### WARNING SIGNS

Red triangles with a white background are warning signs
usually with a supplemental sign attached

Accident hazard

Traffic lights ahead
Be prepared to stop

Double bend,
first curving to
the right

Watch for ice

### GENERAL SIGNS

Snow chains required
A speed limit of
50km/h applies

Bus lane only

No stopping
on roadway

Direction sign to
the Autobahn
(motorway)

Thanks to the following website for its kind permission to reproduce the above signs:
www.texhwyman.com

# Getting to Bavaria and the Austrian Tyrol

**Airlines – UK**

**British Airways** *Tel: 0870 850 9 850; www.britishairways.com*

**Lufthansa German Airlines** *Tel: 08457 737 747; www.lufthansa.co.uk*

**Discount air tickets**

**STA Travel** *6 Wrights Lane, London, W8 6TA; tel: 08701 600 599; www.statravel.co.uk*

**Trailfinders** *194 Kensington High Street, London W8 7RG; tel: 020 7938 3939; www.trailfinders.co.uk*

**Fly-drive**

*Search on www.virgin.com or www.anyway.com for options*

The best travel deals require planning ahead – or waiting until the last minute. An APEX ('advance purchase excursion') fare is 30–40 per cent cheaper than the full economy fare for a trans-Atlantic or cross-channel flight but subject to restrictions: purchase 21 days ahead of time, a stay of at least two weeks, return in 90–120 days. APEX fares are not fully refundable so cancellation insurance is advisable. The Internet is an excellent source of information and booking for last-minute flights (try *www.cheapflights.co.uk*, *www.opodo.com*, *www.flightcomparison.co.uk*, *www.lastminute.com*, *www.travelselect.com* or *www.flightline.co.uk*).

## From the UK

The advantages of bringing your own car are obvious. Apart from saving on airfare, you have a great deal of flexibility. However, it is approximately 500km to Bavaria from the Channel ports and that means spending two days on the *Autobahn*, there and back, and deducting them from your holiday. London, as the European capital of discount flights, offers many alternatives. British Airways and Lufthansa have flights several times a day to Frankfurt and Munich. Of course, hiring a car requires an extra layer of planning but there are many fly-drive packages on offer from London, Manchester and Birmingham, particularly to Innsbruck and Salzburg.

### Channel crossing
Some cross-channel operators now offer an 'APEX'-type discount for advance bookings. **Eurotunnel** *tel: 0990 353 535; www. eurotunnel.com*; **Hoverspeed** *tel: 08705 240 241; www.hoverspeed.com*; **P&O Ferries** *tel: 0870 242 4999; www.poferries.com*; **SeaFrance** *tel: 08705 711 711; www.seafrance.com*

## Hamburg–Harwich/Newcastle

**DFDS Seaways** (*Scandinavia House, Parkeston, Harwich, Essex CO12 4QG; tel: 08705 333 000; www.dfdsseaways.co.uk*) has year-round services between Hamburg and Harwich. The crossing takes 20 hours. They also run a ferry every four days between Hamburg and Newcastle. Prices vary dramatically according to the time of year. A return fare is normally cheaper than two one-way tickets.

## Train

The train has few advantages – in terms of price or time – if you are travelling to Bavaria and Tyrol from London. Eurostar does travel to Cologne where you could arrange to pick up a rental car. It often fills its empty train seats by offering steep discounts to Paris and Brussels (with the usual limitations – advance purchase and three-week return). A railpass, SelectPass Drive, is available in the United States from Rail Europe (see below) that allows you to combine rail travel with car rental.

**Eurostar UK** *Waterloo Station, London SE1 8SE; tel: 0990 134 909; www.eurostar.com*
**Deutsche Bahn UK** *tel: 08702 43 53 63; deutsche-bahn.co.uk*
**Rail Europe** *tel: 08705 848 848; www.raileurope.co.uk.* In the US, call *1-888-382-RAIL* or consult *www.raileurope.com*

## From the US and Canada

Germany is one of the cheapest of trans-Atlantic destinations, particularly Frankfurt, and, to a lesser extent, Munich. American Airlines, Delta Air, United Airlines and Air Canada all have regularly scheduled flights. LTU usually has the cheapest flights to Frankfurt.

### Airlines
**American Airlines** *tel: 1 800 433 7300; www.aa.com;* **Delta** *tel: 1 800 241 4141; www.delta.com;* **LTU International Airways** *tel: 1 866 266 5588; www.ltu.com;* **Lufthansa** *tel: 1 800 399 5838; www.lufthansa.com;* **United Airlines** *tel: 1 800 538 2929; www.ual.com*

### Search the following websites for low fares and fly-drive
*www.travelocity.com*
*www.expedia.com*
*www.lastminute.com*

### Discount air tickets
In USA, **Council Travel** *tel: 1 800 226 8624; www.counciltravel.com;* **STA Travel** *tel: 1 800 781 4040; www.sta-travel.com*
In Canada, **Travel CUTS** *187 College St, Toronto, Ontario M5T 1P7; tel: 1 888 359 2887; www.travelcuts.com*

**Above**
Bamberg

# Setting the scene

### Geography

Bavaria is the largest *Bundesland* (Federal State) in Germany. It also has an international border with the Czech Republic to the east with which it shares a vast forested range, politically divided into the Bavarian Forest and the Bohemian Forest on the Czech side. Beneath the Bavarian Alps is a delightful, pre-Alpine region of hills and lakes, of which the Chiemsee is the largest. Northern Bavaria has a landscape of broad plains interrupted by ranges of low hills with forests such as the Steigerwald. Many rivers crisscross Bavaria, including the Inn (downstream from Innsbruck), and the Isar, which flows through Munich. All of Bavaria's rivers empty into the Danube as it flows west to east through the state.

The word 'Tyrol' first appeared in 1271. Before that, the region was simply called the 'land in the mountains'. It stretches from its highest peak – the Wildspitze (3772m) – in the southwest to the Wilder Kaiser Mountains in the northeast and from the Lienzer Dolomiten in the southeast to Jungholz, a mountain enclave that can only be reached by car from Germany. In between are the Stubai, Pitz, Ötz, Ziller- and Kitzbühel Alps. The wide valley of the Inn sweeps through its entire east–west length. Since time immemorial, the Inn Valley has been the crossroads of travel between southern and northern Europe. Bavaria and the Tyrol share the Zugspitze (2962m), which is officially the highest mountain in Germany.

### History

It's wrong to generalise too much about Bavarians and Tyroleans. Like the British and Americans, they are divided by the things they have in common, to say nothing of politics and history. Bavaria was an independent country for almost 800 years under the rule of the Wittelsbachs, while the Tyrol was the jewel in the crown of the Habsburgs, a dynasty that ruled much of Europe from the Middle Ages until 1918. Salzburg is a different story. For centuries, it was the capital of a powerful clerical state that stretched to Italy. The Bavarians and Tyroleans have often been at war with each other and with Salzburg, which tried to corner the salt market during the Middle Ages.

Borders are a source of confusion, and, in some cases, bitterness. The 'real' Bavaria is much smaller than its present borders, which includes the descendants of three different Germanic tribes – the Bajuwaren (Bavarians), Swabians and Franconians. The western stretch of the 'Bavarian' Alps is Swabian; its northern part – Franconia – only became part of Bavaria in 1805. The people of Franconia make delicate wines and eat a more refined cuisine than further south. They do not wear *Lederhosen* or yodel. The region historically known as the Tyrol, on the other hand, was larger than it is today. Southern Tyrol was invaded by Italy during World War I and the 1919 Treaty of Versailles ratified its annexation. Two pieces of the province remained within Austria – North and East Tyrol – with no common border.

### Timeline

**44–9 million years ago** The Alps rise up above the floor of the vast Tethys Sea.

**30,000 years ago** Stone Age people live in the cave of Tischoferhöhle near the Kaiser Mountains in the Tyrol.

**2000 BC–700 BC** The Celts give the Alps their name ('Alp' is Celtic for 'mountain' or 'high place'). They have an Iron Age culture at least as early as 700 BC in Hallstatt, near Salzburg; control trades routes in Bavaria; mine salt in Hall; and perform rites on the mountain tops of the Tyrol.

**15 BC–AD 500** The Romans occupy the Tyrol in 15 BC and create the provinces of Noricum and Raetia. Emperor Marcus Aurelius builds the fortress of Castra Regina in AD 179 (present-day Regensburg, *see pages 138–147)* on the Danube river, which forms a natural northern boundary to the Roman Empire until the 5th century.

**550** After the fall of the Roman Empire, Germanic tribes, the Bajuwaren and Alemannen, invade Tyrol and impose the German language on the inhabitants who speak Rhäto-romansh. A dialect of Latin, Rhäto-romansh remains a living language for centuries in the remoter parts of the Tyrol. Today, it is still spoken in a few southern Tyrolean villages.

**1180** Emperor Barbarossa gives Otto of Wittelsbach control of Bavaria.

**1258–95** Graf Meinhard II von Görz-Tirol increases the territory under his rule by inheritance, purchase and marriage. The 'land in the mountains' becomes Tyrol.

**1493–1519** Maximilian I becomes Holy Roman Emperor and makes Innsbruck the centre of his European empire. He expands the Habsburg realm and the Habsburg dynasty becomes the most powerful in Europe.

**1564–95** During the Counter-Reformation, all Protestants are driven out of Tyrol.

**1618–48** During the Thirty Years' War Germany loses over a third of its population. Wealthy cities such as Rothenburg and Dinkelsbühl sink into poverty. The Bavarian cities of Eichstätt and Passau are destroyed (to be rebuilt in baroque style).

**1704–78** Wars of the Austrian, Spanish and Bavarian Succession. During this period, Bavarians occupy the Tyrol and Austrians occupy Bavaria.

**1756** Mozart is born in Salzburg.

**1805–9** Napoleon occupies Bavaria and elevates the ruling electoral prince – Maximilian IV – to the status of 'King of Bavaria'. He greatly expands the borders of Bavaria to include Franconia and parts of Swabia. Bavaria, now a French ally, occupies Tyrol. Andreas Hofer leads a

rebellion against French-Bavarian occupation but is ultimately defeated.

**1815** The Congress of Vienna reunites Tyrol with Austria.

**1816** Salzburg becomes part of Austria.

**1864–86** Ludwig II, later to be called the 'fairytale king', becomes king of Bavaria at the age of 19. He begins to build Neuschwanstein in 1869. Declared insane, he is deposed and dies mysteriously in 1886.

**1894** The first ski races are held in Kitzbühel.

**1915** Italy changes sides in World War I, joining forces with the Allied Powers in return for permission to annex South Tyrol, which it then invades. The Tyrolean Militia, consisting mostly of young boys and old men, stop the Italian advance along the mountain ridge between Stilser Joch and Sexton.

**1918** The defeat of Germany and the Austro-Hungarian Empire in World War I has momentous consequences. The ruling family of Bavaria, the Wittelsbachs, is deposed on 8 November, 1918. Only four days later, the Habsburg Empire, of which Tyrol is a part, ceases to exist. Bavaria briefly becomes an independent republic before being incorporated into the German Weimar Republic. Tyrol and Salzburg join the newly created Austrian Republic.

**1919** Adolf Hitler (1889–1945), an Austrian by birth and former corporal in the German army, gives up his career as an impoverished postcard painter for right-wing politics in Munich. He takes charge of the National Socialist Germany Workers' Party (the members would later be nicknamed Nazis). Hitler attempts to seize power in the so-called Munich Beerhall Putsch. He holds Bavarian State leaders hostage in a beerhall and tries to convince them to join in the overthrow of the Weimar Republic. Although he is convicted of treason, Hitler is released after only nine months in prison.

**1920** The first Salzburger Festspiele ('international music festival') is held in Salzburg.

**1933** Hitler is appointed Chancellor of Germany. He imprisons his political enemies in the first concentration camp at Dachau, near Munich.

**1938–45** German troops march into Austria on 11 March, 1938, and meet no resistance. The Tyrol and Salzburg, along with Austria, become part of the German Reich under the *Anschluss* (Annexation) of 13 March. Tyroleans serve in the German army and provide munitions to the German war effort between 1939 and 1945. Near the end of the war, the Allies bomb Munich, Würzburg, Innsbruck and Salzburg.

**1945–55** American GIs occupy Bavaria and the French take charge of the Tyrol, where they remain until 1955. When Allied and Soviet troops withdraw from Austria, it becomes one of the poorer countries in Europe. Within a little more than a generation, it will enter the ranks of the ten richest countries in the world.

**1957** West Germany is one of the founding members of the European Economic Community (EEC).

**1964, 1976** Innsbruck hosts the winter Olympics twice in 12 years.

**1972** Munich hosts the Summer Games. Israeli athletes are kidnapped and murdered by Palestinians.

**1990** Germany is reunified. Bavaria's northern region, Franconia, suddenly finds itself in the middle of Germany again.

**1991** The discovery of a well-preserved Stone Age man in 1991 on a Tyrolean mountain pass reveals much about the earliest human history in the region.

**1995** Austria becomes a member of the Euopean Union (EU) on 1 January, 1995.

**2000** Austria's right-wing Freedom Party (led by Jörg Haider) forms a ruling coalition with the moderate right People's Party, provoking fears of a tilt to the far-right.

**2002** Chancellor Gerhard Schroeder and the Social Democrats (with coalition partner the Greens) win a second term by the narrowest of margins against conservative Bavarian challenger Stoiber. Schroeder gains votes by opposing US policy on Iraq.

### Culture

Bavaria, Tyrol and Salzburg share a fixation with *Kultur* (culture) and *Heimat* (homeland). The emperors, kings, princes, prince-bishops and dukes who wielded power through the centuries created a vast *Kulturgut* – a 'cultural heritage'. Scattered throughout the region are palaces, abbeys, splendid churches, forbidding castles and historic residences built by wealthy *Bürger* ('citizens'). Even small towns will sometimes astonish with their fabulous art collections. Prosperity in the post-war years and major subsidies for the arts have nourished this tradition.

*Heimat*, by contrast, includes the infinitely humbler world of mountain peasants, miners, cheese-makers, metal workers, glass-blowers and hunters. If you spend much time in a local *Heimatmuseum*, you will get a feeling for their desperate need to innovate in order to make ends meet: they peddled canaries, cultivated and wove flax, hawked snake oil, forged spoons and yodelled for strangers. You can even walk through the buildings they lived in. It is easy to move wooden buildings and there are fascinating collections of them on display in open-air museums.

### Art and architecture

Despite five centuries of occupation and settlement by Romans, there are only a few interesting Roman ruins in the region such as Aguntum near the town of Lienz (in Ost Tyrol) and the frontier fortifications in Bavaria's Altmühl Valley. After the Roman period, the earliest surviving architecture dates from the Carolingian period (9th century). The first great building boom to leave a major mark began in the 10th century with the erection of vaulted churches, some of them immense, made of stone. Inside, frescoes illustrated the Bible to a mostly illiterate congregation. This Romanesque style (10th to 12th centuries) united geometry – rectangles, cubes, semicircular arches – with an unprecedented ambition to build upwards.

## Folk music

Bavarians and Tyroleans have a venerable folk music tradition. Unfortunately, it is often misrepresented in kitschy, made-for-tourist shows. Yodelling is a good example. Traditionally, yodelling was not just humorous but used to express all kinds of emotions, at a wedding or a funeral. In general, the chances are much better of hearing authentic Alpine music if local groups (*Gesangsverein* or *Volksbildungswerk*) are involved and the performance takes place in a community hall rather than a hotel.

## Gothic and Renaissance

Architects continued with the vertical programme and found that they could support more weight with a pointed arch. Buttresses allowed for bigger windows that were filled with stained glass. *Hallenkirchen* – 'Hall-churches' are characteristic of the late-Gothic style in southern Germany and Austria. Their nave and aisles are the same height and only separated by pillars, as in Munich's **Frauenkirche** and the **St Georgskirche** in Dinkelsbühl on the *Romantische Strasse*, or the **Pfarrkirche zu Unserer Lieben Frau** in Schwaz. In general, late-Gothic architecture remained resolutely sober – there was no Flamboyant style, as in France. The Tyrol has several Gothic churches with double naves in which two different congregations, miners and merchants, could worship in the same building – separated by a wooden wall. The influence of France gradually transformed Gothic painting and sculpture in Bavaria and the Tyrol. The suffering of Christ was portrayed in ever more human terms. Masons started carving anatomically correct limbs and bodies, and dressed them in robes with folds that resembled real fabric. The transition is particularly notable in the **Dom** of Bamberg. Tilman Riemenschneider (1460–1531), who lived and worked in Würzburg, Bavaria, is often regarded as the greatest German sculptor of the late-Gothic period (he worked in both wood and stone), followed closely by the great woodcarver Veit Stoss (1447–1533) from Nürnberg. Architecturally, the influence of the Renaissance was weak in Bavaria and Austria, with a few exceptions such as the **Michaelskirche** in Munich, and the city of Salzburg, where the prince-archbishops, inspired by Italian models, tried to build a 'new Rome' at the foot of the Alps. However, the Renaissance saw the emergence of a new spirit in German painting – an intense but brief Golden Age was dominated by the work of Dürer and Grünewald, Cranach and Holbein. The most important examples of Renaissance sculpture are the figures surrounding the **tomb of Maximilian I** in Innsbruck.

## Baroque and rococo

Beginning in the middle of the 17th century, the baroque style swept everything before it, setting off a building boom in Bavaria, Tyrol and Salzburg. The interior decorators were kept busy, too. Any community with money invested in lavish baroque facelifts of existing Gothic or Romanesque churches. The baroque style is passionate, sensual and theatrical. It roughly coincided with the resurgence of the Catholic Church and served as agitprop for the Counter-Reformation. The dome, oval and circle regained a certain primacy but were eventually overwhelmed by decorative effects – 3-D *trompe l'œil*, hidden sources of light, twisted pillars, painted marble and monumental altarpieces. In baroque palaces, mirrors were used to create an illusion of infinity. Salzburg's **Kollegienkirche**, by Johann Bernhard Fischer Erlach (1656–1723), was a ground-breaking

## Folk costumes

The people of Bavaria and the Tyrol wear a remarkable range of *Trachten* (folk costumes), particularly on Sundays and holidays. The traditional garments vary by region and town. If you knew what to look for, you could tell, at a glance, that a person wearing *Tracht* was married or single, a hunter or a farmer, living in the mountains or in a town, and even where – Munich, Zillertal, Ost Tirol, Allgäu or the Bavarian Forest. *Trachten* are a labour of love that require countless hours of sewing and stitching to make.

achievement. The greatest architect of this period in Germany was Balthasar Neumann (1687–1753). His best work can be seen in the **Residenz** in Würzburg and the **Vierzehnheiligen** church near Bamberg.

The rococo style pushed the decorative elements of baroque to their showiest limit, adding garlands, medallions and vegetation. It demonstrated a brave willingness to experiment with asymmetry. The **Wieskirche** in Bavaria is arguably the greatest religious rococo building, while the hunting lodge of **Amalienburg** by François Cuvilliés, just outside Munich, is the most impressive secular rococo building. In Austria, rococo was called 'Maria-Theresia Baroque'.

### Neo-classicism and the 19th century

After the waning of rococo, there was a severe swing of the pendulum. A sober style, neo-classicism relies heavily on columns and pediments. Ludwig I of Bavaria spent his entire reign erecting neo-classical buildings, squares and monuments in Munich. The last half of the 19th century witnessed the revival and/or importation of other architectural styles. Ironically, the Romantic obsession with the Gothic era led to the completion of some Gothic edifices, after a building pause of several centuries. The spires of Regensburg cathedral, for example, achieved their present height in 1880. Numerous Bavarian and Tyrolean castles were restored or rebuilt from ruins, often in a style that was truer to romantic fantasy than medieval reality. One major extravagance was the neo-Gothic **Neues Rathaus** in Munich, built in a Flemish style of Gothic that had never existed in German-speaking Europe. But nothing in the neo-genre could rival the fantasy castles of 'mad' King Ludwig II (*see pages 54–61*).

### Modern times

A courageous group of artists, based mostly in Munich, set out to change the world of painting in the early 20th century. *Der Blaue Reiter* ('the Blue Rider') movement was founded in 1911 by Wassily Kandinsky (1866–1944) and Franz Marc (1880–1916) and later included August Macke (1887–1914) and the Swiss painter Paul Klee (1879–1940). They asserted the primacy of colour, line and shape over subject matter. Unfortunately, Marc and Macke didn't live to develop their ideas – both were killed in World War I. Kandinsky, however, eventually saw their initiative through to its logical conclusion and became one of the first abstract painters.

The local tourist office is always a good source of information about festivals. Some are mentioned in individual chapters of this book. Here is a brief overview:

**January/February**
*Fasching* (carnival) celebrations can begin as early as January though the main events occur during the week leading up to Shrove Tuesday. There are costume parades, feasts and clowning. It is celebrated with particular enthusiasm in Munich; also in Bavarian Swabia, Franconia, Salzburg and Innsbruck. There are 'processions of ghosts' in Imst (*Schemenlaufen*, every four years), Telfs (*Schleicherlaufen*, every five years) and Nassereith (*Schellerlaufen*, every three years).

**March/April**
Palm Sunday processions.
Shepherds' Dance (Sundays between Easter and September) in Rothenburg.

**May/June**
*Gauderfest* (1–2 May) is in Zell am Ziller, Tyrol.
*Corpus Christi* processions take place all round the region.

**July/August**
*Schützen* and *Feuerwehrfeste* in the Tyrol (militia and fire department festivities).
The *Bayerische Olympiade* ('Bavarian Olympics') are an annual event somewhat like the Highland Games in Scotland except that they take place at a different venue each year in Oberbayern (Upper Bavaria). *Lederhosen*-clad men engage in epic events such as finger-wrestling, hoisting crates of beersteins or snuff-sniffing.

**September/October**
*Viehscheid* or *Almabtrieb* is an autumn cattle-drive from the high Alpine pastures. It is celebrated all over the Alps, particularly in Bavarian Swabia, and Pfunds and St Johann in Tyrol.
Wine festivals (September/October) in Würzburg and surrounding wine villages.
*Oktoberfest* (late-September/early October) in Munich.

**November/December**
*Christkindlmarkt* ('Christmas markets') are common throughout the region during Advent. They are set up in front of Munich's city hall and the Salzburg cathedral, and brass bands and choirs play carols. You can shop for handmade gifts such as tree ornaments made of wood and straw or wool; you can also mix with locals who ignore the cold and stand around eating *Bratwurst* or *Reiberdatschi* (potato pancakes) and drinking *Glühwein* (hot wine mixed with spices and, on request, rum). Most churches have concerts leading up to and on Christmas Day.
*Krippen* (Christmas nativity scenes) are displayed in Bamberg's churches (in Bavaria) and in villages around Innsbruck such as Thaur, Absam, Mutters, Axams and Zirl.

# Highlights

The regional German tourist boards have created dozens of 'theme roads', such as the famous *Romantische Strasse* ('Romantic Road'), which was first promoted as a tourist route in the 1920s. Not all the routes are well signposted or easy to follow and, in places, the themes outnumber the roads. For example, in a 47km stretch of the *Romantische Strasse* from Bad Mergentheim to Rothenburg, tourists cross paths, unwittingly, with these other 'romantic roads': the Castle Road, the Swabian Wine Road, the Franken Wine Road, the Swabian Poets' Road, and the Bockbeutel (Goat's Scrotum, a kind of wine bottle) Road. Two recent additions are *Die Glasstrasse* (Glass Road) in the Bavarian Forest and the *Strasse der Kaiser und Könige* (Route of Emperors and Kings) between Frankfurt and Vienna, much of which passes through Bavaria along the Main and Danube rivers. One of the advantages of having a car is that you can create your own 'theme' road – choosing subjects and places that appeal and connecting them by way of sleepy *Landstrassen* rather than the *Autobahn*.

## Best attractions (*page numbers in brackets*)

Art museum – *Alte Pinakothek (Munich, 42)*
Beer – *Bamberg (120), Munich (42)*
Cathedrals – *Bamberg (122), Regensburg (140), Passau (162), Salzburg (168)*
Castles – *Ambras (216), Harburg (95), Hohensalzburg (170), Neuschwanstein (56), Veste Coburg (131)*
Cemeteries – *Petersfriedhof (Salzburg, 172)*
Christmas markets – *Munich (42), Rothenburg (102), Salzburg (168), Sommerhausen (114)*
Cities – *Munich (42), Regensburg (138), Salzburg (168)*
Forests – *Bavarian Forest (158), Zirbenwald above Innsbruck (219)*
Geology – *Altmühl Valley (90), Gschnitz Valley (223), Ötz Valley (226), Hohe Tauern National Park (265)*
Glaciers – *Pasterzengletscher (278)*
Gorges – *Altbachklamm (88), Breitachklamm (62), Wolfsklamm (206)*
Historic towns – *Bamberg (120), Hall (199), Rattenberg (201), Regensburg (138)*
Islands – *Herreninsel (75) and Fraueninsel (74) in Chiemsee*
Lakes – *Chiemsee (72), Hintersee (87), Königssee (84), Piburgersee (230)*
National Parks – *Berchtesgaden (82), Bavarian Forest (158), Hohe Tauern (265)*
Markets – *Viktualienmarkt (Munich, 47), Grünmarkt (Salzburg, 174)*
Monasteries – *Banz (133), Weltenburg (152), Stams (242)*
Open-air museums – *Kramsacher (205), Museumsdorf Bayerischer Wald (162)*
Pageants – *Drachenstich (Furth im Wald, 165), Gauderfest (Zell am Ziller, 193)*
Palaces – *Residenz (Würzburg, 107), Weissenstein (near Bamberg, 128), Hellbrunn (near Salzburg, 178)*
Rathaus – *Bamberg (120), Ochsenfurt (113), Staffelstein (133)*
River cruises – *Passau (162), Regensburg (138)*
Roman ruins – *Aguntum (262)*
Science museum – *Deutsches Museum (51)*
Sculpture – *Bamberg cathedral (122), Innsbruck Hofkirche (211)*
Treasure – *Wittelsbach family jewels in the Residenz (Munich, 47)*
Wine – *Würzburg and surrounding villages (107)*
Woodcarving – *altar of the Virgin Mary by Tilman Riemenschneider (Creglingen, 101)*
Zoo – *Alpine zoo (Innsbruck, 208)*

## Ratings

Architecture ●●●●●

Art ●●●●●

Entertainment ●●●●●

Museums ●●●●●

Music ●●●●●

Food and drink ●●●●○

Parks ●●●●○

Nature ●●●○○

# Munich

There is a special chemistry in Munich between international openness and Bavaria's rambunctious *joie de vivre*. It has a famous opera house filled with German high society, world-class art collections, a 100,000-strong army of students, a huge foreign population, a software industry and Germany's major film studio. A nostalgic place, it is the former capital of a former kingdom with countless monuments from its long history as a European power. But Munich is also a *Millionendorf* – 'a village with a million people'. Locals really do wear *Lederhosen* and feathered hats and even wealthy, style-conscious Müncheners sport chic versions of Bavarian *Tracht* (folk costume). Bavarian beer reigns supreme and hamburgers, sushi and fajitas, though welcome, are not about to replace the local *Schweinhax'n* (pork knuckle) and *Weisswurst* (veal sausage). Space and time in Munich don't conform to urban norms. Its English Garden is larger than New York's Central Park and the vastness of the Alps is less than an hour away. The four seasons are interrupted by more important events such as the opera festival, Founding Day, carnival, bock-beer time, and the *Oktoberfest*. The pace is slow for a major city and only the tourists seem to be in a hurry.

## Sights

**Franz-Josef Strauss Airport** tel: (089) 9752 1313; e-mail: info@munich-airport.de; www.munich-airport.com.

**Alte Pinakothek** €€
Barer Strasse 27;
tel: (089) 238 050;
e-mail: info@pinakothek.de;
www.alte-pinakothek.de.
Open Tue–Sun 1000–1700,
Thur until 2000.

### Alte Pinakothek✧✧✧

Rarely has a ruling family been as acquisitive or persistent in their art collecting as the Wittelsbachs. The result is one of the world's great art collections, amassed over a period of 400 years. The Alte Pinakothek, purpose-built as an art gallery for Ludwig I by the 19th-century architect Leo Klenze, contains 800 paintings. Highlights include Leonardo da Vinci's earliest extant painting, the *Madonna with a Carnation* (1473), and Albrecht Dürer's finest works – *Self-Portrait with Fur-Trimmed Robe* (1500) and *The Four Apostles* (1526). There are also paintings by his contemporaries, Albrecht Altdorfer and Matthias Grünewald; masterpieces by Botticelli, Fra Filippo Lippi and Raphael; Rubens by the roomful – look out for his *Drunken Silenus*; the *Land of Cockaigne* (1566) by Pieter Breughel; and Flemish and Dutch masterpieces by Van Dyck and Rembrandt.

Hessstrasse

Schellingstrasse

Prof.-Huber-Platz

Veterinärstrasse

Neue Pinakothek

Theresienstrasse

Barer Strasse

Türkenstrasse

Amalienstrasse

Ludwigstrasse

Raulbachstrasse

Königinstrasse

Alte Pinakothek

Theresienstrasse

Pinakothek der Moderne

Gabelsbergerstrasse

Englischer Garten

Städtische Galerie im Lenbachhaus

Königsplatz

Prinz Ludwig Strasse

Schönfeldstrasse

Karolinen-platz

Brienner Strasse

Oskar von Miller Ring

Jägerstrasse

Kard. Döpfner Strasse

Von der Tann Strasse

Bavarian National Museum

Max Joseph Strasse

Pl. d. Opfer d. Nationalsoz.

Ottostrasse

Brienner Strasse

Ludwigstrasse

Galeriestrasse

Prinzregentenstrasse

Wagmüllerstrasse

Ottostrasse

Jungfernturmstr.

Hofgartenstrasse

Residenz

Seitzstrasse

St.-Anna-Strasse

Prannerstrasse

Salvatorstrasse

Palace and Museum

Franz Josef Strauss Ring

Pacellistrasse

Promenade-platz

Theatinerstrasse

Wurzerstrasse

Karl Scharnagl Ring

Burkleinstrasse

Robert Koch Stras

Michaelskirche

Löwengru

Maffeistrasse

Schrammer-str.

Maximilianstrasse

Maximilianstrasse

Sternstrasse

Neuhauser Strasse

Schäfflerstrasse

Frauenkirche

Weinstrasse

St Michael's Church

German Hunting and Fishing Museum

Marien-platz

Sparkassenstrasse

Hildegardstrasse

Hernnstrasse

Thomas-Wimmer-Ring

Knöbelstrasse

Adelgundenstrasse

Thierschstrasse

Färbergraben

Rindermarkt

Church of the Holy Ghost

S 1-8 Im Tal

Joseph-italstrasse

Sendlinger Strasse

Oberanger

Rosental

Viktualienmarkt

Frauenstrasse

Rumfordstrasse

Thierschstrasse

Isar

Isar

Unterer Anger

Blumenstrasse

Klenzestrasse

Buttermelcherstrasse

Baaderstrasse

Zweibrückenstrasse

Steindorfstrasse

Am Gaster

Blumenstrasse

Müllerstrasse

Cornelliusstrasse

Gärtner-platz

Kohlstrasse

Erhardtstrasse

Rosenheimer Strasse

Holzstrasse

Fraunhoferstrasse

Klenzestrasse

Cornelliusstrasse

Deutsches Museum

0    200m

0    200 yards

ⓘ **Hauptbahnhof**
*Bahnhofplatz 2;*
*tel: (089) 2333 121;*
*www.bahn.de. Open Mon–Sat*
*0900–2000, Sun 1000–1800.*

**Tourist Information**
*Neues Rathaus, Marienplatz 8;*
*tel: (089) 2333 313;*
*Open Mon–Sat 1000–2000,*
*Sun 1000–1600.*

They sell a **München Welcome Card** that allows unlimited travel on all public transport within Munich and reductions of 25–50 per cent on city sightseeing tours, bicycle rental and admission to castles, museums and the zoo.

### Frauenkirche✷

The 500-year-old Church of Our Lady is the symbol of Munich. Completed in the Middle Ages, it was all but destroyed in World War II. Its twin onion-shaped domes dominate the city skyline and, until recently, the city's building code prohibited construction higher than its towers. As you enter the church, look for the *Teufelstritt*, the dark imprint of a large footstep – said to be the Devil's – in the church floor.

### Königsplatz✷✷

The neo-classical Propyläen (gateway) dominates this square as a symbol of the relationship between Bavaria and Greece. Ludwig I supported Greece in its struggle for independence against Turkey in the early 19th century and one of his sons, Otto, later sat on the Greek throne. Ludwig's enthusiasm for Greece was such that he fantasised about making Munich the 'Athens on the Isar' and enlisted the help of architect Leo Klenze. A hundred years later, Hitler exploited the grandiose square for his Munich rallies. The classical art collections of the Wittelsbach family are divided between the square's two museums. The **Glyptothek✷**, on the east side of the square, is an Ionic structure with a marvellous enclosed courtyard, surrounded by Greek and Roman sculpture. Its Corinthian cousin on the west side, the **Antikensammlungen✷**, contains Greek and Roman vases, glass and silverware, and Greek and Etruscan gold jewellery.

**Glyptothek €**
*Königsplatz 3; tel: (089) 286 100. Open Tue–Sun 1000–1700, Thur until 2000. Entrance free on Sun.*

**Antikensammlungen €**
*Königsplatz 16; tel: (089) 598 359. Open Tue–Sun 1000–1700, Wed until 2000.*

**Left**
Michaelskirche

## Marienplatz*

Marienplatz has been the centre of events since Munich was founded: the site of tournaments, royal weddings, public executions, riots, rebellions and political rallies. Locals still use it as the main venue for Christmas festivities, *Fasching* (carnival), and the Founding Day Festival. The square is named after its column of the Virgin Mary, erected in gratitude for the retreat of a hostile Swedish army during the Thirty Years' War (1618–48). The massive **Neues Rathaus*** (Town Hall) is a fake, built between 1867 and 1909 in 'pastry cook Gothic' style. Tourists love it for the **Glockenspiel**, the mechanical clock that re-enacts the 16th-century wedding festivities of Duke Wilhelm V and Renata von Lothringen (at 1100, 1200 and 1700). The **Altes Rathaus*** lies on the west side of the square; almost completely destroyed in World War II, it was rebuilt and now doubles as a conference hall and toy museum. Munich's most important contribution to Bavarian cuisine, the *Weisswurst* (a white veal sausage) was invented in the Peterhof Gaststatte on the southside of the square.

## Maximilianstrasse*

Munich's 'luxury mile' stretches east from Max-Joseph-Platz to the shore of the Isar river where the massive Maximilaneum looms across the water (it houses the Bavarian Parliament). Along the way you can buy something from Giorgio Armani, Christian Dior, Hermès, Guy Laroche, or local talents such as jeweller Hemmerle or tailor Rudolf Moshammer. Maximilian II, the son of Ludwig I, had the street reconstructed – and named after him – in the latter half of the 19th century. His oversized bronze statue occupies a lonely pedestal near the end. The stately buildings are neo-Renaissance in style with some Gothic detailing thrown in. The exquisite *Jugendstil* building at No 26 houses the **Münchener Kammerspiele**, the city's most avant-garde theatre, and the **Museum für Völkerkunde** (No 42) has an important collection of anthropological exhibits.

## Michaelskirche*

The Michaelskirche was the obsession of 16th-century Duke Wilhelm V, the man whose wedding is celebrated by the Marienplatz clock. Built by architects and artisans from Italy and the Netherlands, the original church tower collapsed during construction and Wilhelm took it as a sign that God wanted a dome instead. The one he built is second in size only to St Peter's in Rome. The expense was so great that Bavaria nearly went bankrupt. Wilhelm agreed to abdicate but continued to pay for the project out of his own pocket, earning himself much Jesuit adulation and the nickname 'the pious'. It became a model for a hundred other churches in southern Germany. Wilhelm and 30 assorted Wittelsbach sovereigns are buried in the crypt – including the 'fairytale' King Ludwig II.

**Neue Pinakothek**
€€ *Barer Strasse 29;
tel: (089) 2380 5195;
www.neue-pinakothek.org.
Open Tue–Sun 1000–1700,
Thur until 2000.*

**Pinakothek der
Moderne** €€ *Barer
Strasse 40; tel: (089) 2380
5360; www.pinakothek-der-
moderne.de. Open Tue–Sun
1000–1700, Thur and Fri
until 2000.*

### Neue Pinakothek✲✲

The original Neue Pinakothek, an architectural cousin of the Alte Pinakothek, was destroyed in World War II. The post-modern replacement by Alexander von Branca has won over the hearts of art lovers, particularly for the spaciousness and exquisite lighting of the interior. The first rooms are filled with paintings by David, Gainsborough, Goya and Turner, but the real excitement begins in Room 18. What follows is a wide spectrum of Impressionists and post-Impressionists – Monet, Manet, Cézanne, Gauguin and Van Gogh. There are also representative works by Egon Schiele and Gustav Klimt.

### Pinakothek der Moderne✲✲

Munich's new modern art museum is an important international centre for contemporary art, architecture and design. It houses four major collections: the State Gallery of Modern Art, the New Collection for design, the Architecture Museum, and the State Collection of Graphic Art.

**Residenz €€**
*Residenzstrasse 1;*
*tel: (089) 290 671;*
*fax: (089) 2906 7225;*
*e-mail: info@bsv.bayern.de.*
*Open daily Apr to mid-Oct*
*0900–1800; mid-Oct to Mar*
*1000–1600.*

**Lenbachhaus €**
*Luisenstrasse 33; tel: (089)*
*2333 2000; fax: (089) 2333*
*2004; www.lenbachhaus.de.*
*Open Tue–Sun 1000–1800.*

## Residenz**

Bavaria's rulers, the Wittelsbachs, lived in the Residenz from 1385 until 1918. The palace is so huge that it takes two guided tours (morning and afternoon) to see everything. Sadly, it was almost completely destroyed in the war and most of the building is, in reality, only a little over 30 years old, but all the art work and interiors are original. It is recommended that you explore it on your own, beginning with the Bavarian crown jewels in the **Schatzkammer**** (Treasury). Its glass cases are full of crowns, diadems, private altars carved of ivory, bejewelled reliquaries, cameos and other precious objects. The single most extraordinary example of the goldsmith's art is the *Statuette of St George* (1590), a golden knight on an agate horse waving a crystal sword and preparing to slay an emerald dragon. A separate ticket is required for the palace itself. Its **Antiquarium*** is the oldest surviving part of the Residenz, built during the Renaissance to display the Wittelsbachs' collection of antiquities. The **Reichen Zimmer*** (Rich Rooms) on the upper floor are a rococo spectacle designed by François Cuvilliés, a Belgian court jester who, in an amazing career change, became a leading designer of the German baroque era. His **Cuvilliés-Theater**** is one of the finest rococo theatres in Europe (also called the **Altes Residenztheater**, the entrance is off the Brunnenhof, and a third ticket is required).

## Städtische Galerie im Lenbachhaus*

The Lenbachhaus, a Tuscan-style villa, was the dream home of the richest portrait painter of late 19th-century Germany, the gifted but academic Franz von Lenbach (1836–1904). It now belongs to the city of Munich and houses the City Art Gallery. Lenbach would be horrified by the pale blue neon sign hanging above his doorway that says (in English): 'Can you imagine the opposite?', and a permanent exhibition of paintings by Kandinsky, Klee, Marc and other members of the *Blaue Reiter* (Blue Rider) movement – artists who broke every rule in his book. The gallery also mounts interesting exhibitions of contemporary art.

## Viktualienmarkt*

The Viktualienmarkt (Food Market) has the best of everything: fresh fruit and flowers, fish from many seas, game, cases of wine, pyramids of eggs and forest mushrooms. Alleys such as Heiliggeiststrasse are full of family-run delicatessens. On one side, there are 15 butchers competing to display the choicest pigs' feet, calf brains and beef tongue and to sell the best *Würste*. The market is a great place for lunch, either sitting beside the *bayerische Maibaum* (Maypole) under the old chestnut trees or in one of the *Gaststätte* (inns). Lots of booths sell *Bratwurst* and *Weisswurst*, which you can then take along to the *Biergarten*. Café Frischut-Schmalznudel, on the market, serves the best *Ausgezogene* (a kind of heavy doughnut) in town.

# Accommodation

**Hotel Am Markt** € *Heiliggeiststrasse 6; tel: (089) 225 014; fax: (089) 224 017.* A friendly hotel with a great location near the Viktualienmarkt. The halls are wallpapered with photographs of opera singers.

**Hotel Vier Jahreszeiten Kempinski** €€€ *Maximilianstrasse 17; tel: (089) 21250; fax: (089) 2125 2000; e-mail: reservation.hvj@kempinski.com; www.kempinski-vierjahreszeiten.de.* One of Germany's grandest hotels where you might meet Luciano Pavarotti in the elevator on the way up to the rooftop swimming pool. For all the luxury, the management is friendly and relaxed.

**Opera** €€ *St-Anna-Strasse 10; tel: (089) 2104 940; fax: (089) 2109 477; e-mail: reception@hotel-opera.de; www.hotel-opera.de.* This hotel is a labour of love in a tranquil location off chic Maximilianstrasse. All 28 rooms are perfect and the inner courtyard is an oasis of flowers, palm trees, marble columns and bronze busts.

**Pension Frank** € *Schellingstrasse 24; tel: (089) 281 451; fax: (089) 2800 910; e-mail: pension.frank@gmx.net; www.angelfire.com/de/pensionfrank/indexe.html.* Cheap and cheerful. Baths are down the hallway as is the shared kitchen.

**Romantik Hotel Insel Mühle** €€ *Von-Kahr-Strasse 87; tel: (089) 81010; fax: (089) 8120 571; e-mail: insel-muehle@t-online.de; www.inselmuehle-muenchen.de.* The 16th-century mill-turned-hotel is in a leafy park near Nymphenburg with a *Biergarten* on the millstream.

# Food and drink

**Andechser am Dom** € *Weinstrasse 7a; tel: (089) 298 481.* No Munich brew rivals the monastery beer of Andechs. This is the only place that serves it straight from the tap. The kitchen uses the monks' recipes and monastery game, vegetables, mushrooms and cheese.

**Dallmayr** € *Dienerstrasse 14/15; tel: (089) 213 510; www.dallmayr.de.* A legendary gourmet delicatessen.

**Halali** €€ *Schönfeldstrasse 22; tel: 285 909.* Seated beneath stuffed birds of prey, diners here rejoice in truly noble variations on Bavarian regional cooking using the freshest produce, fish, game, forest mushrooms. Reservations essential.

**Hunsingers Pacific** €€ *Maximiliansplatz 5; tel: (089) 5502 9741. Open Mon–Sat 1100–0100, Sun until 1630.* The fixed-price lunch and dinner menus are some of the city's top culinary bargains.

**Lenbach Palais** €€ *Ottostrasse 6.* Munich is a notoriously trendy place full of *schiki-mickis* ('beautiful people'), gossips, fashion victims and wannabes. This *Jugendstil* villa is their watering hole. Take a seat in the café or at the bar. Don't bother with the restaurant.

**Lyra €** *Bazeilles-strasse 5; tel: (089) 486 661 (Haidhausen, S-Bahn Rosenheimerplatz). Open daily 1700–0100.* An evening here begins with Greek food, garlicky starters, succulent lamb or grilled fish and can end at 0100 dancing to live Greek music.

**Sum €** *Marienplatz 11; tel: (089) 2369 1447.* Buy fresh Thai specialities and eat standing up at one of the elbow-high tables.

**Tantris €€€** *Johann-Fichte Strasse 7; tel: (089) 361 9590; www.tantris.de. Open Tue–Sat 1200–1500, 1800–0100.* This restaurant has collected the most stars and toques of any restaurant in Munich thanks to the Tyrolean chef Hans Haas. Some might find the black and orange décor an acquired taste.

**Weisses Bräuhaus €** *Baumkirchnerstrasse 5; tel: (089) 4316 381; www.weissesbrauhaus.de. Open daily 0800–2400.* The most famous place to eat the Munich speciality *Weisswurst* (poached veal sausages). By tradition, they are eaten before noon; the *Weissbier* and other Bavarian specialities are good any time.

**Below**
The Englischer Garten

# Entertainment

Munich has two major orchestras, one of Germany's best opera companies, dozens of theatres, and a hot jazz and techno music scene. Local listings magazines *Münchner Stadtmagazin* (available from newsagents) and the free *In Munich* provide concert information. The single best source of tickets and information is the **München-Ticket GmbH** with desks in both the tourist information offices (*see page 44 for contact details; www.muenchenticket.de*).

The **Kunstpark Ost**, in the Haidhausen district (*S-Bahn Ostbahnhof Grafingerstrasse 6; tel: (089) 4900 2928; www.kunstpark.de*), is an ex-factory converted into Europe's largest nightlife zone. The labyrinth of bars, clubs, discos and all-night restaurants pulses from Thursday to Saturday, 2000 to dawn. Its **Babylon** is Munich's largest disco while the **Colosseum** specialises in rock music. The **Ultraschall** is arguably Germany's best techno club and the **Bongo Bar** ('roaring twenties' atmosphere) fills up with over-30s listening to soul music.

**Above**
Marienplatz

# Suggested tour

**Total distance:** 3.5km. Detours add another kilometre.

**Time:** 1–3 days. The actual walking time (not counting detours) is only 2 hours but could add up to days depending on the amount of time spent in museums, palaces, churches and parks. Try to be at Marienplatz when the Glockenspiel strikes at 1100 or 1200. The English Garden and Deutsches Museum each require half a day unless you are on horseback or roller skates.

The medieval gate of **Karlstor** is a convenient place to begin a tour of the **Altstadt** (Old Town). The first 200m introduce you to one of its seeming contradictions: deep Catholic roots versus rampant consumerism. Department stores face off baroque churches and bag-toting shoppers, street musicians and tourists form a gauntlet. As you enter Neuhauser Strasse, there is a *Jugendstil* fountain to the left, graced by a nude satyr spitting water. Also on the left, a dozen metres further, the **Bürgersaalkirche** contains the tomb of Rupert Mayer, a Jesuit priest who denounced Hitler as early as 1923 and suffered in a concentration camp. Across from the church is a turn-of-the-century beerhall, the **Augustinerbräu**, decorated with seashells and full of locals. Only a few steps further is one of the most interesting churches in Germany: the **MICHAELSKIRCHE** ❶ was erected by a 16th-century egomaniac, the Wittelsbach Duke Wilhelm V; nothing like it existed north of the Alps. The massive statue in front of the church – an archangel spearing Satan – is a metaphor for the Counter-Reformation and its intended victims, the Protestants. At the end of the next block, the **Deutsches Jagd- und Fischereimuseum** (Hunting and Fishing Museum) displays antique guns and stuffed animals in the airy space of a former Augustinian church. Turning into Augustinerstrasse, you will find yourself at the foot of Munich's most famous landmark, the **FRAUENKIRCHE** ❷ (Church of Our Lady). After leaving the church, go left and continue walking past it. Follow one of the narrow streets heading east to arrive at **MARIENPLATZ** ❸, the 'living room' as locals call it.

**Detour:** From the square, follow Rosentstrasse until it quickly becomes Sendlinger Strasse, one of the city's most charming shopping streets. It takes about 5 minutes to reach the **Asamkirche**, which is on the right. Behind the rough raw rock portal is a Catholic Aladdin's cave, a 'Sacred Theatre' with a cast of thousands – angels, cherubs, saints, virgins and patriarchs. Architecture, sculpture, painting and stucco are fused into a single late-baroque hallucination. Watch out for the golden skeleton of Death getting ready to cut the String of Life.

**Peterskirche** is just south of the square. Though it is one of the oldest buildings in Munich (11th century), the interior is mostly baroque. The tower, 300 steps up, has a magnificent view of the Alps on a clear day. On leaving Peterskirche, follow the street downhill; on the way you will have a view of the Heiliggeistkirche (Church of the Holy Ghost). At the foot of the hill you will come to the **VIKTUALIENMARKT ❹**, the perfect place for a cheap meal or the makings of a picnic. Buy a *Bratwurst* or a *Schinkensemml* (a roll with ham) from one of the butchers, or hearty soup from the Münchner Suppenküche.

**Detour:** Pass in front of the Heiliggeistkirche and turn right down Talstrasse to the Isartor; cross Isartorplatz into Zweibrückenstrasse and you will find yourself on the bank of the Isar river. The world's largest science and technology museum – the **Deutsches Museum** – lies on the narrow Isar island in the middle of the river. Around 18,000 exhibits explain how things work, from the lightbulb to the nuclear reactor.

Cross Talstrasse and duck left into the passage beneath the Altes Rathaus where you will pass the door to the Toy Museum. An immediate right takes you into Burgstrasse, a street that follows the line of the oldest city walls. Veer right again at No 10 through an arch to reach Ledererstrasse; cross Sparkassenstrasse, then turn left into Orlandostrasse. The **Hofbräuhaus** is the city's oldest beerhall; it is also the only one that sells T-shirts. Don't eat there. Continue up Orlandostrasse to **MAXIMILIANSTRASSE ❺**, Germany's most elegant shopping street. Go left on Maximilianstrasse to Max-Joseph-Platz, bordered by the massive portico of the Nationaltheater (where the Bavarian State Opera company performs) and, on the north side, the rusticated wall of the **RESIDENZ ❻**. Going north from Max-Joseph-Platz, the Residenzstrasse leads to **Odeonsplatz**. From here, you have a view down **Ludwigstrasse**, an ostentatious boulevard of neo-classical buildings that begins at the **Feldherrnhalle** (Field Marshall's Hall), a copy of the Loggia dei Lanzi in Florence. This square was the site of Hitler's Beerhall Putsch in 1923, a violent fiasco that caused the deaths of several policemen and 16 of Hitler's 600-strong gang of thugs. During the Nazi era, a bronze memorial and guard of honour marked the spot; every passer-by had to raise an arm and give a Hitler salute or else. The square's other Italianate building, the **Theatinerkirche** (Theatiner Church), was built in 1663 to please a homesick Italian princess who married into the Wittelsbach family.

**⓫ Schloss Nymphenburg €**
Tel: (089) 17908; e-mail: info@bsv.bayern.de. Open Apr to mid-Oct 0900–1800, mid-Oct to Mar 1000–1600.

**Amalienburg €** Tel: (089) 17908. Open Apr to mid-Oct 0900–1800, mid-Oct to Mar 1000–1600.

**Detour:** The **English Garden**, Munich's famous park, is only 10 minutes' walk across the Hofgarten, on the opposite side of Prinzregentenstrasse. The park (all 360 hectares of it) is famous for its beer gardens (**Chinesischer Turm**, **Seehaus**, **Hirschau** and **Aumeister**) and nude sunbathers. It also has shaded paths, brooks, ponds and swans.

From Odeonsplatz, take a long walk down Brienner Strasse, once used for princely carriage rides from the Residenz to the summer palace of Nymphenburg. In a later era, the Gestapo headquarters stood at the crossroads of Türkenstrasse (on the site of the Bayerische Landesbank); the square is now named Platz der Opfer des National Sozialismus ('square of the victims of National Socialism'). The obelisk at Karolinenplatz commemorates 30,000 Bavarian soldiers who were sent to fight with Napoléon in Russia and never came back. Ludwig I, whose ambition was to make Munich look more like Athens, commissioned the monumental gateway and Greco-Roman buildings of **KÖNIGSPLATZ ❼** . The charming 19th-century villa, the **LENBACHHAUS ❽** is across from **Königsplatz** in Luisenstrasse. From there, stroll back in the same direction through the park behind the Glyptothek to Arcisstrasse, and go left. After Gabelsbergerstrasse. the vast 19th-century **ALTE PINAKOTHEK ❾** is on the right and the thoroughly 20th-century **NEUE PINAKOTHEK ❿** is across the street. The new **PINAKOTHEK DER MODERNE ⓫** is located just behind the Alte Pinakothek.

**Below**
Schloss Nymphenburg

## Also worth exploring

The magnificent **Olympiapark** is a masterpiece of modern architecture built for the ill-fated Olympic games in 1972. It has a new museum, **Olympic Spirit**, that uses virtual reality to allow visitors, no matter how unfit, to experience athletic agony and ecstasy as they run white water in a kayak, ski the grand slalom or sprint the 100m.

Once a royal summer residence, **Schloss Nymphenburg♦** contains Ludwig I's famous 'Gallery of Beauties' – portraits of his ex-girlfriends – and a park and gardens along the Nymphenburg Canal (used for ice skating in the winter). The real highlight is the hunting lodge of **Amalienburg♦♦**, by François Cuvilliés (see page 47), one of Germany's most original rococo buildings.

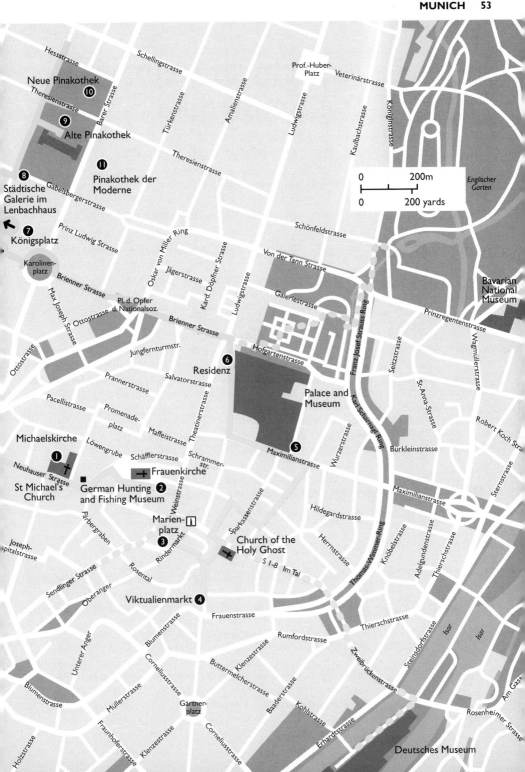

Hessstrasse

Schellingstrasse

Prof.-Huber-Platz

Veterinärstrasse

Neue Pinakothek
**10**

Theresienstrasse

Barer Strasse

Türkenstrasse

Amalienstrasse

Ludwigstrasse

Kaulbachstrasse

Königinstrasse

**9**

Alte Pinakothek

Theresienstrasse

**11**

Pinakothek der Moderne

**8**

Städtische Galerie im Lenbachhaus

Gabelsbergerstrasse

**7**

Königsplatz

Prinz Ludwig Strasse

Oskar von Miller Ring

Jägerstrasse

Kard. Döpfner Strasse

Ludwigstrasse

Schönfeldstrasse

Von der Tann Strasse

0        200m

0        200 yards

Englischer Garten

Karolinen-platz

Brienner Strasse

Max Joseph Strasse

Ottostrasse

Pl. d. Opfer d. Nationalsoz.

Brienner Strasse

Galeriestrasse

Franz Josef Strauss Ring

Prinzregentenstrasse

Wagmüllerstrasse

Bavarian National Museum

Ottostrasse

Jungfernturmstr.

Hofgartenstrasse

Seitzstrasse

St-Anna-Strasse

Robert Koch Str.

Prannerstrasse

Salvatorstrasse

Pacellistrasse

Promenade-platz

**6**

Residenz

Theatinerstrasse

Palace and Museum

Karl Scharnagl Ring

Burkleinstrasse

Sternstrasse

Michaelskirche

Löwengrube

Maffeistrasse

Schäfflerstrasse

Schrammer-str.

**5**

Maximilianstrasse

Wurzerstrasse

Maximilianstrasse

**1**

Neuhauser Strasse

St Michael's Church

German Hunting and Fishing Museum

**2**

Weinstrasse

**+** Frauenkirche

Sparkassenstrasse

Hildegardstrasse

Thomas-Wimmer-Ring

Knöbelstrasse

Adelgundenstrasse

Thierschstrasse

Färbergraben

Marien-platz **i**

**3**

Rindermarkt

Church of the Holy Ghost

Hermstrasse

Joseph-spitalstrasse

Sendlinger Strasse

Oberanger

Rosental

**+**

S 1-8  Im Tal

Viktualienmarkt **4**

Frauenstrasse

Rumfordstrasse

Thierschstrasse

Isar

Isar

Unterer Anger

Blumenstrasse

Corneliusstrasse

Buttermelcherstrasse

Klenzestrasse

Baaderstrasse

Steinsdorfstrasse

Zweibrückenstrasse

Am Gas

Blumenstrasse

Müllerstrasse

Gärtner-platz

Kohlstrasse

Erhardtstrasse

Rosenheimer Strasse

Holzstrasse

Fraunhoferstrasse

Klenzestrasse

Corneliusstrasse

Deutsches Museum

## Ratings

| | |
|---|---|
| Castles | ●●●●● |
| Nature | ●●●●● |
| Scenery | ●●●●● |
| Walking | ●●●●● |
| Children | ●●●●○ |
| Mountains | ●●●●○ |
| Art and craft | ●●●○○ |
| History | ●●●○○ |

# Neuschwanstein and the Ammergau

The Ammergau mountain range is the sparsely inhabited corner of the Alps where Ludwig II – the 'fairytale king' of Bavaria – grew up and built the castles of Linderhof and Neuschwanstein. Only two roads traverse it, offering a generous view of the scenery that inspired him. After Schwangau, the village at the foot of Neuschwanstein castle, a *Landstrasse* follows the wild Lech river into Austria, travels the length of the fiord-like Plansee and returns to Bavaria via the pass known as the Ammersattel. The Graswang (valley) is surrounded by peaks rising to more than 2000m and makes a suitable backdrop for Schloss Linderhof, the only one of Ludwig's castles that was actually completed. On the way back to Schwangau, the route passes through Oberammergau, the village of woodcarvers and the Passion Play. A slight detour leads to the Wieskirche, Bavaria's most famous rococo church.

## OBERAMMERGAU*

ⓘ **Tourismus Information** *Eugen-Papst-Strasse 9a; tel: (08822) 92310; fax: (08822) 923 190; www.oberammergau.de*

◑ The next Passion Play will be performed in the year 2010 between May and October.

Oberammergau is one of the most visited villages in the Bavarian Alps, a place where tradition, tourism and religion seamlessly intertwine. Its most famous tradition is the Passion Play, performed (with only a couple of interruptions) every ten years since 1634 when it began as a form of thanksgiving for the end of the 1633 plague. Over a thousand locals take part in this re-enactment of Christ's Passion that lasts most of a summer day. The town has many fine examples of another tradition – *Luftmalerei*. During the Counter-Reformation, a period of almost theatrical religious zealotry, people began to paint scenes from the Bible on their homes. The **Pilatushaus**, in Verlegergasse, is perhaps the finest example here. Even before the Passion Play, Oberammergau was known for its *Herrgottschnitzer*, woodcarvers who specialise in crucifixes, cherubs and Nativity scenes. Its **Heimatmuseum** has a remarkable collection of hand-carved Christmas scenes, many of them dating from the 18th century.

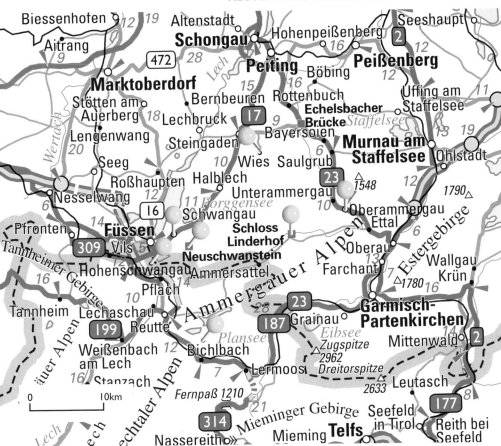

## PLANSEE**

This remote, heavily wooded lake is a world away from the crowded car park of Neuschwanstein (*see page 56*). It is enclosed on all sides by the Ammer mountain range and linked by a small canal to nearby Heiterwanger See; both are heavily stocked with fish. Fresh trout is on the menu in shoreside restaurants, as well as game from the lakeside woods. It is an ideal spot for people who want to explore the wilder side of the Ammergau region. There are only a couple of hotels and campsites in the area.

## SCHLOSS HOHENSCHWANGAU**

The ruins of Burg Schwanstein were rebuilt in neo-Gothic style between 1832 and 1836 by King Maximilian II, the father of Ludwig II, who spent much of his youth here with his beautiful but

**Schloss Hohenschwangau**
€€€ *Tel: (08362) 930 830; fax: (08362) 9308 320; for reservations online see* www.hohenschwangau.de. *Open daily Apr–Sept 0900–1800, Oct–Mar 1000–1600.*

emotionally distant mother, Queen Marie (he later nicknamed her 'the Colonel of the Third Artillery Regiment'). Huge wall murals depict scenes from the legends of romantic chivalry, particularly those pertaining to the *Schwanenritterordens* (Knightly Order of the Swan), and there is a motley collection of *objets d'art* that the family received as gifts from other royal families and Bavarian communities. Unlike Neuschwanstein (*see below*), the place feels like it was once someone's home. Ludwig's bedroom has night-sky constellations on the ceiling that he would illuminate by a 19th-century version of remote control before going to sleep.

# SCHLOSS LINDERHOF✦✦✦

**Schloss Linderhof**
€€ www.linderhof.de. *Open daily Apr–Sept 0900–1800, Oct–Mar 1000–1600.*

Linderhof is perhaps the strangest of all Ludwig's castles and the only one that he ever finished. The setting, in the remote Graswang Valley, is even more isolated than Neuschwanstein. Built as a private homage to Louis XIV, it is a sycophantic imitation of French baroque and rococo architecture. A bronze statue of the Sun King on horseback dominates the vestibule. The bedroom impresses by its sheer size, with its vast blue velvet bed and the ceiling fresco of Apollo driving his sun-chariot across the sky. Ludwig had his dining room equipped with a 'magic table' that worked like a lift. The servants would lower it into the downstairs kitchen, load it up with delicacies and then hoist it back to the dining room, where Ludwig liked to eat by himself, dressed as Louis XIV. In the English garden, a gilt fountain shoots 32m into the air every hour; and there are fantasy pavilions and stage sets intended for performances of scenes from Wagner's operas. The peacock throne in the Moorish pavilion is a typical Ludwig fantasy: three coloured birds of enamelled wrought iron sit atop a radiant silk-covered divan.

# SCHLOSS NEUSCHWANSTEIN✦✦✦

**Schloss Neuschwanstein**
€€€ *Tel: (08362) 930 830; fax: (08362) 930 820; for reservations online see* www.neuschwanstein.de. *Open daily Apr–Sept 0900–1800, Oct–Mar 1000–1600.*

An American tourist once asked a tour guide if Ludwig built his castle after a visit to Disneyland. For the record, Ludwig built his fantasy castle between 1869 and 1886. Only 20 out of 70 rooms were complete at the time of his death. In 1868, the 23-year-old King wrote to Wagner: 'I intend to rebuild the old castle ruins of Hohenschwangau by the Pöllat Gorge in the genuine style of the old German knightly fortresses...the spot is one of the most beautiful that one could ever find'. The old ruins were dynamited and replaced by a five-storey castle built in mock-Romanesque style, surmounted by whimsical turrets and pinnacles. A stage designer – not an architect – drew up the plans, and the interior feels like a series of stage sets, from the neo-Byzantine throne-room to the artificial stalactite grotto and neo-Gothic bedroom (14 woodcarvers worked on it for five years). Wagnerphiles will feel right at home; many of the rooms are decorated with scenes from *Tannhäuser*, *Lohengrin* and *Tristan und Isolde*. The castle became a museum within weeks of Ludwig's death, and today tourists from all over the world are ushered through in groups of 70 for a 35-minute tour. The ordeal is worth enduring for the views alone: from the castle windows you can see the Alpsee shimmering below, the Pöllat cascading through its chasm beneath the Marienbrücke and the solitary spire of St Koloman rising in the distance from the grassland in the valley.

**Below**
The Peacock Throne at Schloss Linderhof

# SCHWANGAU✢

**ℹ Tourismus Information**
*Münchener Strasse 2; tel: (08362) 81980; fax: (08362) 819 825; e-mail: info@schwangau.de; www.schwangau.de. Open Mon–Fri 0800–1230, 1330–1700.*

**🛏 Alpenhotel Meier €€** *Schwangauer Strasse 37; tel: (08362) 81152; fax: (08362) 987 028; www.alpenhotel-allgaeu.de.* A rustic inn and restaurant with good regional food and fair prices right at the foot of Neuschwanstein.

As proud as they are of 'their' Ludwig, locals will quickly point out that Schwangau has more to offer than Ludwig's castles. There are four lakes nearby and the **Wallfahrtskirche St Koloman**. This ancient pilgrimage church honours an early Christian Irish martyr. The **Tegelbahn✢✢** (cable car) whisks you up 1720m to a former royal hunting lodge (now a restaurant) for great views and, in winter, some very good ski runs (the longest is 4.2km). The blue-grey **Alpsee✢**, at the foot of Hohenschwangau, is remarkably peaceful despite the tourist hordes on the hill above. Ludwig II used to swim its length; it takes about an hour to walk around it.

## Accommodation and food in Schwangau

Schwangau is full of family-run hotels and pensions that are a lot cosier and better value than the hotels in nearby Füssen, where most tourists spend the night. The Kurverwaltung Schwangau will help with reservations. They also have a list of camping sites.

**Hotel-Restaurant Rübezahl €€** *Am Ehberg 31; tel: (08362) 8888; fax: (08362) 81701.* A little hard to find but worth it. Most rooms have views of Neuschwanstein and all have solid, rustic-style furniture. The restaurant serves *edelbayrische küche* – creative variations on regional specialities; many ingredients come from the owner's garden and he enjoys guiding his guests on mountain treks.

**Hotel Weinbauer €** *Füssener Strasse 3; tel: (08362) 9860; fax: (08362) 986 113; www.hotel-weinbauer.de.* This solid comfortable family-run hotel is situated right on the road to Ludwig's castles.

**König Ludwig €€€** *Kreuzweg 11; tel: (08362) 8890; fax: (08362) 81779.* Enjoy a fabulous view of Ludwig's castles and the Alps and luxuriate in the hotel's swimming pool and sauna. In addition to Bavarian cooking, the restaurants offers German *nouvelle cuisine*, vegetarian delicacies and a connoisseur's wine list.

# WIESKIRCHE✢✢✢

The 'Church in the Meadow' was constructed to house a grim object of veneration that now occupies the high altar: a wooden statue of Christ manacled to a post and bleeding from repeated whippings. After being carried in several Good Friday processions in the nearby town of Steingaden, it was relegated to an attic. Maria Lory, a local farm girl, asked to take it home with her. On 14 July, 1738, she saw it cry real tears. It was placed in a small chapel so pilgrims could pray to

it. By 1746, their number was so great that a new church was built, the work of architect Dominikus Zimmerman and his brother, Johann, who painted its radiant ceiling frescoes. Plain on the outside, the interior is a symphony of gilded stucco, woodcarvings and luminous frescoes that becomes ever more elaborate as the eye moves upward and reaches the cupola and a vertiginous Second Coming. Dominikus Zimmerman settled in nearby Landsberg so he could live out his life in close proximity to his masterpiece, while his son Franz married Maria Lory. Today, the church seems to catch the overflow from Neuschwanstein with coachloads of tourists queuing up in the car park. Souvenir kiosks and piped organ music add to the theme-park atmosphere.

## Suggested tour

**Total distance:** 110km.

**Time:** 1 long day, or 2 leisurely days.

**Links:** From Füssen, the B16 – the *Romantische Strasse* – travels north through Augsburg, Rothenburg and Würzburg (*see pages 90–109*). A stretch of the *Deutsche Alpenstrasse* heads along the B310 west through the Allgäu Alps to Lindau (*see pages 62–71*).

**SCHWANGAU ❶** is the best point of departure for this tour. It is important to reach **SCHLOSS NEUSCHWANSTEIN ❷** before the tour groups from Munich storm the place. Be there before it opens at 0900. Arriving later almost guarantees a long wait that can easily exceed two hours in the summer (there are plans for a new reservation system that might help). Save time for **SCHLOSS HOHENSCHWANGAU ❸**, which is just down the hill; it is far less popular so the queues should be shorter.

Return to Schwangau and drive left (west) on the B17 towards **Füssen** ; turn left again where Reutte is signposted just before reaching the town. The *Landstrasse* skirts the Lech river. There is a turn-off after 2km; from there, you can walk out on a footbridge for a view of the **Lechfall** (Lech Falls). The road continues along the course of the river as it churns through the next 12km between the peaks of the Tannheimer mountain range and the sheer Säuling massif. When you enter the city of **Reutte**, you will be funnelled into Bahnhofstrasse; keep driving left and follow the signs for Breitenweg/Plansee. The *Landstrasse* winds up to **PLANSEE ❹** and hugs its north shore. On the way, there are breathtaking views to the south (southwest to southeast) of the summits of Thaneller, Kohlberg, Hochschrutte and Daniel, and of the Ammergauer Alps to the north. At the end of the lake, the road straggles along the bank of the wild mountain stream, the Erzbach, on its way up a 12 per cent gradient to

**Above**
Wieskirche

🌙 **Ludwig der Bayer**
€€ *Kaiser-Ludwig-Platz 10–12, Ettal; tel:
(08822) 915 404; fax:
(08822) 915 420;
www.kloster-cttal.de.* Run by the Benedictine monastery across the street, this hotel is a vibrant place with restaurants, a vaulted beerhall (serving the monks' own brew), indoor swimming pool, sauna, fitness room and bowling alley.

the Ammersattel; beyond the pass, it descends into the lovely Ammertal. The sign appears soon after the border crossing for **SCHLOSS LINDERHOF** ❺. The castle's highlight is really its surroundings – a Renaissance Italian garden within a larger English garden within an alpine valley. After another 11 idyllic kilometres the *Landstrasse* meets B23.

**Detour:** Turn right on the B23 to get to **Kloster Ettal**, at the foot of the Ettaler Mandl, a 1634m massif. Emperor Ludwig der Bayer founded the Benedictine abbey in 1330 but it was mostly destroyed by fire in 1744. The cloister and church were then rebuilt in the rococo style with an impressive dome and **ceiling frescoes**. The abbey brews wonderful beer (there are tours of the brewery) and distils a potent *Ettaler Klosterlikör* from 70 mountain herbs. The complex also includes a woodcarving shop, farm and an excellent hotel-restaurant (Ludwig der Bayer).

Turn left on the B23. It is only 4km northwest to **OBERAMMERGAU** ❻. You then pass through Unterammergau, a farm town once famous for the manufacture of whetstones. The B23 also passes by Bad Kohlgrub, known for its mud baths, on its way to **Echelsbacher Brücke**, Germany's first concrete suspension bridge (1929). The gorge is spectacular but you have to park the car and walk out over the bridge to really see it. The **WIESKIRCHE** ❼ is clearly signposted off the B23 (5km return). It is widely regarded as Bavaria's finest rococo church. Sadly, it is also widely visited and you might have to compete with coaches for parking space. Back on the B23, **Steingaden** is only 2.5km further on. For a look at contrasting styles, it is worth stopping at its massive **Klosterkirche St Johannes**, a Romanesque church with a playful rococo interior. Before reaching Schwangau, take the *Landstrasse* that leads northwest in a beeline for Neuschwanstein. It is only 1km to **St Koloman** – impossible to miss because there is nothing around it on the open plain. If your timing is right, you can catch the sun setting on Neuschwanstein and the mountains of the Ammergau.

## Also worth exploring

The **Zugspitze**, the highest peak in the Bavarian Alps, can be reached from the town of Garmisch, 16km south of Ettal on the B23. There are two ways to the top: a relaxed 65-minute ride from the Garmisch train station on the *Zugspitzbahn* (cog railway), followed by a 10-minute ride on a cable car; or a dizzying 10-minute ride by way of the *Grosskabinenbahn* (funicular) from the alpine lake of Eibsee (10km above the town). It is possible to go up one way and come down another using a combination ticket. The price in winter includes the use of ski lifts.

## The Dream King

King Ludwig II of Bavaria (1845–86) is also known as the 'Fairytale King', the 'Dream King', the 'Last True King' or simply 'Mad Ludwig'. He enjoys a royal cult status that was almost unrivalled before the death of Princess Diana. No doubt, part of the fascination is that Ludwig didn't just live in a fantasy world, he built one too. His castle, **Neuschwanstein**, became the model for Walt Disney's fairytale castles and tourists from all over the world wait patiently for hours to get in. A musical based on his life is set to run forever at the purpose-built **König-Ludwig-Musical-Festspielhaus** in nearby Füssen. Ludwig was the next-to-last member of the House of Wittelsbach, the family that ruled Bavaria for an extraordinary 738 years, from 1180 until 1918. His withdrawal from the affairs of state began after he was forced into a war against Prussia, which Bavaria lost. 'It is necessary to create paradises that allow one to forget the terrible times in which we live', he later commented. Ludwig's ministers plotted to remove him from office and, on 10 June, 1886, had him declared insane by a panel of doctors. He drowned in Starnberger Lake three days later under mysterious circumstances. To this day, no one knows if it was suicide, an accident or murder.

# The Allgäu Alps: Füssen to Lindau

**Ratings**

| | |
|---|---|
| Mountains | ●●●●● |
| Nature | ●●●●● |
| Scenery | ●●●●● |
| Walking | ●●●●● |
| Skiing | ●●●●○ |
| Architecture | ●●●○○ |
| History | ●●●○○ |
| Food and drink | ●●○○○ |

The Allgäu Alps are a 150km-long mountain range bordered by the Upper Bavarian Alps to the east, Austria to the south and the Bodensee to the west. The range was part of the ancient province of Swabia and its dialect and food differ from that of Bavaria. Popular with Germans for its health resorts, uncrowded skiing and summer hiking, this stretch of the Alps offers similar attractions to the Bavarian Alps with fewer crowds, lower prices and less kitsch. Its dairy farms produce some of Germany's best cheeses. Many of its cows are still pastured in the alpine foothills and driven back downhill in early September. The lead cows (one per herd) are adorned with ornamental headdresses and huge clanking bells. Their safe arrival is celebrated in towns and villages all through the region in a festival known as the *Viehscheid*.

## BREITACHKLAMM✧✧

A raging mountain stream, the Breitach, has cut deep through bedrock for 2km to create this legendary gorge, which narrows to a mere 2m in places. Its traditional name was Zwing, because the peasants believed that *Zwinggeister* – nasty spirits – haunted it. The walk is beautiful in winter, when the waterfalls all turn to curtains of ice hanging from the polished walls. Walking the length of the gorge takes 1½ hours to the end and back but the first few hundred metres are as impressive as what follows. Wear waterproof clothing.

## FÜSSEN✧

Füssen is a health resort at the southern end of the *Romantische Strasse* (Romantic Road). It is first mentioned as a Roman fort guarding the *Via Claudia* (the road towards Augsburg where Reichenstrasse is

**ℹ Tourismus Information** *Kaiser Maximilian Platz 1; tel: (08362) 93850; fax: (08362) 938 560; www.fuessen and www.allgaeu-schwaben.com*

today). While the city owes its historical importance to a position high above the Lech river, much of its present prosperity is due to the proximity of Ludwig's castles. A **König-Ludwig-Musical-Festspielhaus** now hosts year-round performances of a musical based on the life of the fairytale king. Despite 2000 years of history, there is not that much to see in Füssen. The **Hohes Schloss** (castle) has a cleverly executed *trompe l'œil* oriel, a Rittersaal (Knight's Hall) and a small art collection. The beautiful public park with views of the Säuling massif is ideal for picnics. In the St Anna-Kapelle (entrance by way of the Stadtmuseum), there is an unusual set of frescoes on the theme of the **Totentanz❖** ('Dance of Death', c 1600).

## GROSSER ALPSEE❖

**ℹ Tourismus Information** *Marienplatz 3, Immenstadt; tel: (08323) 914 176; fax: (08323) 914 195; www.immenstadt.de*

This high mountain lake is one of the best places to pull off the road for a swim. The lakeside village of Bühl has a public beach and a small marina where you can rent a boat. From the south side of nearby Immenstadt, a cable car climbs up to the **Mittag-Ski-Centre❖**, with fine views of the surrounding Allgäuer and Tyrolean peaks and some of the region's best cross-country skiing in winter.

## HINDELANG❖

Hindelang is the gateway to the wide Ostrach Valley and the centre of a cluster of small towns and villages that includes Vorderhindelang, Hinterstein and Bad Oberdorf. Hindelang's rather nondescript St Jodok-Kirche houses one of the Allgäu's artistic treasures – the **Hindelanger Altar❖**, a 16th-century altarpiece by Jörg Lederer. **Bad**

**Oberdorf** is known for its sulphur springs, which are put to good use in the Prinz-Luitpold-Bad hotel (*see below*), and **Hinterstein** is a popular base for mountain climbers. The valley is famous for wild flowers in spring and summer and fit hikers can climb the summits of the **Daumen** (2280m), the **Geisshorn** (2249m) and the **Hochvogel** (2593m).

## Accommodation and food in Hindelang

**Bad-Hotel Sonne** €€ *Marktstrasse 15; tel: (08324) 8970; fax: (08324) 879 499; www.sonne-hindelang.de.* Behind its historic façade, this is a friendly hotel of rustic wood panelling and flower arrangements. It has a pool and sauna and the Chese Schneider restaurant excels at cheese-based Allgäu and Swiss specialities such as fondue and *Kässpatzen* (noodles with cheese and caramelised onions).

**Prinz-Luitpold-Bad** €€€ *Andreas-Gross-Strasse, 1km east of Bad Oberdorf; tel: (08324) 8900; fax: (08324) 890 379; www.luitpoldbad.de.* This is a grand 19th-century hotel and spa that has been meticulously modernised. It has its own sulphur springs, a herbal sauna, steam bath, Jacuzzi and solarium. They even lifted and installed an interior from the Scottish castle of Lanrick.

# KLEINWALSERTAL✦✦

**ℹ Tourismus Information**
*Walserstrasse 64, Hirschegg; tel: (08329) 51140; fax: (08329) 511 421; www.kleinwalsertal.com*

In the 13th century, the Walser – German emigrants from the Upper Valais, which is now in Switzerland – moved into the high, uninhabited valley of the Breitach river. They built traditional Valais-houses in places such as the small hamlet of **Bödmen**, just beyond Mittelberg. Life for the mountain farmers became even more daunting when the territory was transferred to the dukes of Tyrol a couple of centuries later and they suddenly found themselves subjects of Austria, which was on the other side of the impassable Allgäu Alps. A treaty signed in 1891 ended their deep isolation by allowing the region to be economically united with Germany while remaining under Austrian sovereignty. As a result, Kleinwalsertal has Austrian police but a German postal service, using Austrian stamps. Hitler had plans drawn up to bore a route through the mountains and the non-existent road was actually printed on maps. The resorts of **Riezlern**, **Hirschegg** and **Mittelberg** have excellent ski runs and the whole region – including the adjoining runs in neighbouring Oberstdorf (*see page 68*) – is covered by one ski pass. A drive to the end of the valley takes you as far as **Baad**. From there, you will have perfectly awesome views of **Widderstein** (2536m). If you want to carry on, it is a strenuous, 4½-hour hike to the top.

**Opposite**
Lindau Harbour

# LINDAU IM BODENSEE**

**ⓘ Tourismus Information**
*Ludwigstrasse 68; tel: (08382) 260 030; fax: (08382) 260 026; www.lindau-tourismus.de. Open Nov–Mar Mon–Fri 0900–1200 and 1400–1700; Apr–mid-Jun and mid-Sept–Oct Mon–Fri 0900–1300 and 1400–1800, Sat 1000–1400; mid-Jun–mid-Sept Mon–Fri 0900–1800, Sat and Sun 1000–1400.*

Lindau traces its history to Roman times; it received the status of Free Imperial City in 1275, conferring lucrative trading privileges. Most of its beautiful *Bürger* houses were built in the 15th century with money acquired in trade between the German region of Swabia and Italy. A marble lion erected by Bavarian King Ludwig I in 1856 adorns the tiny harbour. The lighthouse, built in the same year, has spectacular views. In the distance, the Swiss and Liechtenstein Alps form the backdrop to the lake. You can see the 'three sisters' – mountain peaks in Liechtenstein – on a clear day.

The 15th-century **Altes Rathaus**, with its playful ensemble of frescoes, gables and *trompe l'œil* detail is on Reichsplatz, near the harbour. It also has an external staircase of painted timber. The **Haus zum Cavazzen**, a former baroque palace on Marktplatz, houses the city's art gallery and local history museum. On the other side of the island, the stark Romanesque **Peterskirche** sits neglected just inside the ancient city wall next to the **Diebsturm** (Thief's Tower, 1350). The oldest church in the Bodensee region, it is decorated with the only surviving frescoes of Hans Holbein the Elder, depicting the life of St Peter. Unfortunately, they are in poor condition made even worse by 19th-century repainting.

## Accommodation and food in Lindau

It is delightful to stay overnight in Lindau but also expensive and not necessarily tranquil. The tourist office keeps a list of small hotels and pensions near the lake – many of them in lovely rural surroundings – and will help with reservations.

**Gasthof-Pension Grüner Baum €** *Bodenseestrasse 14, Oberreitnau; tel: (08382) 5552; fax: (08382) 945 736.* This recently renovated, good-value pension has its own *Biergarten* and sauna. It is a short drive from Lindau Island.

**Reutemann und Seegarten €€** *Seepromenade; tel: (08382) 9150; fax: (08382) 915 591.* These two hotels form one establishment and offer 19th-century hotel tradition with 20th-century comfort and a panorama of the Bodensee and the Alps.

**Weinstube Frey €€** *Maximilianstrasse 15; tel: (08382) 5278.* The historic dining room upstairs is a charming place to sample fish from the Bodensee, poached (*blau*) or pan-fried (*Müllerin*), and to drink the crystal clear, tart wines of local vintners.

**Zum Sünfzen €** *Maximilianstrasse 1; tel: (08382) 5865.* This converted 14th-century house in the Altstadt is good for dining out on venison stew or fish. It also has its own butcher's shop, which makes and sells a delectable *Weisswurst*.

**Left**
Lindau: Altes Rathaus

# OBERSTDORF*

**ⓘ Tourismus Information**
*Marktplatz 7; tel: (08322) 7000; fax: (08322) 700 236; e-mail: info@oberstdorf.de; www.oberstdorf.de.*

**ⓒ Wiese €€**
*Stillachstrasse 4a; tel: (08322) 3030; fax: (08322) 3135; www.hauswiese.de.* A family-run hotel with rustic Allgäu-style furnishings. Every room has a balcony.

Seven noble mountain valleys fan out from Oberstdorf like spokes from a wheel, making it an ideal base for hiking and skiing. You can count them while being whisked up to the **Nebelhorn**** by cable car. From the top, the view sweeps from the Zugspitze through the Austrian and Swiss Alps. An alternative way down is the easy trail past two alpine lakes, the Gaisalpseen.

Alpine roses and rare flora cover the area around **Fellhorn**** (also accessible by cable car) from mid-June to mid-July. For skiing, Oberstdorf is cosier, cheaper and less crowded than places such as Garmisch. High-adrenalin pursuits include hang-gliding, mountain-biking, kayaking and bungee-jumping from the **Heini-Klopfer-Schanze** (world cup ski-jump).

The **Oberstdorf Eislaufzentrum** is Germany's largest ice-skating complex and the venue for the Oberstdorf International Figure Skating Championships (27–30 August). Some visitors to Oberstdorf come here in order to take a *Kneippkur*, a form of hydrotherapy and diet regime developed by 19th-century parson Sebastian Kneipp (1821–97). It relies on the combined healing properties of water, grass, sunshine and pure mountain air.

Oberstdorf has a village festival in August. The *Oberstdorfer Viehscheid* (in September) is a pastoral procession of local cows, decked out in flowers and ornamental bells, on their way back from pastures in the Alps.

# PFRONTEN*

**ⓘ Tourismus Information**
*Vilstalstrasse 2; tel: (08363) 69888; fax: (08363) 69866; e-mail: info@pfronten.de; www.pfronten.de*

Pfronten came into being as a federation of 13 villages in the Middle Ages with its own constitution in broad Pfrontener Valley. It likes to refer to itself as the 'sun terrace' of the Allgäu Alps. It is popular as a base for hiking and cross-country skiing in the nearby Tannheim mountains. You can take the cable car to the summit of **Breitenberg*** (1870m) or chair lifts up to the **Hochalpe** (1600m) for mountain walks and cross-country and downhill skiing. The formidable ruined castles of **Eisenberg*** and **Hohenfreyberg**** are 7km northeast of Pfronten (and a 20-minute walk from the car park). Their **Burgenmuseum** has a motley collection of archaeological finds from the castles.

Five Pfronten hotels have given a new meaning to the expression 'to take a roll in the hay'. They offer a *Heukur*, or 'Hay' therapy. Biochemists and herbologists have demonstrated that sleeping in hay from (unfertilised!) alpine meadows can work wonders, particularly if it is heated first by steam. The lucky hotel guests lie and sweat in sacks of steaming hay for 30 minutes at a time and evidence suggests that it is an effective treatment for skin diseases, arthritis, insomnia, and rheumatism.

# Suggested tour

**Burghotel €€** *Just 50m below the Falkenstein ruin; tel: (08363) 914 540; fax: (08363) 9145 444; e-mail: schlachter@online-service.de; www.schlossanger.de.* The balcony of this 100-year-old hotel almost defies gravity, perched on a sheer outcrop of rock, but the solid cooking in its restaurant is an effective antidote to vertigo.

**Total distance:** 112km.

**Time:** 1 day, 2 days with all the detours.

**Links:** The B310 (part of the **Deutsche Alpenstrasse**) meets the **Romantische Strasse** at Füssen (*see page 62*).

As the B310 leaves **FÜSSEN ❶** it passes along a lake, the Weissensee, and a plateau with a fine view of Füssen and Säuling mountain (2041m) in the rear-view mirror.

**Detour: Schloss Falkenstein** is signposted shortly before the town of Pfronten. You are supposed to buy a parking ticket before you start up the road from the *Automat* at the crossroads where it begins. The lonely, inaccessible crag with Germany's highest castle ruin was rarely visited until Ludwig II had the road constructed. It is mostly a one-lane road and not for the faint of heart. It might be a feat of engineering but there is no guardrail between you and the precipice. Many visitors prefer to walk up instead. Ludwig intended to build his ultimate fantasy castle – the Gralsburg – on the site of the ruin at the top and it was meant to surpass anything he had ever done (a model is on display at Neuschwanstein, *see page 56*). The ruin itself is nothing more than four crumbling walls; the views, on the other hand, are even more spectacular than from Neuschwanstein. The Tannheimer range, the Ammergau mountains, Füssen and the lakes further south – they are all there at your feet. Just 50m below the ruin, the **Burghotel** proudly serves *Ludwigbräu,* a beer brewed in honour of the Dream King.

The next stop is **PFRONTEN ❷**. Take the turn-off just before Nesselwang – northwest of Pfronten on B309 – to reach the **Wallfahrtskirchlein Maria Trost**, a famous pilgrimage church with rococo frescoes. Continue past Grüntensee and Wertach. A few kilometres after, the B310 leads into the B308. The panoramic view at the top (turn off where **Kanzel** is signposted) takes in the Ostrach Valley. After the mountain village of **Oberjoch**, the **Jochstrasse**, the curviest stretch of the *Deutsche Alpenstrasse* (German Alpine Road), begins the first of 106 hairpin turns down to the valley and the town of **HINDELANG ❸**. The next major town, **Sonthofen**, lies in a basin at the foot of the Grünten peak in the Iller Valley. It was a training centre for one of Hitler's élite units, the *Ordensburg*, and was heavily bombed during the war. Its Gothic **Pfarrkirche St Michael** survived and is worth a look.

**Detour:** Nearby **Rettenberg** offers a 4.2km ski-run, and a scenic gorge, the **Starzlachklamm**, can be reached by driving up to the village of Winkel (just past Burgberg).

Turn south on the B19, a road that leads through magnificent mountain valleys and into the Tyrolean Alps (where it becomes the B201).

**Getting out of the car:** One of the region's most impressive walks is through the **BREITACHKLAMM GORGE** ❹, which you reach by a *Landstrasse* that turns off just before **OBERSTDORF** ❺.

Oberstdorf is one of the best points from which to explore the area. Drive further south into the Tyrolean enclave of **KLEINWALSERTAL** ❻ and through the towns of Riezlern and Mittelberg before dead-ending in Baad. Retrace your route back to Bavaria and the B308 (via the B19) and follow the signs for Immenstadt. Just west of the town, the road skirts the shore of the **GROSSER ALPSEE** ❼. Past the health resort of Oberstaufen, watch for a sign for a village called **Paradies**. The Café Paradies has a grandiose view of the Austrian Alps. Further west, the Allgäu Alps begin to give way to rolling hills. After the town of Scheidegg the road winds its way through the densely wooded ravine of **Rohrachtobel** then flattens out into open farmland on its way to **LINDAU IM BODENSEE** ❽. Lindau gets crowded during the summer and there is only one large car park on the island. It is easier to park on the mainland and walk across to the island.

## Also worth exploring

From the town of Fischen, on the B19, it is possible to take a steep mountain road that snakes along the Schörnberger Ache over Riedbergpass (the grade going up and down is 16 per cent) to the high mountain valley of Balderwang. You cross the Austrian border before reaching Hittisau. From there, you can return to the *Deutsche Alpenstrasse* by driving north on the 205.

**Above**
Lindau: Altes Rathaus

## Allgäu cheese

The rich pastures of Allgäu are home to half a million cows that produce 25 per cent of Germany's cheese. Cheese was not actually introduced into the region until the middle of the 19th century by Dutch and Swiss cheesemakers. They created wonderful, Allgäu-style Emmenthaler and Limburger, but another famous cheese was the result of serendipity on the part of two farmers, Josef and Anton Kramer. They messed up the formula for Limburger cheese and put the sorry result in a cellar to see if it would improve with time. When they took it out a half year later, the first heavenly piece of *Weisslacker* saw the light of day. No visit to Allgäu is complete without eating a mouthful.

# The Chiemgau

## Ratings

| | |
|---|---|
| Scenery | ●●●●● |
| Skiing | ●●●●● |
| Architecture | ●●●●○ |
| Nature | ●●●●○ |
| Outdoor activities | ●●●●○ |
| Walking | ●●●●○ |
| Children | ●●●○○ |
| History | ●●●○○ |

The Chiemgau region contains an assortment of Upper Bavarian landscapes – glacial lakes and moorland, rolling pre-Alpine hills, gentle river valleys, wild mountain streams and alpine summits. At its heart is the Chiemsee, the largest and most beautiful of Bavaria's lakes. Its charm was not lost on Ludwig II who built a vast fantasy palace on one of its islands. Nearly 2000 years ago, the resourceful Romans ran a road along its northern shore to link their settlements at Salzburg and Augsburg. The same road, with more pot-holes and detours, became the *Güldene Salzstrasse* (Salt Road) in the Middle Ages. Early Christian monks built monasteries on lake islands in the region that served as points of light for culture and learning. The mountains above the Chiemgau have some of Bavaria's best skiing and hiking and are linked by the *Deutsche Alpenstrasse* (German Alpine Road).

## CHIEMSEE✦✦

**ⓘ Tourismus Information** *Felden 10, Bernau am Chiemsee; tel: (08051) 96555; fax: (08051) 9655 530; www.chiemsee.de. Open Mon–Fri 0900–1900; Sat–Sun 1000–1600.*

**ⓒ** *In summer, a steam train travels between the Prien train station and the ferry terminal at Prienstock where boats leave for the islands.*

Bavarians like to call the Chiemsee the Bavarian 'Sea'. In reality, the sea is an enormous glacial lake, which is rich in such fish as lake trout, pike, whitefish and eel. Some 250 bird species nest on its shores. From the gentle hills of the north shore, there are spectacular views of the Chiemgauer Alps to the south – including the prominent peaks of the Kampenwand, Hochgern, Hochfelln, Rauschberg and Sonntagshorn.

Ludwig II so loved the lake that he chose it as the site of his ultimate folly, the construction of a copy of the Versailles palace on the **Herreninsel✦✦** (Gentlemen's Island). A second island, the **Fraueninsel✦✦** (Ladies' Island) has an 8th-century nunnery. Passenger ferries crisscross the lake, stopping at the islands and Prien, Gstadt, Seebruck and Chieming; a combination ticket allows you to visit them all. The lake is popular for swimming (the best beach is at Chieming), sailing and windsurfing.

## Accommodation and food on the Chiemsee

**Gasthof zur Linde €** *Fraueninsel im Chiemsee 1; tel: (08054) 90366; fax: (08054) 7299.* Built to house pilgrims 600 years ago, it became the gathering point for a 19th-century colony of artists attracted to the ever-changing light around the island. The rooms have simple but comfortable furnishings. A vast linden tree shades the *Biergarten*, and the dining room, the *Fischstüberl*, serves lake fish, fresh and smoked.

**Hotel Wassermann €€** *Ludwig-Thoma-Strasse 1, Seebruck; tel: (08667) 8710; fax: (08652) 871 498; email: info@hotel-wassermann.de; www.hotel-wassermann.de.* Most of the hotel's generous-sized rooms have balconies (overflowing with geraniums in summer) and dramatic views of Chiemsee and the Chiemgauer Alps. The Stocker family are energetic hosts who rent bicycles and organise bike tours.

**Yachthotel Chiemsee €€€** *Harrasser Strasse 49, Prien; tel: (08051) 6960; fax: (08051) 5171; www.yachthotel.de.* The region's top sport hotel is right on the lake, with a little fleet of sailing boats. It has facilities for all sorts of high- and low-impact athleticism.

# Fraueninsel✢✢

The 'Ladies' Island' is a small community of nuns and fisherfolk who keep cottage gardens with fruit trees and sunflowers. Celts and Romans once lived on the island. Benedictine nuns founded a monastery in AD 780 and are still here. Today, the nuns run a boarding school and brew their traditional *Klostergeist* ('Spirit of the Convent'). You can drink it in the Klostercafé or its *Biergarten*. The Island's whitewashed church has a Romanesque portal with a Gothic vault and tombstones showing vivid details from the lives of its abbesses. A flurry of hand-written notes hangs behind the altar addressed to St Irmengard. She was the great-granddaughter of Charlemagne and lived on the island in the 9th century. Adjoining the church is an octagonal bell tower with a 16th-century onion dome; across its graveyard is the **Torhalle**, an ancient chapel with Carolinian frescoes in the upper storey. Walking along the island shore one day, Munich artist Max Haushofer was so overcome by its beauty he decided to stay on and was joined by a colony of painters and writers in 1828. Many of these artists used to stay in the Gasthof zur Linde (*see page 73*), which is still one of the region's most charming hotels.

# HERRENINSEL✦✦

**Neues Königsschloss**
€€ *Herrenchiemsee;*
tel: (08051) 68870; fax:
(08051) 688 799;
*www.herren-chiemsee.de.*
Open daily Apr–Sept
0900–1800; Oct
0940–1700; Nov–Mar
0940–1600. A small
museum inside the palace
explores the life of Ludwig II
and exhibits models of all
his buildings – including the
dream castles he did not
build (*same hours as palace*).

**Chiemsee-
Schifffahrt Ludwig
Fessler** € *Seestrasse 108,
Prien;* tel: (08051) 6090;
*www.chiemsee-schifffahrt.de.*
Ferry line to the
Herreninsel island.

Ludwig II was ahead of his time in his environmentalism. One of the reasons he bought Herreninsel, the largest of the three islands on Lake Chiemsee, in 1873 was to end its deforestation. However, his main purpose was to find the perfect setting for his **Neues Königsschloss**✦✦ – a new and improved copy of Versailles with larger rooms and a more spectacular staircase. It is not hard to understand why some of his ministers thought he was mad. After bankrupting the state to build the castles of Linderhof and Neuschwanstein, he spent the Wittelsbach family fortune erecting a palace at least equal in size and magnificence to the French original – and only spent a couple of weeks there. The 20-minute ferry from Prien-Stock takes you to a long wooden jetty and signs lead the way past a 12th-century chapel and the refurbished buildings of a former monastery (now housing a small museum and an inn). You can walk (20 minutes) or ride in a horse-drawn carriage across sloping meadows and through a stand of woods. A formal garden suddenly spreads out before you with the seemingly endless façade of the schloss. A guided tour of the palace takes you through the **Audience Hall**, **Bedroom**, **Dining Room** and **Gallery of Mirrors**, which Ludwig used to have illuminated with 2000 candles. At the time of his death, only 20 rooms were finished out of a total of 70.

# KLOBENSTEINPASS✦✦

A mountain torrent flows down from the Kitzbühel Alps past several towns on its way to Chiemsee – Kitzbüheler Ache, Kössener Ache and Tiroler Ache. After it passes the town of Kössen in Austria, the Ache plunges into a deep chasm that has served as a border between Bavaria and the Austrian province of Tyrol since 1506. Two pilgrim's chapels hang from a cliff deep in the gorge: the 1696 **Wallfahrtskapelle Maria Klobenstein**✦, which contains a mysterious black Madonna; and a smaller one, with an entrance cut through the rock. From the chapels, a footpath leads to a bridge and into a misty ravine called **Entenlochklamm**✦.

# REIT IM WINKL✦

The town prides itself on being Germany's No 1 Ski Village. There are 50km of downhill pistes for all levels, including some World Cup runs. A single ski pass covers a huge area called **Winklmoosalm**✦✦ (1160–1900m) that includes Scheibelberg, Möseralm and – across the border in Austria – the Steinplatte. The cross-country skiing is equally impressive. The same mountains serve as a starting point for hikes to the top of the Fellhorn and Dürrnhorn. You can take the cable car up to Walmberg, with its views of the Kaiser mountain range, and walk the Peterhofrundweg to Kössen. The most beautiful view of the Chiemgauer range is from the **Hindenburghütte** (Untere Hemmersuppenalm).

### Accommodation and food in Reit im Winkl

**Landgasthof Rosi Mittermaier** €€ *Chiemseestrasse 2a; tel: (08640) 1012; fax: (08640) 1013; www.landgasthof-rosi-mittermaier.de.* This chalet-style hotel has wonderful views of the surrounding *Bergwelt* and an excellent restaurant with a wide-ranging menu. Owner Rosi Mittermaier was a star of the 1976 Innsbruck winter Olympics.

# RUHPOLDING*

The first tourists arrived in Ruhpolding in the 1930s. Despite its popularity, it still manages to maintain many of its traditions, crafts and folklore, which are represented in two small museums. The eastern part of the town has a lovely collection of old wooden buildings with carved balconies smothered in geraniums; many are decorated with *Luftmalerei* (frescoes). A cable car ascends to **Rauschberg*** (1671m), which might look familiar. It was used as a set in the Hollywood war movie, *Where Eagles Dare*. The town's pride and joy is the baroque **Pfarrkirche St Georg**** (Parish Church of St George), without a doubt one of the most beautiful churches in the Alps. The panoramic view from its graveyard chapel is the finest in the valley. Its most venerated object is 500 years older than the church itself: the austere but brightly painted **Ruhpolder Madonna**. She evokes gentle, maternal compassion.

# Suggested tour

**Total distance:** 161km with detours.

**Time:** 1–3 days.

**Links:** Heading east from Ruhpolding, the B305 (another section of the *Deutsche Alpenstrasse*) enters Berchtesgadener Land and the spectacular uphill climb that begins the route of the next chapter (*see page 87*). The intersection of B172 with B176 overlaps with the tour of the Kaiser Mountains described on *pages 186–9*.

This driving tour of the Chiemgau begins with a boat ride to its famous islands, **HERRENINSEL** ❶ and **FRAUENINSEL** ❷. The ferries only take pedestrians. There is ample, paid parking in a car park next to the landing in **Prien**. After visiting the islands, retrieve your car and drive along the north shore. For the best views of the lake and the Alps to the south, stop at the **Malerwinkel** ('painter's corner'), a hill between Breitbrunn and Gstad. **Seebruck** was an ancient Roman crossroads and is popular today for water sports. It has a collection of Roman mosaics in its **Römermuseum Bedaium** and a charming lakeside promenade.

**Detour:** Take a *Landstrasse* 6km north (signposted Seeon/Obing). The onion-domed church towers of the **Kloster Seeon** rise up from a peninsula in the Kloster lake. The peninsula was an island when it was founded in AD 994. Once famous for illuminated manuscripts and music, today the abbey is a fascinating complex of a thousand years of architecture, from Romanesque to baroque. If the thought of all that building makes you thirsty, stay for a glass of beer in the abbey's inn.

The road now heads east and angles away from the lakeshore. If you want to swim, turn off after 10km on the *Landstrasse* to Chieming; otherwise, continue down an uneventful stretch of road leading to **Traunstein**, an important city in the Middle Ages that was largely destroyed by fire in the 18th and 19th centuries. Its main link to the past is a medieval procession and sword dance held on Easter Monday – the **Georgtritt**. If it is not Easter, take the B306 south to **Siegsdorf**, a rustic village on the Weisse Traun river. Turn right (south) on the *Landstrasse* that runs along it and carry on upstream. One of the landmarks of the Bavarian Alps – the **Pfarrkirche St Georg** – heralds your arrival in the town of **RUHPOLDING** ❸, which lies in the large basin of the Weisse Traun Valley. Beyond the town, take the *Deutsche Alpenstrasse* (B305). The road skirts a series of glacial lakes (Lödensee, Mittersee and Weitsee) that are perfect for a picnic. A little further on, you pass the road leading up to the **Winklmoosalm**, an extensive network of ski-runs and hiking trails. The B305 veers down a narrow valley, the Schwarzlofertal, regains a few metres in elevation and takes a blind turn through **REIT IM WINKL** ❹. From here, you are spoiled for choice between two roads that follow the course of alpine streams back in the direction of the Chiemsee. The B305 – via Ober- and Unterwössen – is more direct and intensely scenic, but for real alpine drama follow the B172 and the signs to **Kössen** , which is in the Austrian Tyrol, at the foot of the **Zahmer Kaiser** mountain range. On the way you will

**Right**
Fraueninsel

**Residenz Heinz Winkler €€€**
Kirchplatz 1, Aschau im chiemgau; tel: (08052) 17990; fax: (08052) 179 966; www.residenz-heinz-winkler.de. Once an annexe to the ancient castle, the building has been converted into one of Germany's top hotel-restaurants (complete with Michelin stars and Estée Lauder Skincare Centre).

have to grip the wheel for a few bends along a wild tributary of the Grosse Ache and take a right turn off the B172 north on to the B176. The resort town is popular for hang-gliding and cross-country skiing. The road now winds into the wild, romantic gorge created by Tiroler Ache on its way to the **KLOBENSTEINPASS ❺**. It was blasted through the rock in 1967 along with the tunnel that marks the (unmanned) border crossing. Back in Bavaria, the countryside becomes more pastoral. The ancient cemetery at St Remigius in the peaceful village of **Schleching** is a good place to pause and reflect. From the village, follow the signs for Marquartstein. Before you get there, you will return to the B305, which strings together the pretty villages of Marquartstein, Grassau and Bernau.

**Detour:** Aschau, perhaps the most charming town in the Chiemgau, lies 12km southwest of Bernau. Its **Schloss Hohenaschau** is a brooding medieval castle that was given an ecstatic baroque facelift in the 17th century and *Jugendstil* additions in the 19th. Inside, the **Preysingsaal** and **Schloss Kapelle** are gems of Italian baroque décor and the **Rittersaal** is an atmospheric venue for summer chamber music concerts. The town invites aimless wandering; at every turn, you will bump into medieval patrician homes and offices – a *Rentei*, *Gerichtsschreiberhaus* (courthouse), *Amtshaus* (tax collector) or the *Marstall* (royal stables). A cable car hoists hikers and skiers up to the **Kampenwand**✥✥ (upper station, 1460m), which has extraordinary views of the Chiemsee below.

From Bernau, continue on the B305 through flat terrain towards Prien.

**Detour:** A very small detour is required to visit a remarkable group of **frescoes** in the village church of **St Jakobus**. Just south of Prien, watch for a small brown sign that says **Urschalling**. The signpost is not easy to see because it is in the shadow of a bus stop; look for the antique shop on the right-hand side of the road. Turning left, you climb a narrow country road straight up to a village on a knoll. The tiny white church suddenly appears from behind a quaint inn, the Messner. Go behind the inn, ignore the farmyard (a rope keeps visitors separate from the chickens), and step inside. The chapel is packed with vividly restored, late-Romanesque and early-Gothic frescoes telling the story of the Fall from Grace, the Life of Jesus, the story of St James and the apocalyptic visions of St John.

**Prien** itself is a pleasant town that serves as a gateway to the region (with traffic jams in summer). There is no particular reason to linger unless you are staying at one of the lakeside hotels, except perhaps to visit the **Pfarrkirche Mariä Himmelfahrt**. In the 18th century, the baroque painter Johann Baptist Zimmermann adorned its ceiling with a frescoed re-enactment of the sea battle of Lepanto 1571, a violent subject that was nevertheless pious since it depicts a Christian navy defeating a Turkish one.

## Also worth exploring

Few foreign tourists ever visit **Wasserburg am Inn**, a town folded inside a sharp oxbow curve of the Inn river and, seemingly trapped in a time warp. The almost perfectly preserved town was at the centre of events in the Middle Ages, lying on the ancient salt route between Bad Reichenhall and Munich on the Inn river, which was used as a waterway between the Adriatic and the Danube. The best way to explore the city is to walk over the Inn bridge through the imposing Brucktor and then to **Marienplatz**, the nexus of an ancient maze of streets.

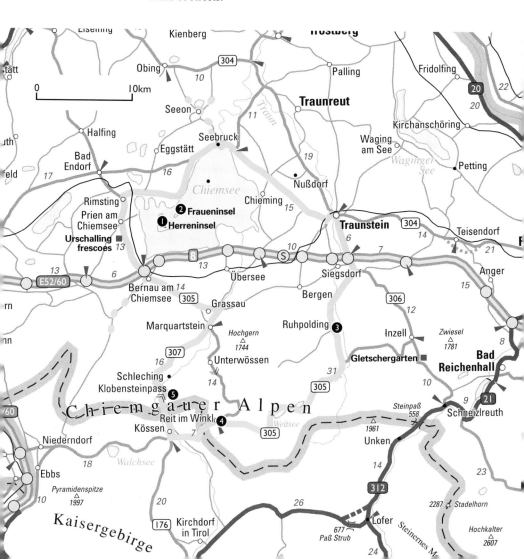

# Berchtesgadener Land

## Ratings

| | |
|---|---|
| Geology | ●●●●● |
| Hiking | ●●●●● |
| Mountains | ●●●●● |
| National parks | ●●●●● |
| Scenery | ●●●●● |
| Skiing | ●●●●○ |
| History | ●●●○○ |
| Food and drink | ●●○○○ |

This southeastern corner of the Bavarian Alps, surrounded by Austria on three sides, has been called the Yellowstone Park of the German Alps. 'He whom God loves is dropped into Berchtesgadener Land' wrote a 19th-century novelist. Getting there by car is a little more difficult. Only two winding roads connect it to Germany through a narrow 10km corridor. This route starts from the classy spa town of Bad Reichenhall, climbs the steepest stretch of the *Deutsche Alpenstrasse*, circles one of Bavaria's most beautiful Alpine lakes, touches the shore of another and cruises Germany's highest mountain road for panoramic views of the Bavarian and Austrian Alps and the city of Salzburg. There are many possible excursions: deep gorges with thundering waterfalls; an underground salt mine; boat rides on the fiord-like Königssee; and the town of Berchtesgaden itself, once the summer home of the royal Wittelsbach family.

## BAD REICHENHALL*

**ℹ Kur- und Verkehrsverein**
*Wittelsbacherstrasse 15;*
*tel: (08651) 606 303;*
*fax: (08651) 606 311;*
*www.bad-reichenhall.de*

Bad Reichenhall owes its long history, which began with the Celts, to salt. Immensely valuable in the Middle Ages, the 'white gold' brought great wealth. The water wheels and pumps of the old salt mine are still functioning as an impressive exhibit in the **Heimatmuseum**. Maximilian II of Bavaria came in 1848 for a cure and brought his entire court with him. Almost overnight, Bad Reichenhall became fashionable. In 1900, the town was anointed *Bayerisches Staatsbad* (Spa of the Bavarian State). Today, there are a wide range of treatments such as *Untersberger Moor* (black mud) baths, brine heliotherapy (combining salt water and sunlight), and steam inhalations using sap from dwarf pines. A testament to the importance of this city in the Middle Ages, the **Münsterkirche St Zeno** is the largest Romanesque basilica in Bavaria. Bad Reichenhall has its own philharmonic orchestra and hosts an annual Mozart Week in the spring. The awesome **Predigtstuhl** (1613m) can be reached by Germany's oldest cable car (1928).

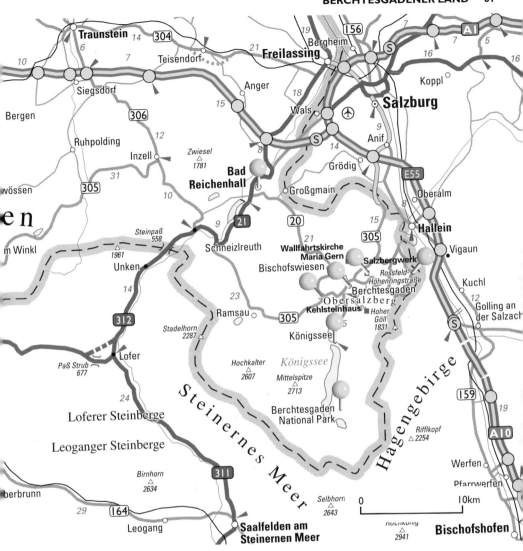

## Accommodation and food in Bad Reichenhall

**Hotel Steigenberger Axelmannstein €€€** *Salzburgerstrasse 2–6; tel: (08651) 7770; fax: (08651) 5932; www.bad-reichenhall.steigenberger.de.* One of Germany's grandest hotels, with its own luxurious spa-treatment centre and elegant park. Nostalgia comes at a price.

# BERCHTESGADEN*

**ⓘ Tourismus Information**
e-mail: info@tourismus-berchtesgaden.de;
www.berchtesgaden.de

**ⓗ Königliches Schloss Museum €€**
Schlossplatz 2; tel: (08652) 947 980; fax: (08652) 9479 812; www.haus-bayern.com. Open Sun–Fri Easter to mid-Oct 1000–1300 and 1400–1700; mid-Oct to Easter 1100–1400.

Woodcarvers in Berchtesgaden are known for their dolls, toy horse-carriages and Spanschachteln, brightly painted wooden boxes. They are for sale at **Berchtesgadener Handwerkskunst** (Marktplatz 24) and **Holzschnitzerei Hans Schuhegger** (Schlossplatz 7).

The Augustinian monks who founded the town of Berchtesgaden described the region as 'a vast solitude inhabited by wild beasts and dragons'. Things started to look up when salt was discovered in 1190 and mining it brought great prosperity. It was also the source of friction with neighbouring Salzburg, the major producer of salt in the Alps. The **Königliches Schloss Museum*** occupies the palace where the Augustinian prince-provosts lived. They ruled the region as an independent clerical principality until it was secularised in 1810; their palace then became the summer residence and hunting lodge of Bavaria's royal family, the House of Wittelsbach. The museum has an excellent collection of German woodcarving, including pieces by Tilman Riemenschneider and Veit Stoss, displayed in a Gothic dormitory. The Romanesque cloister is the principal relic of the medieval priory; the wild beasts and dragons described by the monks seem to have found their way on to its strangely carved columns. The adjoining **Stiftskirche St Peter und Johannes*** has been the town landmark since the 13th century; it contains the tombstones of the prince-provosts.

## Accommodation and food in Berchtesgaden

There are hundreds of pensions, guesthouses and private homes in Berchtesgadener Land. They are the best value for a longer stay (there is usually a three-night minimum). The tourist offices keep an up-to-date list and will make reservations.

**Hotel-Pension Floriani €** Königsseer Strasse 37; tel: (08652) 66011; fax: (08652) 63453; www.hotel-floriani.de. This hotel is tucked away in a quiet street a few minutes from the train station. It is newly renovated in light pastel colours and most rooms have balconies. Owners Wilfred and Ursula Conserti are gracious, English-speaking hosts.

**Hotel Vierjahrszeiten €€** Maximilianstrasse 20; tel: (08652) 9520; fax: (08652) 5029; website www.berchtesgaden.com/vier-jahreszeiten. A hotel with archetypal hunting-lodge décor right in the heart of Berchtesgaden's Old Town. The affable owner and chef, Herr Miller, speaks excellent English. He serves savoury game dishes in his restaurant, named after the patron saint of hunters, St Hubertus.

# BERCHTESGADEN NATIONAL PARK***

The southern half of Berchtesgadener Land is a national park accessible only by foot and boat. It offers some of the wildest, most beautiful hiking in the German Alps. In all, there are 150km of trails with high mountain huts for overnighting. Two easy, popular trails

ℹ️ **Nationalpark-Haus Berchtesgaden,**
*Franziskanerplatz 7; tel: (08652) 64343; www.nationalpark-berchtesgaden.de. Open daily 0900–1700.*

**Nationalpark Informationsstelle Königssee** (in the former Königssee train station) *Seestrasse 17; tel: (08652) 62222. Open mid-May to mid-Oct 0900–1700.* Both centres have maps and guides.

are the 2km path from St Bartholomä to the Watzmann-Ostwand (East Wall) and the trail that connects the southern end of Königssee to Obersee. The region is famous for alpine flowers such as gentian, Alpine rose, colt's foot, columbine, alpine dwarf boxtree, saxifrage, rockrose and mountain orchid.

**Right**
Marktschellenburg, in the Berchtesgaden National Park

# KÖNIGSSEE❖❖❖

Germany's deepest, pristine lake is 8km long, up to 1.2km wide and 190m deep. It was created by glacial melting in the last Ice Age at the foot of Mount Watzmann (2713m), Germany's second-highest mountain. The Königssee is the official end of the *Deutsche Alpenstrasse* (German Alpine Road). There are no roads around the lake. Electric boats ferry tourists noiselessly back and forth, stopping first at the chapel of **St Bartholomä**❖; on the way there the boat stops, the captain blows his horn and an echo rebounds seven times from the face of Watzmann and the surrounding peaks. St Bartholomä rests on a narrow peninsula. It might look familiar since it appears on millions of calendars and postcards. Mount Watzmann and its 2000m granite massif rise above the copper-domed chapel and the gentle meadows that encircle it. According to local legend, the two big and seven smaller peaks of the Watzmann range represent a king, his queen, and their children who were turned into stone as punishment for being cruel to their subjects. Nearly a hundred climbers have died trying to scale its east face since the first successful ascent in 1881. Most visitors turn back at St Bartholomä, but the boat continues on to the end of the lake and more spectacular scenery. From the end, at Saletalm, it is only a 15-minute walk to the Königssee's sister lake, the **Obersee**❖❖, and its 300m waterfall.

# OBERSALZBERG✥

**Tours:** David Harper of **Berchtesgaden Mini Bus Tours** (*same address as the tourist office in Berchtesgaden, tel: (08652) 64971; fax: (08652) 64863; www.eagles-nest-tours.com*) offers a detailed 4-hour tour of all the sites associated with Hitler and the Nazi Party. Space is limited to eight participants per tour so make reservations.

High in the mountains east of Berchtesgaden at the southern end of the Rossfeld-Höhenringstrasse is the little village of Obersalzberg. It is because of Obersalzberg, dubbed the 'cradle of the Nazi Party', that the name Berchtesgaden has grim associations with the Nazi era. Hitler purchased the Berghof, his private home, after becoming chancellor in 1933. Members of the party élite, including Hermann Goering, Martin Bormann and Albert Speer moved into the neighbourhood. The Nazis erected a 3m-high fence with three heavily guarded access roads, and constructed a vast underground network of lodgings. By then, the idyllic alpine village had became the heavily fortified, southern headquarters of the Nazi Party. Statesmen such as Neville Chamberlain visited Hitler in the Berghof in the late 1930s, hoping to convince him not to invade the Sudetenland. The house was heavily bombed during World War II and levelled by US troops in 1952. Contrary to what most guidebooks say, there are still many Nazi-era buildings standing in the area (most are completely nondescript) and much of the underground complex remains. There is every indication that Hitler intended to make his last stand at Obersalzberg rather than Berlin. He had built a sprawling underground fortress (6km of tunnels) with sealed vents to protect against gas attacks, vast stocks of provisions, an underground projection room, and a cell for his dog. A small part of it is open to the public at the **Hotel zum Türken.**

# ROSSFELD-HÖHENRINGSTRASSE✥✥✥

**Rossfeld-Höhenringstrasse** €€ *The northern half is open all year round.*

Germany's second-highest alpine road (the highest is Kehlstein) was the brainchild of Martin Bormann in the 1930s, but it was not actually finished until the 1950s. The toll road ascends to 1600m, beginning at either Oberau or Obersalzberg. It runs along the Rossfeld ridge, which separates Bavaria from Austria. From the parking place at the top your view sweeps from the Hohen Göll massif to Kehlstein, the Tennen- and Dachstein ranges, Untersberg (local legend claims Charlemagne is asleep beneath it), Berchtesgadener Land and, on a clear day, the city of Salzburg. The road has two strategically located *Berggasthöfe* (mountain lodges) for *Koffee* and *Kuchen* (coffee and cakes) with a view.

# SALZBERGWERK✥✥

The Berchtesgaden region, miserably poor in the Middle Ages, entered a period of prosperity thanks to the mining of salt. Tourists have been visiting the dark underworld of the salt mine since the 19th century. Despite the theme-park atmosphere, it is still a working salt-mine.

**Salzbergwerk €€€**
*Bergwerkstrasse 83;
tel: (08652) 60020;
fax: (08652) 600 260;
e-mail: info@geheimnisvolle-
salzwelt.de;
www.salzbergwerk-
berchtesgaden.de.
Open May–15 Oct daily
0900–1700; 16 Oct–Apr
Mon–Sat 1130–1530.*

**Below**
Berchtesgaden, looking towards
the Waltzmann cliff

Most of the year, if you arrive much later than 0900, you have to queue up and might easily wait two hours to get in. You will be asked to put on miner's clothes: a baggy jacket and trousers and a leather kidney-warmer (women will find it easier if they don't wear a skirt). The staff insist on shooting (and offering to sell) photos before a tiny train carries you deep into the earth down a long tunnel. After getting off, you are invited to slide down a 30m chute (there are stairs, too) that drops into a vast chamber veined with salt crystals. A short film about the extraction of salt is followed by a tour of a disused shaft complete with a 19th-century brass pump that never missed a beat in its century of operation. A series of exhibits with German-language captions leads you through the history of salt production and a second chute descends to a mysterious underground salt lake, crossed by wooden ferryboat. A funicular and train bring you back to the mine entrance.

# Suggested tour

**Total distance:** 90km. The detour to Almbachklamm adds 10km.

**Time:** A full day.

**Links:** Berchtesgaden can readily be combined with a visit to Salzberg (*see page 168*). It is less than 20km away.

The route begins in **BAD REICHENHALL** ❶, the stately spa town that lies at the foot of the Predigtstuhl (1613m). Heading west, cross the Saalach river and follow the signs for Kirchberg, Thum and Reuth. The road passes beneath the ruined castle of Karlstein and along a lake, the Thumsee, before it links up with the formidable *Deutsche Alpenstrasse*. Turn south (right) and prepare for a steep (11 per cent) ascent between the Latten range to the left and the Reiteralpe to the right up to Schwarzbachwacht pass. On the other side of the pass is a roadside car park. From there you will have a fantastic view of Hochkalter (2608m) and Watzmann (2713m). The road begins a gradual descent that becomes quite steep (15 per cent) before it reaches the valley of the Ramsauer Ache ('River').

**Detour:** Turn off the B305 at **Ramsau**. After only a few hundred metres the road passes one of the region's most photographed places – the **Ramsauer Pfarrkirche**. Many painters have stared at it from the *Malerwinkel* ('painter's corner') – a bench on the opposite side of the stream between the two wooden bridges – including amateur landscape artist General Dwight D Eisenhower, who came to Berchtesgaden for a few days after Germany's final surrender. At the western edge of **Ramsau**, the Zauberwald ('Magic Forest') begins. It owes its fairytale qualities to the ancient trees that throw long shadows in the afternoon, and moss-covered boulders jumbled in fantastic shapes. Carry on through the forest by way of Hinterseestrasse to **Hintersee**, then circle the lake. The surrounding peaks of Reiteralpe, Hochkalter and Hoher Göll are mirrored in its emerald-green water, while massive rocks rise out of the water on its northern shore. The lake inspired many German artists at the turn of the century who used to meet at the lakeside inn, the Gasthof Auzinger.

Return to the B305 and go right (east). An enchanted length of road follows, one of the best stretches of the *Deutsche Alpenstrasse*, along the Ramsauer Ache. To get to **KÖNIGSSEE** ❷, take the country road – signposted Schoenau a. K. (a. K. stands for am Königssee) rather than the B20, which is often miserably congested. Use the B20 on your way back and take a right turn at the main train station, then a left further on, to drive up to the hilltop town of **BERCHTESGADEN** ❸. The main road is subject to traffic jams and street parking is hard to find; fortunately, there is an underground garage. The town's most popular attraction, the **SALZBERGWERK** ❹, is 1km northeast of the Old Town, clearly signposted from the B305. Continue on the B305 in

## Berchtesgaden and National Socialism

Berchtesgaden was Hitler's 'Wahlheimat' – the place he called home – for over 20 years. One of the reasons, perhaps, was the fact that his real homeland, Austria, was easily visible on a clear day from the village of Obersalzberg, above Berchtesgaden. His mentor, Dietrich Eckart, used the village as a hideout in 1923 and Hitler visited him there incognito as Herr Wolf. When Hitler was released after nine months in prison just in time for Christmas in 1924, he came to Obersalzberg. It was there that he wrote part two of *Mein Kampf*. Indeed, Hitler spent at least a couple of months each year at Obersalzberg between 1923 and 1936, with shorter stays between 1936 and 1942 that became longer again during 1943 and 1944.

sync with the Berchtesgadener Ache for 4km, turning right at the sign for the circular **ROSSFELD-HÖHENRINGSTRASSE** ❺ , Germany's second-highest mountain road. Get on it going north and savour every kilometre of one of Europe's best engineered and most panoramic highways. It is wider and grander and reveals more than any other mountain road in Bavaria. At the top, you can see every landmark in the region and Salzburg just over the Austrian border (from here on the road is sometimes closed in winter). It then descends in a series of dramatic curves to **OBERSALZBERG** ❻ .

**Getting out of the car:** Germany's highest mountain road is not accessible to private motorists. It was carved deep into the mountain in a mere 13 months and rises at a 27 per cent grade for 6.5km before reaching the base of the **Kehlsteinhaus**, or 'Eagle's Nest', as it is known to most foreigners. After the bus ride, visitors walk through a tunnel that leads 124m deep into solid rock, then they are whisked up an equal distance – in 41 seconds – by a massive, brass-lined elevator. It might come as a disappointment to some that the 'Eagle's Nest' had no military purpose whatsoever: it was just a conference room with a view. It is a daring feat of engineering and, for what it is worth, a document of National Socialism architecture. Hitler's adviser and private secretary, Martin Bormann, had it built for his boss at extraordinary expense for his 50th birthday. The *Führer* was afraid of heights but still forced himself to the top so he could receive – and impress – foreign dignitaries. He also liked to have himself photographed while standing on the precipice. Today, it is always flooded with foreign tourists who seem weirdly star-struck by its associations with history's most evil man; but the expensive price of admission goes to charity and the view across the Alps is sublime (open May–Oct).

To complete the circle, continue on the Rossfeldstrasse back to Oberau (don't take the road signposted for Berchtesgaden) and return to the B305.

**Detour:** Turn right on the B305 and drive 5km east. **Altbachklamm** is on the left, announced by a brown sign. It is one of the most stunning gorges in the region and its best pools and waterfalls are only a 15-minute walk from the roadside.

Turn left on the B305 and retrace the route until it is intersected by the B20, which will take you north. Bischofswiesen is the first major town. From there, the road follows the Bischofswiesen Ache through a high mountain valley to **Pass Hallturm** between Untersberg (east) and the Latten range (west). It is possible to have a last look at Watzmann (2713m) in the rearview mirror. There are ruins, too. The pass was once fortified by the powerful prince-provosts to keep the Bavarians out. A challenging series of curves leads downhill to Bayerische Gmain and **Bad Reichenhall**.

## Also worth exploring

Located in a spectacular high mountain valley, the **Wallfahrtskirche Maria Gern** is the most beautiful church in Berchtesgadener Land. It was built between 1709 and 1724 on an elliptical floor plan, replacing an earlier chapel. Its most precious object is the deeply venerated Madonna (1666) above the altar by Wolfgang Huber. Joseph Schmidt from Salzburg did the stucco work and Christoph Lehrl painted the ceiling frescoes. Everything else was done by local people in a collaborative labour of devotion: the altar, the woodcarved figures, the side altars and wrought ironwork. For many, the most interesting aspect of the church is its collection of votive offerings.

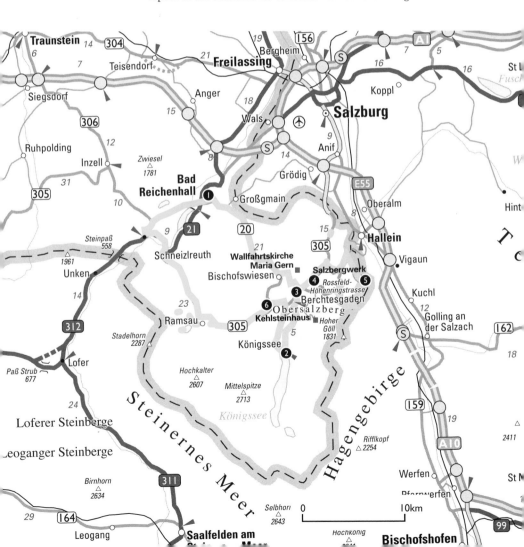

# The Ries Crater and the Altmühl Valley

**Ratings**

Architecture ●●●●●

Castles ●●●●●

Geology ●●●●●

Nature ●●●●○

Outdoor activities ●●●●○

Scenery ●●●●○

Walking ●●●●○

Food and drink ●●○○○

The Ries Crater is a flat basin of wheat fields crossed by straight roads such as the famous *Romantische Strasse* (Romantic Road), which strings together historic walled towns and castles. At first glance, all of its highlights seem to be architectural, but the terrain, boring to the untrained eye, suddenly becomes fascinating with the knowledge that it was created by a meteor. The Altmühl Valley, by contrast, is one of Germany's most scenic river valleys, a series of vast loops through the Franconian highlands carved first by the primeval Donau and later by the Altmühl river; there are quarries for fossil hunting and limestone outcrops crowned by feudal castles. The area is almost undiscovered by foreign tourists.

## ALTMÜHLTAL NATURPARK✦✦✦

**❶ Altmühl Valley Nature Park Information Centre** *Notre Dame I, Eichstätt; tel: (08421) 98760. The helpful staff have maps of hiking trails and cyclepaths but they don't make room reservations.*

**❽ Fahrradgarage,** *Herzoggasse 3, Eichstätt, tel: (08421) 2110; www.fahrradgarage.de, rents canoes and bicycles.* **San-Aktive Tours,** *Nürnberger Strasse 48, Gunzenhausen; tel: (09831) 4936, has canoes.*

The Altmühl Valley Nature Park is Germany's largest (3000sq km) and one of its most varied. The valley formed the shoreline of a vast lake 150 million years ago and its bedrock is riddled with fossils. The central stretches of the valley are the most scenic with limestone crags, thick woods and lush meadows. There are hundreds of caves in the limestone rock; Stone Age people used many of them as homes. The Naturpark is ideal for canoeing, cycling and hiking, and almost every town has a place where you can hire bicycles or canoes.

### Accommodation in Altmühltal Naturpark

There are private guesthouses and camping grounds throughout the Altmühl Valley. Enquire at the **Nature Park Information Centre**.

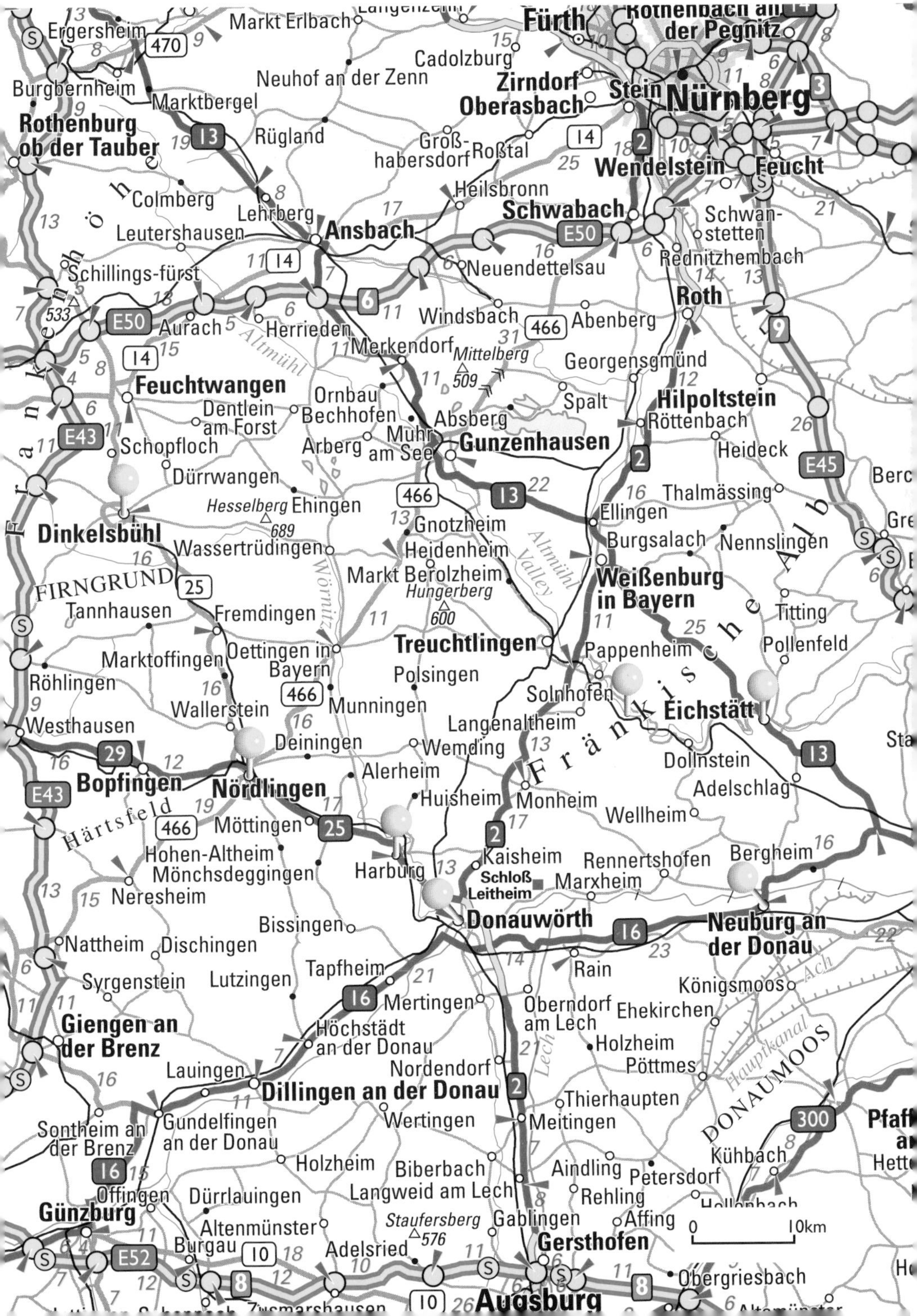

Ergersheim
Markt Erlbach
Langenzenn
Fürth
Rothenbach an der Pegnitz
470
Burgbernheim
Neuhof an der Zenn
Cadolzburg
Zirndorf
Oberasbach
Stein
Nürnberg
3
Marktbergel
Rothenburg ob der Tauber
13
Rügland
Groß-habersdorf
Roßtal
14
Wendelstein
2
Feucht
Colmberg
Lehrberg
Heilsbronn
Schwabach
Schwan-stetten
Leutershausen
Ansbach
E50
Roth
21
Schillings-fürst
14
Neuendettelsau
Rednitzhembach
533
E50
Aurach
Herrieden
6
Windsbach
466
Abenberg
Roth
14
Merkendorf
Mittelberg
31
Georgensgmünd
9
Feuchtwangen
Ornbau
Bechhofen
Absberg
Spalt
Hilpoltstein
Dentlein am Forst
Gunzenhausen
Röttenbach
Heideck
26
E43
Schopfloch
Arberg
Mühr am See
2
E45
Dürrwangen
Thalmässing
Berc
Dinkelsbühl
Hesselberg
689
Ehingen
Gnotzheim
Ellingen
Burgsalach
Nennslingen
Gre
FIRNGRUND
Wassertrüdingen
466
13
Heidenheim
Weißenburg in Bayern
S
25
Tannhausen
Fremdingen
Markt Berolzheim
Hungerberg
600
Titting
Röhlingen
Marktoffingen
Oettingen in Bayern
Treuchtlingen
Pappenheim
25
Pollenfeld
Westhausen
466
Munningen
Polsingen
Solnhofen
Eichstätt
29
Wallerstein
Deiningen
Langenaltheim
Dollnstein
13
E43
Bopfingen
Nördlingen
Wemding
Monheim
Adelschlag
Sta
Härtsfeld
466
Möttingen
Huisheim
Wellheim
25
Hohen-Altheim
Mönchsdeggingen
Harburg
Kaisheim
Rennertshofen
Bergheim
16
Neresheim
Schloß Leitheim
Marxheim
Nattheim
Dischingen
Bissingen
Donauwörth
Neuburg an der Donau
16
22
Syrgenstein
Lutzingen
Tapfheim
Rain
Königsmoos
Ach
Giengen an der Brenz
16
Mertingen
Oberndorf am Lech
Ehekirchen
DONAUMOOS
Höchstädt an der Donau
Holzheim
Pöttmes
Lauingen
Nordendorf
Thierhaupten
300
Sontheim an der Brenz
Gundelfingen an der Donau
Dillingen an der Donau
2
Wertingen
Meitingen
Kühbach
Pfaff
Offingen
16
Holzheim
Biberbach
Aindling
Petersdorf
Hett
Günzburg
Dürrlauingen
Langweid am Lech
Rehling
Affing
Hollenbach
E52
Altenmünster
Staufersberg
576
Gablingen
8
Burgau
10
Adelsried
Gersthofen
Obergriesbach
8
Zusmarshausen
10
Augsburg
Altenmünster

0    10km

# DINKELSBÜHL❖❖

ℹ️ **Tourismus
Information**
*Marktplatz; tel: (09851)
90240; fax: (09851) 552
619; e-mail:
touristik.service@
dinkelsbuehl.de*

**Above**
Dinkelsbühl

Dinkelsbühl has the medieval character of Rothenburg (*see page 102*) without the flood of tourists. Beneath its 17 towers is a city which remains in the Middle Ages. From the bridge leading to the 13th-century Wörnitz Tor, the walled city seems to float on the River Wörnitz and the waters of its moat. The town's landmark is the late-Gothic **Münster St Georg**❖❖. Although its tower was never finished, it is considered one of Germany's finest hall-churches – a design in which the aisles and nave are the same height. The nearby Weinmarkt is dominated by the 16th-century **Deutsches Haus**, an exuberant medieval residence. A narrow alleyway leads to the massive 17th-century **Schranne** ('granary'). Today, it is a festival hall and one of the venues for the annual *Kinderzeche* (in the third week of July), a commemoration of the most important event in the town's history. The Protestant Swedes conquered the Catholic town in 1632 and were preparing to plunder it (*see Eichstätt, page 94*) when a crowd of weeping children surrounded the Swedish commander's horse and a young woman thrust her child into his arms. He spared the town. As part of the festival, there are also parades, fireworks, medieval dances and open-air concerts by the *Knabenkapelle* (boys' choir) dressed in 18th-century uniforms. From the Schranne, a choc-a-bloc row of half-timbered façades – Nördlinger Strasse – angles its way to the Nördlinger Tor. Just past the gatehouse is the mill that ground the city's grain in the 15th century – the Stadtmühle – fortified with pike loopholes and a moat. It is a surreal home for the **Museum der Dritten Dimension**✳, with state-of-the-art exhibits that play tricks on your eyesight. Don't miss the 3-D nudes on the third floor.

### Accommodation and food in Dinkelsbühl

**Deutsches Haus** €€ *Weinmarkt 3; tel: (09851) 6058; fax: (09851) 7911; www.deutsches-haus-dkb.de.* There is not a more beautiful half-timbered house on the *Romantische Strasse* and the hotel inside is full of period furnishings. The restaurant contributes solid cooking and a varied wine list of Franconian vintages.

**Eisenkrug** € *Dr-Martin-Luther-King-Strasse 1; tel: (09851) 57700; fax: (09851) 577 070; www.hotel-eisenkrug.de.* This pink 17th-century house on the Weinmarkt has big canopied beds, generous portions in its regional restaurant and a wine bar in the vaulted cellar. It even has a few parking places.

# DONAUWÖRTH✳

**ⓘ Tourismus Information**
*Rathausgasse 1; tel: (0906) 789 150; e-mail: tourist-info@donauwoerth.de. Open Apr–Sept Mon–Fri 0900–1200, 1300–1800; shorter hours in winter.*

**Käthe-Kruse-Puppen-Museum** €
*Tel: (0906) 789 185; e-mail: museen@donauwoerth.de. Open Tue–Sun 1100–1700; shorter hours in winter.*

The town occupies a steep hillside where the River Wörnitz meets the Donau. The **Reichstrasse**✳ is one of the most beautiful streets in Bavaria, with its collection of patrician dream houses built by wealthy merchants in the Middle Ages: the **Baudrexlhaus** (No 1); the Renaissance **Stadtzoll** (No 2); the 13th-century **Café Engel** (No 10) that once served as a *Meistersingerschule*; the **Stadtkommandantenhaus** (No 32); and the **Tanzhaus**, with an archaeological museum on the third floor. The Gothic Liebfrau parish church also rises up from Reichstrasse; the nearby **Heiligkreuz** (Holy Cross) church is one of the finest examples of the 'Wessobrunn School', a rococo architectural style. The **Käthe-Kruse-Puppen-Museum**✳ at Plegstrasse 21a is a delightful collection of classic handmade dolls.

# EICHSTÄTT❖❖

**ⓘ Tourismus Information**
Domplatz 8; tel: (08421) 98800; fax: (08421) 988 030; e-mail: tourismus@eichstaett.btl.de. Open Apr–Oct Mon–Sat 0900–1800, Sun 1000–1300; Nov–Mar Mon–Thur 1000–1200 and 1400–1600, Fri 1000–1200.

**ⓗ Wilibaldsburg €**
Burgstrasse 19. Open Apr–Sep Tue–Sun 0900–1800; Oct–Mar Tue–Sun 1000–1600.

**Museum Berger €**
Harthof 1; tel: (08421) 4663; fax: (08421) 905 591; e-mail: g.h.berger@t-online.de. Open Apr–Sept Tue–Sun 0900–1800; Oct–Mar Tue–Sun 1000–1600.

**ⓒ Adler €€** Marktplatz 22–4; tel: (08421) 6767; fax: (08421) 8283; e-mail: adler.stigler@t-online.de. The top address in Eichstätt with contemporary comforts behind its big baroque exterior.

Eichstätt is the most important city of the Altmühl Valley and its history goes back at least as far as the Celts. The seat of Germany's largest Catholic university, it has been a bishopric since English missionary St Wilibald built a monastery here in the 8th century. The baroque city you see today looks much as it did in the 17th century when it rose from the ashes left by a rampaging Swedish army in 1634. The two main squares are Marktplatz and Domplatz. The **Dom❖** (cathedral), despite its baroque façade, reflects the city's long history in its Romanesque and Gothic elements. Look for the **Pappenheimer Altar❖❖❖** (c 1490) in the north aisle, one of the great masterpieces of German religious sculpture. Its 10m of delicately carved limestone depict members of all the classes and trades of medieval life gathered around Christ on the Cross. The **Mortuarium❖** is interesting for its stained-glass windows by Hans Holbein the Elder. Across the river, at a lordly distance above the town, sits the 17th-century **Wilibaldsburg❖**, the former residence of Eichstätt's prince-bishops. Today, it houses two museums: the **Historisches Museum** (local history); and the **Jura Museum** (palaeontology and geology of the Altmühl Valley), www.jura-museum.de. The **Museum Berger❖**, located at the base of a quarry 4km west of the city (off the B13), has a rich collection of geological and palaeontological finds, including a copy of the famous *Archaeopteryx*, the fossil of a dinosaur with claws and feathered tail – a missing link between reptiles and birds. The original was discovered near Eichstätt in 1877 and purchased by a German industrialist (now on display in Berlin). Visitors who are keen to find fossils for themselves can rent chisels and hammers from the museum.

**Right**
The Pappenheimer Altar

# NEUBURG AN DER DONAU✧✧

**Schloss Neuburg €**
*Residenzstrasse 2; tel:
(08431) 8897; fax: (08431)
42689. Open Tue–Sun
Apr–Sept 0900–1800;
Oct–Mar 1000–1600.*

Although Roman in origin, Neuburg's Golden Age began in 1505 when it suddenly became the capital of a small, newly created principality – the Junge Pfalz (Young Palatinate), which was carved out of the territory of the Wittelsbachs. Its first ruler, Palatine Count Otto-Heinrich, was one of the great personalities of the German Renaissance and obsessed with building. We have him to thank for Neuburg as well as a ruined wing of the castle in Heidelberg, where he moved in 1556 after becoming a Prince-Elector. He had the **Schloss Neuburg**✧ constructed between 1527 and 1538. The courtyard is very Italianate with arched loggias and black-and-white sgraffito paintings of princes, Old Testament Patriarchs and Greek deities.

# NÖRDLINGEN✧✧

**Nördlingen
Tourismus
Information** *Marktplatz 2;
tel: (09081) 84116; e-mail:
verkehrsamt@noerdlingen.de*

**Rieskrater-Museum**
*€ Eugene-Shoemaker-
Platz 1; tel: (09081) 2738
220; e-mail:
rieskratermuseum@
noerdlingen.de. Open Tue–Sat
May–Oct 1000–1630;
Nov–Apr 1000–1200,
1330–1630.*

**Flamberg Hotel
Klösterle €€** *Beim
Klösterle 1; tel: (09081)
88054; e-mail:
noerdlingen@astron-hotels.de.
A former Franciscan
monastery now converted
into an elegant hotel.*

Fifteen million years ago, an asteroid struck the earth's surface creating a basin 25km in diameter and 1500m deep. The energy released was equivalent to 250,000 Hiroshima atom bombs. It took several million years to fill up the basin, now known as the Rieskrater (the region's fertile soil has earned it the nickname 'Bavaria's Bread Basket'). Scientists reconstructed this dramatic event in the earth's history in 1974 after studying rock samples taken from deep in the earth near Nördlingen. Convinced that the region might share characteristics with the moon, NASA sent Apollo 14 and 17 astronauts to do field training here. Information about the region's astonishing meteoric past can be found in the **Rieskrater-Museum**✧, housed in a medieval barn.

The town of Nördlingen looks more medieval than lunar. Its ancient **Stadtmauer**✧ (town walls) form a nearly perfect circle within the eroded circular print of outlying crater hills. It takes almost an hour to walk around their 3km circumference; the best place to begin is the oldest gatehouse, the **Reimlinger Tor**✧. The town's crowning glory is the late-Gothic church of **St Georgskirche**✧✧. Its 89.5m-high Daniel Tower has 365 steps and commanding views of the town and Ries Basin.

# SCHLOSS HARBURG✧✧✧

**Schloss Harburg**
*€€ Tel: (09080)
96860; e-mail burg-
harburg@fuerst-
wallerstein.de. Open mid-
Mar to Oct Tue–Sun
1000–1700.*

Harburg is the most impressive 'real' castle on the Romantic Road (with all due respect to Neuschwanstein further south). The name means 'Muck Castle', a reference perhaps to the muddy Wörnitz river that it overlooks. First mentioned in 1050, it is one of the oldest and largest castle complexes in southern Germany. To reach the inner courtyard you have to pass beneath an imposing portcullis. The oldest building is a 12th-century keep, the **Diebsturm** (Thieves Tower); other structures include the 16th-century **Kastenhaus** (that served as stables and armoury) and the **Burgtvogtei**, formerly the castle manor and now a small hotel (the **Burgschenke**, *tel: (09003) 1504*). You can walk along part of the parapet that is intact. The art collection of the Earls of Oettingen, acquired over five centuries, is on view in the **Fürstenbau**✤: illuminated manuscripts, carved ivory, miniatures, tapestries, musical instruments, sculpture and paintings.

## SOLNHOFEN✤

**Bürgermeister-Müller-Museum €**
*Bahnhofstrasse 8; tel: (09145) 832 030; fax: (09145) 832 050. Open Apr–Oct daily 0900–1700; Nov–Mar Sun 1300–1600.*

**Below**
Dinkelsbühl

Little Solnhofen prides itself on being 'a world in stone' – and with good reason. Its limestone quarries have provided an astonishing array of Ice-Age fossils and continue to do so. Stop off at the local tourist office and ask to hire a hammer and chisel to hunt fossils for yourself. Solnhofen is also the birthplace of lithography – stone-block printing – invented by Alois Senefelder in the 19th century. His first lithographs are on display in **Bürgermeister-Müller-Museum**✤, along with the region's most important collection of fossils.

# Suggested tour

**Total distance:** 195 km.

**Time:** A whole day.

**Links:** The B25 is part of the *Romantische Strasse* and heads further north to Rothenburg and Würzburg (*see pages 102 and 106*).

Starting at **DINKELSBÜHL** ❶, take the B25 for a straight drive through wheat fields to **Wallerstein** where the road just manages to squeeze past the Pestsäule (1722–5), a pillar carved with saints and the Holy Trinity that was meant to ward off the plague. The town's pride and joy is an exquisite baroque palace and English garden that belonged to the princes of Oettingen-Wallerstein. There is a 360-degree view of the Ries Basin from a rock above the Fürst Wallerstein Brauhaus. It is only another 6km to **NÖRDLINGEN** ❷; if time allows, park outside the city walls and explore it on foot. The road further south is uneventful until it comes to **SCHLOSS HARBURG** ❸; arriving from the north you don't have a good view of it but it is clearly signposted. There are two car parks for the castle; the lower one involves a short uphill walk.

**Detour:** The best view of the castle requires a slight detour. From the lower car park, take the right-hand downhill road, veering into the Old Town of Harburg and carry on right along the Wörnitz river until the edge of town; cross the bridge, turn left and drive along the riverbank back in the same direction about 200m. You will see an ancient stone bridge – walk out on to it and bring your camera.

Get back on the B25 and head south. After 7km, watch for signs for the city centre of **DONAUWÖRTH** ❹. Drive directly into town and descend a steep hill (you will be funnelled into Kapellestrasse). Just before the bridge over the Donau, take the country road signposted **Leitheim/Marxheim** and follow it along the river.

**Detour:** Turn west instead and continue on the B16 to reach the village of **Blindheim**, about 16km. The terrain is boring but people with a vivid historical imagination will appreciate the lonely memorial to one of the most important battles in European history. On 13 August, 1704, the forces of Austria, Holland and England, fighting under the command of John Churchill, the Duke of Marlborough, decimated a Franco-Bavarian army in a surprise attack that decided the outcome of the War of the Spanish Succession. In the town of **Höchstädt**, 6km further west, the Heimatmuseum's diorama re-enacts the battle with 9000 tin soldiers (the actual number of combatants was 112,000).

The next town is **Leitheim**, where the road passes by a whimsical rococo palace – **Schloss Leitheim** – built in 1690 as the summer home of a pleasure-loving abbot from nearby Kaisheim; today, it is used in summer as a stately venue for classical concerts. The *Landstrasse* continues along the Donau and passes in and out of tiny

**Fürst Wallerstein Brauhaus €** *Berg 78, Wallerstein; tel: (09081) 7075; fax: (09081) 7048; www.fuerst-wallerstein.de. Sit over a glass of Wallersteiner Landsknecht Bier on the sunny terrace and contemplate the surrounding Ries moonscape. Sauerbraten and Swabian specialities such as Maultaschen (resembling big ravioli) are on the menu.*

Rennertshofen (at the southern end of the Wellheim Valley). NEUBURG AN DER DONAU ❺ is on the south side of the Donau; it is advisable to settle for parking in the lower town and visit the historic Old Town on foot. The road north, the B13, is clearly signposted for EICHSTÄTT ❻. The next 36km are an amazing lesson in geology. After an 11km bend in the Altmühl river you will dip into the town of **Dollnstein**, embedded in the northern end of the Wellheim – a dry valley through which the Donau flowed during the last Ice Age. The town is encircled by high defensive walls beneath a ruined castle (**Burg Tollenstein**, immortalised in the opera *Parsifal*); its Romanesque parish church has a cycle of vivid Gothic frescoes. The road then grapples with a set of dramatic Jurassic-era loops known as the **Zwölf Apostel** (Twelve Apostles). **SOLNHOFEN** ❼ is on the valley floor below one of them.

**Detour:** Take the turn-off for **Pappenheim** – just 2km. In one of the narrowest places in the valley, the former seat of the Earldom of Pappenheim is bottled up in an oxbow loop of the river. The tableau of collapsed castle walls, encroaching wooded hillsides and fortified riverbank make it one of the most romantic towns in the Altmühl Valley. It never completely recovered from the destruction of the Thirty Years' War (1618–48) that left its **Burg** in ruins, though many towers still stand. On the north side of the river, the 9th-century **Pfarrkirche St Gallus** is one of the oldest Carolinian buildings in Germany though it has undergone a few modifications since. The first tombstones in the **Judenfriedhof** (Jewish Cemetery) were laid in the 12th century.

The next major town, **Treuchtlingen**, has its own thermal springs, the **Altmühltherme**, an indoor complex with pools, sauna and solarium. If there is no time to soak, return to the Ries Crater zone on the country road to **Oettingen** (clearly signposted but with two spellings, Öttingen and Oettingen). On the way there are a lot of gentle twists, dips and curves before it all finally flattens out. From Oettingen, another *Landstrasse* takes you to the B25 and north back to Dinkelsbühl. Alternately, you can drive south on the B486 to Nördlingen.

## Also worth exploring

**Audi Museum Mobile €** *Tel: (0841) 8937 575; www.museummobile.de. Open Mon–Sat 1000–2000. Changing interactive exhibitions on topics like design, safety and the environment. You can also tour the Audi factory.*

A prosperous industrial city on the Donau (18km southeast of Eichstätt), Ingolstadt is the headquarters of Audi, which has an award-winning historical car museum. In the city's historic core, the church of **Maria-de-Victoria** reveals the world's largest flat **ceiling fresco**, a *trompe-l'œil* wonder by the Asam brothers that depicts the progress of the Christian faith. If you stand in the right place (a circle marks the spot) the ceiling looks three-dimensional and the figure of Moses changes shape as you walk beneath him. The **Bayerishes Armeemuseum** (Bavarian Army Museum) occupies the vast chambers of a medieval fortress with exhibits from 500 years of warfare. Ingolstadt was the city that promulgated Germany's Beer Purity Law in 1516 and the local brews proudly maintain the tradition.

Ergersheim
Markt Erlbach
Langenzenn
Fürth
Rothenbach an der Pegnitz
470
Cadolzburg
Burgbernheim
Neuhof an der Zenn
Zirndorf
Stein
Nürnberg
3
Marktbergel
Oberasbach
Rothenburg ob der Tauber
13
Rügland
Groß-haberdorf
Roßtal
14
2
Colmberg
Heilsbronn
Wendelstein
Feucht
Lehrberg
Schwabach
E50
Leutershausen
Ansbach
Schwan-stetten
13
14
Rednitzhembach
21
Schillings-fürst
Neuendettelsau
Roth
533
E50
6
Windsbach
466
Abenberg
9
Aurach
Herrieden
Merkendorf
Mittelberg
Georgensgmünd
E43
14
15
Feuchtwangen
509
Hilpoltstein
Dentlein am Forst
Bechhofen
Ornbau
Absberg
Spalt
Röttenbach
26
Schopfloch
Arberg
Muhr am See
Gunzenhausen
Heideck
E45
Dürrwangen
2
Hesselberg
Ehingen
466
13
Thalmässing
Dinkelsbühl
689
Gnotzheim
Ellingen
Wassertrüdingen
Heidenheim
Burgsalach
Nennslingen
FIRNGRUND
25
Markt Berolzheim
Weißenburg in Bayern
Tannhausen
Fremdingen
Hungerberg
Titting
Röhlingen
Marktoffingen
Oettingen in Bayern
Polsingen
Pappenheim
Pollenfeld
Westhausen
466
Munningen
Solnhofen
Eichstätt
6
29
Wallerstein
Deiningen
Wemding
Langenaltheim
Dollnstein
13
Bopfingen
Nördlingen
Alerheim
Monheim
Adelschlag
E43
466
Möttingen
25
Huisheim
Wellheim
Bergheim
Hohen-Altheim
Harburg
Kaisheim
Rennertshofen
Mönchsdeggingen
Schloß Leitheim
Marxheim
Neresheim
Nattheim
Dischingen
Bissingen
Donauwörth
Neuburg an der Donau
Syrgenstein
Lutzingen
Tapfheim
Rain
16
Königsmoos
Giengen an der Brenz
Mertingen
Oberndorf am Lech
Ehekirchen
Höchstädt an der Donau
Nordendorf
Holzheim
Pöttmes
Lauingen
Dillingen an der Donau
Wertingen
Meitingen
Thierhaupten
300
Sontheim an der Brenz
Gundelfingen an der Donau
Holzheim
Biberbach
Aindling
Petersdorf
Kühbach
Günzburg
Altenmünster
Langweid am Lech
Rehling
Affing
Hollenbach
Offingen
Staufersberg
Gablingen
576
10
Burgau
Adelsried
Gersthofen
Obergriesbach
Jettingen-Schennach
Zusmarshausen
Augsburg
Altmühl
Wörnitz
Altmühl Valley
Fränkische Alb
Härtsfeld

0    10km

# The Romantic Road: Würzburg to Rothenburg ob der Tauber

**Ratings**

| | |
|---|---|
| Architecture | ●●●●● |
| Art | ●●●●● |
| Castles | ●●●●● |
| History | ●●●●● |
| Wine | ●●●●● |
| Children | ●●○○○ |
| Nature | ●●○○○ |
| Scenery | ●●○○○ |

One of Germany's most popular tourist attractions, the *Romantische Strasse* (Romantic Road) was an ancient route used by Romans, crusaders, traders and pilgrims. The stretch of road from Würzburg to Rothenburg ob der Tauber reflects the many centuries when Germany was a patchwork of territories divided between bishops, princes and city-states. It begins in the vainglorious Residenz of Würzburg beneath Europe's largest fresco and stops along the way at Schloss Weikersheim, a Renaissance pearl erected by the hedonistic Hohenlohe princes. The end point is the Rathaus of Rothenburg, a Free Imperial City in the Middle Ages. Its patrician homes still radiate the civic pride and prosperity of enterprising burghers, and massive fortifications remind us how they kept the world at bay.

## BAD MERGENTHEIM❖

**ⓘ Deutschordens-
schloss €€** *Schloss
16; tel: (07931) 52212. Open
Tue–Sun 1000–1700.*

Contemporary conspiracy theorists could never invent a story as bizarre as the history of the Knights of the Teutonic Order. A religious and military society founded in Jerusalem, it had already conquered Prussia and made war on Poland when it moved its headquarters to Bad Mergentheim. The Knights built a Renaissance castle, the **Deutschordensschloss**❖❖, with a vertiginous spiral staircase (the Berwart-Treppe) and sumptuously decorated rooms. The Grand Masters of the order resided there from 1525 until the order's dissolution by Napoleon in 1809 (the order was revived in passivist form with Papal approval and still exists in Vienna). Today, the castle contains a Museum of the Teutonic Order of Knights where you can study the details of its convoluted history, and sleep on them in its hotel. The local mineral springs, first used by the Celts, had been silted up and long forgotten when a shepherd rediscovered them in 1826. Since then the town has become a health resort.

# CREGLINGEN*

**🌙 Heuhotel Ferienpension €**
*Weidenhof 1; tel: (07933) 378; fax: (07933) 7515; www.ferienpension-heuhotel.de.* If you fancy sleeping in freshly turned hay, visit this 'hay hotel'.

In 1384, a peasant ploughing a field found the Host (consecrated bread of the Eucharist) beneath a clod of earth, and the **Herrgottkirche** was built on the very spot where the miracle occurred. Towards the end of the 15th century, Tilman Riemenschneider was commissioned to carve a new altar for it. The **altar of the Virgin Mary**** , which he finished in 1505, is considered by many as his greatest work. It owes its remarkable state of preservation to the Protestants, who boarded it up when the church passed into their hands and left it that way for 300 years. The life of the Virgin Mary is depicted in a set of reliefs on the wings, in the niches and on the base of the altar; the central scene shows Mary going to heaven. At the bottom of the altar, Riemenschneider portrayed himself as the scholar in the middle of the group in the right-hand relief of the *predella* (altar platform).

In Germany, there is no object, however humble, considered unworthy of a museum. The **Fingerhutmuseum** is a case in point. Housed in an old watermill across from the church is a collection of 2000 thimbles, including one that belonged to Goethe's girlfriend, Charlotte von Stein. The town itself has an interesting collection of half-timbered houses at the corner of Tor and Lindleinsstrasse. From there, the Romstrasse leads to the best one of all, the 15th-century Romschlössle.

# DETWANG*

The coachloads of tourists on their way to Rothenburg generally bypass tiny Detwang, despite its idyllic location in the scenic **Obertaubertal** (Upper Tauber Valley). The village can be the beginning of a delightful detour (*see page 108*). The Romanesque **St Peter und Paul Kirche** dates back to AD 1000 and is a peaceful place in which to contemplate Tilman Riemenschneider's **Heiligen-Kreuz-Altar*** ('crucifixion altar'), originally created for the Michaelkapelle in Rothenburg. Side panels portray Jesus in the Garden of Gethsemane and the Resurrection. Just before the Tauber-Brücke (bridge), in the direction of Vorbach, a shady *Biergarten* reverberates with live music on weekends.

# ROTHENBURG OB DER TAUBER***

**ℹ Rothenburg Tourismus Service**
*Marktplatz 2; tel: (09861) 404 800; e-mail: info@rothenburg.de; www.rothenburg.de*

A powerful and wealthy city in the Middle Ages, Rothenburg never recovered from the devastation of the Thirty Years' War (1618–48) until modern times. Today, it is regarded by some as Germany's best preserved medieval town and by others as a nightmare of kitsch. A tour of the city ramparts (the full circuit takes half an hour) reveals what all the excitement is about: en route you will see not just a few highlights but a complete city of half-timbered buildings beneath gabled roofs, decorated façades, turrets, spires and dizzying ramparts. After the walls, head straight for the Gothic **St Jakobskirche**** (St James Church), the city's greatest artistic treasure that is strangely overlooked by the hordes of tourists. In the Middle Ages it was full of pilgrims seeking out a famous relic – drops of Christ's blood encased in a cross of crystal. Tilman Riemenschneider carved the **Heiligblut*** (Holy Blood) altar to house the precious object. It was a bold work for its time in which Judas, rather than Christ, seems to be the central figure. The nearby **Rathaus*** is one of the finest Renaissance buildings in southern Germany (except for the tower, which is Gothic and well worth climbing for the view if you can scale the ladder at the top). Its Imperial Hall and dungeons are open to the public, too. When the Catholic General Tilly captured Protestant Rothenburg during the

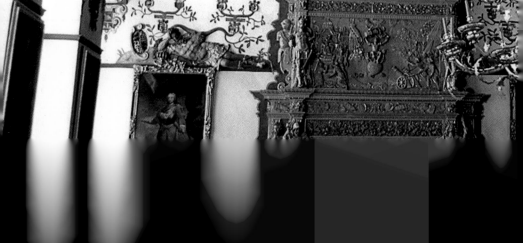

**Mittelalterliches Kriminalmuseum €**
Burggasse 3; tel: (09861) 5359; fax: (09861) 8258; www.kriminalmuseum. rothenburg.de. Open Apr–Oct daily 0930–1800; Nov, Jan and Feb, daily 1400–1600; Dec and Mar 1000–1600.

**Käthe Wohlfahrt**
Herrngasse 2; tel: (09861) 4090; fax: (09861) 409 410; www.wohlfahrt.com (see website for other locations). Open Mon–Sat 0800–2000, Sun 1100–1700. One-stop, year-round shopping for German Christmas ornaments.

**Previous page**
Rothenburg's town walls
**Below**
The Rittersaal, Schloss Weikersheim

Thirty Years' War in 1631, the citizens begged him not to raze it. No doubt as a joke, he said he would spare the town if a citizen could drain a *Meistertrunk* (a 3-litre tankard of wine) in one gulp. Georg Nusch, a former Mayor of Rothenburg, stepped forward and performed the miraculous quaff, downing the entire tankard in about ten minutes and sleeping it off for three days afterwards. The incident is re-enacted by the figurines of the Rathaus clock on the hour, from 1100 to 1500 and again at 2100 and 2200. Among Rothenburg's museums, the **Mittelalterliches Kriminalmuseum**＊ (Medieval Crime Museum) can hardly fail to impress. The strange collection of 'Shame Masks' – used for public humiliation – is the most fascinating part. Torture devices from Spain are invariably the cruellest.

## Accommodation and food in Rothenburg ob der Tauber

Staying overnight in Rothenburg is not as expensive as you might think and it gives you the chance to get up early and explore the town before it is overrun by day-trippers.

**Burg-Hotel €€** *Klostergasse 1–3; tel: (09861) 94890; fax: (09861) 948 940; www.burghotel.rothenburg.de.* A tiny hotel perched on the city walls. Most rooms have heart-stopping views of the Tauber Valley.

**Romantik Hotel Markusturm €€** *Rödergasse 1; tel: (09861) 20980; fax: (09861) 2692; www.markusturm.rothenburg.de.* This inn is right at the foot of a 13th-century tower and a few paces from the Town Hall. The English owner and chef Herr Berger is almost as good as his cooking.

**Glocke €** *Am Plönlein 1; tel: (09861) 958 990; fax: (09861) 9589 922; www.glock-rothenburg.de.* Just down the street from the city's most photogenic corner, this inn is popular with locals for its cooking and wine cellar.

# WEIKERSHEIM❖❖❖

**ⓘ Verkehrsamt Weikersheim**
*Marktplatz 12; tel: (07934) 992 575; e-mail: info@weikersheim.de; www.weikersheim.de*

**ⓗ Schloss Weikersheim €**
*Info-tel: (07934) 8364. Guided tours daily Apr–Oct 0900–1800; Nov–Mar 1000–1200, 1330–1630.*

**ⓒ Laurentius €€**
*Marktplatz 5; tel: (07934) 91080; fax: (07934) 910 818; www.hotel-laurentius.de. This hotel-restaurant is just a stone's throw from Schloss Weikersheim.*

**Schloss Weikersheim**❖❖❖ is a princely Midsummer Night's Dream come true. Despite the medieval moat, the Renaissance castle was really built for pleasure, as was the baroque garden with its rollicking stone dwarfs and sexy goddesses. The **Rittersaal** (Knights' Hall) has a 40m suspended ceiling adorned with hunting scenes and life-size sculptures of animals. In summer, the old walls and windows vibrate with music when the castle is a podium for seven weeks during the **Jeunesses Musicales**, an International Festival for Young Musicians. Wine is served by the glass from huge old vats in the cellar.

## Tilman Riemenschneider (1460–1531)

Destined for great things, the sculptor Tilman Riemenschneider arrived in Würzburg in 1483 without a penny in his pocket. He married a rich widow – the first of four wives – and set up shop. Arguably the greatest German sculptor of the late-Gothic period, he worked in both wood and stone (and was the first woodcarver to reject the use of paint). He also pursued a successful political career and was twice elected Bürgermeister of Würzburg. His downfall came near the end of his long life in the aftermath of the Peasants' Revolt (1524–5). He sympathised with the long-suffering peasants and convinced the city not to intervene on the side of the archbishops and feudal lords. The revolt was put down with unspeakable brutality and Riemenschneider was imprisoned in 1525. Court records show that he was tortured in the second degree – meaning that his tormentors bound his hands behind his back, tied weights to his legs and hoisted him into the air until both shoulders dislocated. He never worked again.

# WÜRZBURG✦✦

ℹ **Congress &
Tourismus**
*Falkenhaus am Markt; tel:
(0931) 372 398;
www.wuerzburg.de. Open
Jan–Mar Mon–Fri
1000–1600, Sat 1000–1300;
Apr–Dec Mon–Fri
1000–1800, Sat 1000–1400;
Apr–Oct Sun 1000–1400.*

Würzburg is the capital of Franconia's *Weinland*. Powerful *Fürst-Bischöfe* (prince-bishops) ruled the city and the surrounding Franken region for centuries until the arrival of Napoleon in 1806. Statues of 12 of them line the Alte Mainbrücke (the Old Main Bridge) at the foot of the **Festung Marienberg✦**, the castle where they lived for more than 500 years (now housing the **Mainfränkisches Museum✦**). The source of their wealth was wine, which came from vineyards such as Stein, at the northern end of town. Franconian wine was the wine of the German emperors and of Free Imperial Cities such as Nürnberg and

**⇄ Frankfurt Airport** *is only 1 hour 20 minutes from Würzburg. Tel: (01805) 3724 636; www.frankfurt-airport.de*

**⊞ Mainfränkisches Museum €** *Tel: (0931) 205 940; www.mainfraenkisches-museum.de. Open Apr–Oct Tue–Sun 1000–1700, Nov–Mar 1000–1600.*

**Residenz €** *Residenzplatz 2; tel: (0931) 355 170; fax: (0931) 51925; e-mail: sgvwuerzburg@ bsv.bayern.de. Open daily Apr–Oct 0900–1800, Nov–Mar 1000–1600.*

**Opposite**
Würzburg

**Wine tasting**

Three great wine producers offer wine tasting in Würzburg: the **Bürgerspital** (*Theaterstrasse 19; tel: (0931) 3503 448; www.buergerspital.de*); the **Juliusspital** (*Juliuspromenade 19; tel: (0931) 3931; www.juliusspital.de*); and the **Hofkeller** (*Residenzplatz 3; tel: (0931) 30509 23; www.hofkeller.de*). **Haus des Frankenweins**, right on the river near the Old Crane Kellerstube, Kranenkai 1, sells wine from all over the region. *Riesling* and *Silvaner* from the local Stein vineyards are justly famous. *Kerner* is an intriguing new variety (produced by grafting the vines of red *Trollinger* and *Riesling*).

Rothenburg. The most powerful family in Würzburg's history, the Schönborns, suffered from a chronic case of *Bauwurm* – 'building worm' – diagnosed as an uncontrollable urge to build. In 1720, the new Prince-Bishop, Johann Philipp von Schönborn, showed remarkable foresight in commissioning young Balthasar Neumann (1687–1753) to build him a *Schloss über die Schlösser* ('a palace of palaces'). A military engineer by training, Neumann was destined to become Germany's greatest baroque architect. The **Residenz♦♦♦** that he built for Schönborn was one of the architectural wonders of the 18th century: a U-shaped palace with a 167m façade, a monumental staircase and Europe's largest ceiling fresco – painted by the Venetian Giovanni Battista Tiepolo – that opens up like a sky above the visitor's head.

## Accommodation and food in Würzburg

Hotels in Würzburg are much more expensive than in neighbouring towns such as Sommerhausen, Iphofen or Volkach (*see pages 113 and 114*), and many charge extra for parking. Book ahead in autumn.

**Auf dem Steinberg €€** *Auf dem Steinberg; tel: (0931) 97020; fax: (0931) 97121; www.steinburg.com*. This 19th-century villa sits atop a hillside vineyard with imposing views of the city, the Würzburger Stein vineyard and the Festung Marienberg. It has a swimming pool, sauna and plenty of parking. Hungry locals from Würzburg seek out the restaurant.

**Hotel-Gasthof Zur Stadt Mainz €€** *Semmelstrasse 39; tel: (0931) 53155; fax: (0931) 58510; www.hotel-stadtmainz.de*. The Schwarzmann sisters are simply phenomenal. They treat hotel guests and devoted regulars in their restaurant (some have been coming for decades) like family. In the dining room, among the bric-à-brac and family photos, you will eat the best of Franconian cooking.

**Hotel Rebstock €€€** *Neubaustrasse 7; tel: (0931) 30930; fax: (0931) 3093 100; www.rebstock.com*. Chic Laura Ashley-style rooms lurk behind the historic rococo façade of this Old Town hotel. The *Weinstube* and more formal restaurant rely on the same talented chef for refined variations of Franconian cuisine.

## Suggested tour

**Total distance:** 100km; 112km with detour.

**Time:** 4 hours' driving, 8 hours for the main route, 9 with the detour. Those with limited time should concentrate on the Residenz in Würzburg, the castle in Weikersheim, the Herrgottkirche in Creglingen and Rothenburg.

**Links:** At the end of this route, the Romantic Road continues south on the B27 for 343km all the way to Füssen (*see page 62*). Würzburg is only 1 hour's drive from Frankfurt.

Leaving **WÜRZBURG** ❶, it doesn't make much difference whether you take the B27 or the *Autobahn* A3/A81 to the Tauber Valley, which you reach at **Tauberbischofsheim**, a typical Franconian wine town with a nice collection of half-timbered houses in its high street and a landmark tower, the Türmersturm (1250).

**Detour:** A lovely country road begins at **Gerlachsheim**, with a look at the stone bridge that spans the Wittigbach, and the onion-towered abbey church with a rococo interior. The road veers 6km past half-timbered farmhouses and water mills. After Grünsfeld (only 3km) turn to **Grünsfeldhausen**. You will soon reach the Romanesque **Achatiuskapelle** – an ancient church of two octagons propping up a single tower. Its purpose is a complete mystery but the nearby spring might have been used for healing or baptisms.

Carry on past Lauda-Königshofen to **BAD MERGENTHEIM** ❷ where you can visit the castle and museum of the German Teutonic Order.

**Detour:** The village of **Stuppach** is just 6km from Bad Mergentheim (going in the direction of Schwäbisch Hall). When experts peeked under a layer of 19th-century paint at the beginning of the 20th century, the village church found itself in possession of a rare masterpiece by Mathias Grünewald, one of the great artists of the late Middle Ages, whose experiments in light and colour anticipated modern schools of painting. The **Stuppacher Madonna** is his vision of paradise (*The Madonna im Garten, open Mar–Apr daily 1000–1700; May–Oct 0900–1700; Nov–Feb 1100–1600*).

Continue on the B27 to **WEIKERSHEIM** ❸. There is convenient free parking right near its Renaissance castle. Even if there is not time for a guided tour, take a walk through the playful baroque garden. After **CREGLINGEN** ❹ the Tauber Valley becomes narrow and the road intimate. You just squeeze by the quaint half-timbered farmhouses of Archshofen, Tauberzell and Bettwar and might have to brake for children and geese. The main road to Rothenburg bypasses **DETWANG** ❺ by a couple of hundred metres.

**Detour:** From Detwang, a rustic country road hugs the Tauber river and skirts the mills that once provided Rothenburg with flour, and the **Topplerschlösschen**, a Romanesque tower with a tiny moat built in 1388 as a summer home for mayor Heinrich Toppler. Follow the river further for a number of bends before crossing the **Doppelbrücke** (double bridge) and enter Rothenburg via the **Spitalbastion** (the road is closed to automobiles in the afternoon on Sundays and holidays).

Continue up the winding B27 to world-famous **ROTHENBURG OB DER TAUBER** ❻.

## Also worth exploring

Once the residence of the Franconian line of Hohenzollern princes, **Ansbach♦♦** (35km east of Rothenburg ob der Tauber) is a dreamy little town packed with medieval quaintness and baroque flair. Gabriel de Gabrieli turned the gloomy fortress of **Markgrafenschloss** into a baroque fairytale complete with a two-storey **Prunkraum** (Art Gallery), and **Spiegelkabinett** (Hall of Mirrors). The **Kachelsaal** (Porcelain Hall) has a collection of 2800 porcelain tiles. One of Bavaria's most famous modern works of art, the *Anscavallo* – a massive cubistic horse – dominates the square in front of the palace.

# A tour of wine heaven

**Ratings**

| | |
|---|---|
| Villages | ●●●●● |
| Vineyards | ●●●●● |
| Wine | ●●●●● |
| Architecture | ●●●●○ |
| Scenery | ●●●●○ |
| Food and drink | ●●●○○ |
| History | ●●●○○ |
| Nature | ●●●○○ |

The mysterious affinity between Catholicism and wine is summed up in the history of Würzburg and its surrounding towns. Monks first planted wine grapes here in the 8th century; in terms of quantity, production reached its height in the 16th century, with Würzburg's prince-bishops in control of most of the vineyards. They pushed cultivation to an extraordinary level of 100,000 hectares (today, quality takes precedence over quantity, with only about 6000 hectares of vineyards). No other wine region in Germany possesses such a density of medieval towns and villages and they have more than a hundred wine festivals between May and November. As the local proverb says, 'life is good in Franconia's wine heaven'. The region's country roads loop through vineyards and forests, skirt ancient city walls and pass beneath feudal towers. The distances are short but there is much to see. A tour of Franconia's cellars could take many days and it is hard to say which is most impressive, the architecture, local hospitality or wines by the glass.

## CASTELL✣

**🏛 Fürstlich Castell'sches Domäneamt** *Schlossplatz 5; tel: (09325) 401; fax: (09325) 980 789; www.castell.de.* An estate that goes back to the 11th century, famous for its honeyed dessert wines.

**Gerhard Roth** *Büttnergasse 11; tel: (09325) 373; fax: (09325) 528; www.weingut-roth.de.* The organic estate of Herr Roth supplies Franken with outstanding *Spätburgunder* (light red) wines.

After the Reformation, Castell became a Protestant enclave in an overwhelmingly Catholic region, but, like its neighbours, it continued to live and prosper from the wine trade. It remained the seat of its own tiny principality for centuries and still has the feel of a place apart. The Old Town straggles up a steep slope of the Steigerwald where the Grafen (Earls) of Castell ruled from castles (now ruined) on a high ridge. The **Neues Schloss** (1686–90) and its stately garden date from a more civilised time. The **Pfarrkirche** (1784–92) is admired as an early example of the neo-classical style.

### Food in Castell

**Weinstall €** *Schlossplatz.* A restaurant that adjoins the wine estate of Castell'sches Domäneamt and serves estate wines and solid regional fare. Closed Thursdays.

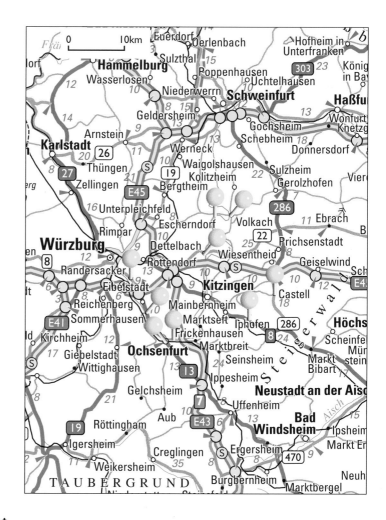

## DETTELBACH❖

**ⓘ Tourismus
Information**
*Rathausplatz 1; tel: (09324)
3560; fax: (09324) 4981;
www.dettelbach.de*

In 1484, when Dettelbach was elevated to the status of a city, it built the walls and 36 towers that you see today and, six years later, its splendid Gothic **Rathaus❖**, which also serves as a covered bridge over the Dettel river. Many sections of the wall now shelter shops, restaurants and wine cellars. Perhaps the ideal way to see it is simply to wander up and down the steep streets at random. You will easily identify the **Pfarrkirche St Augustin** by its two uneven towers. The church of **Maria im Sand❖** (1610–13), still an object of real devotion, is surrounded by vineyards. Inside, the baroque artist Michael Kern carved the entire genealogy of Christ on its extraordinary pulpit.

### Food in Dettelbach

**Himmelstoss €€** *Bamberger Strasse 3; tel: (09324) 4776.* Creative touches by chef Kuffer – cassoulet of oxtail and cabbage, sauerkraut quiche, carp bouillon with mussels – bring something new to local ingredients and recipes. His gracious wife manages the dining room and small inner courtyard. The wine comes from the restaurant's own estate.

# ESCHERNDORF✥

**Weingut Egon Schäffer** *Astheimer Strasse 17; tel: (09831) 9350; www.weingut-schaefferi.de. Open Mon–Sat 0800–1900 (best to call ahead for appointment).* The estate makes celestial Silvaner as well as *Birnen* (Pear) schnapps and wine vinegar.

**Weingut Michael Fröhlich**
*Bocksbeutelstrasse 41; tel: (09831) 2847; fax: (09831) 71360.* In addition to the fine Silvaner, try their pale reds made from *Schwarzriesling* (a type of Pinot grape).

**Zehnthof-Weinstuben**
*Hauptstrasse 2; tel: (09381) 1702; fax: (09381) 4379.* This is a great place to try *Meefischle* (Main fish) and wine from up the hill.

The inhabitants of this village live at the foot of a steep hill – named *Lump* – that they are devoted to body and soul. It may not sound like much but it happens to be one of the choicest bits of wine real estate in Germany and certainly brings a lump to the throat of anyone who has ever tasted its Silvaner and Riesling wines. The whole village rolls up its sleeves for the harvest in autumn and an odour of crushed grapes hangs in the air. They celebrate with a wine festival every weekend in September and October (before and after the stresses of the harvest).

# FRICKENHAUSEN✥

The way in and out of Frickenhausen is the same as it was five centuries ago – through one of four gates (Ochsenfurter, Oberes, Marktbreiter and Wassertor). Few towns even in this historic region can offer such a complete immersion in the past. Its dry white wines are produced on the south-facing slope of the Kapelleberg.

# IPHOFEN❖❖

📍 **Johann Ruck**
*Marktplatz 19;*
tel: *(09323) 800 800;*
*www.ruckwein.de.*
Herr Ruck has won
universal respect for his
loyalty to traditional
methods of winemaking
and the extraordinary
wines that it produces.

**Weingut Hans
Wirsching** *Ludwigstrasse
16; tel: (09323) 87330;
www.wirsching.de.* This wine
estate has been in the
same family for 15
generations and produces
classic Franken wines,
which were chosen during
visits by the Pope and
Queen Elizabeth.

Iphofen has been called a 'Rothenburg in miniature', but it has something more than history and architecture – it has the age-old culture and business of wine. The town's vines thrive in the soil of the nearby hillsides. The best known vineyards – Kalb, Julius-Echterberg and Kronsberg – produce sensual Silvaner and earthy Riesling. Where the vines end, the Steigerwald begins, a dense forest that provides wild game for the region's cooks. The fine market square has an oversized, three-storey baroque **Rathaus** and the **St Veitskirch**, noted for its late-Gothic stained-glass windows and the *Beautiful Madonna of Iphofen*, carved by Tilman Riemenschneider (*see page 105*). Its most famous landmark is the **Rödelseer Tor**, a crazy half-timbered gatehouse that seems to collapse before your very eyes.

## Wine festivals and towns

The wine towns around Würzburg hold over 100 Weinfeste between May and October. In many places, a Wine Queen is elected, not just for her beauty – she must know her wine. There is no better opportunity to savour Franconian food and sample local vintages.

Paradoxically, a visit to 'wine heaven' requires discipline. It is important not to rush for there is a lot to see in a small geographical area. On the other hand, it would be easy to halt at the first town, have a couple of glasses of wine and let the day slip away. Last but not least, drivers must resist temptation – German laws are very strict where drinking and driving are concerned (see page 28).

# OCHSENFURT❖

For a vivid example of what an old Franconian high street looked like in the 15th and 16th centuries, visit Hauptstrasse in Ochsenfurt. Its gabled half-timbered houses line the street between the gates of the Klingentor and Oberemtor and the most interesting building of all is the **Neues Rathaus**❖ ('new' Town Hall, 1488–99) crowned by an odd mechanical clock. Every hour two oxen butt heads, a figure of Death flips an hourglass and a carved wooden man peeks out the window. What does it mean? The oxen represent the founding of the city, the wooden man is a symbol for its proud citizenry, and Death, of course, reminds us where it all leads.

# Randersacker*

**Weingut Martin Göbel** *Friedhofstrasse 9; tel: (0931) 709 380; www.weingut-martin-goebel.de.* A visit to the cemetery is a must because this wine estate is just beyond it. The family has been in the business since the 17th century and knows how to make robust Silvaner. The Rieslaner, a dessert wine, is sumptuous.

This is a town of family-owned wine estates and first-class vineyards – Teufelskeller, Pfülben, Marsberg and Sonnenstuhl – whose limestone soils produce Riesling, Silvaner and Traminer. Beneath its narrow streets and half-timbered houses is an unrivalled network of wine cellars. Above ground, the most interesting building is the **Fürstbischöfliche Zehnthof*** (Prince-Bishops' tithe house).

### Food in Randersacker

**Bären €** *Würzburgerstrasse 6; tel: (0931) 70510; fax: (0931) 706 415.* This sturdy old inn has a leafy inner courtyard where you can eat and drink Franconian-style in summer.

# Sommerhausen*

Thanks to a colony of artists living here, Sommerhausen is home to art galleries and one of the Germany's most aesthetic Christmas markets. The country's smallest theatre is located in the **Torturmtheater** (50 seats), founded by Luigi Malpiero and now under the direction of actor and painter Veit Relin. It was the birthplace of Franz Pastorius, who founded the first German settlement in the United States in 1683 (Germantown, now part of Philadelphia). In Hauptstrasse, there is a small **Schloss**, a **Rathaus** and **Pfarrkirche**.

### Accommodation and food in Sommerhausen

**Weinhaus Düll €€** *Maingasse 5; tel: (09333) 220; fax: (09333) 8208; www.weinhaus-duell.de.* Travellers have been sleeping and dining in this inn since the 16th century. The restaurant menu is based on local game and vegetables, wild berries and Sommerhausen wines.

**Mönchshof €** *Mönchshof 7; tel: (09333) 758; fax: (09333) 974 710; www.moenchshof-brennerei.de.* Set in its own courtyard, this modest inn offers comfortable rooms above a medieval cellar. The owners proudly serve local wines and the schnapps is home-made.

# Volkach**

**Tourismus Information** *Rathaus 1; tel: (09381) 40112; e-mail: tourismus@ volkach.de; www.volkach.de*

Depending on which direction you arrive from, you can enter Volkach through a 13th-century gatehouse or a 16th-century gatehouse. The city's battered walls encircle a medley of historic buildings. The half-timbered **Rathaus** (1544) is the easiest to find. In the tiny Schelfengasse lurks its most elegant building: the 15th-century **Schelfenhaus** (No 1), decorated by a baroque artist named Vogel ('bird'), who left a sculpted bird as his business card. **Maria im Weingarten Pilgerkirche** (Our Lady of the Vineyard Pilgrimage Church) houses the **Rosenkranz-madonna**∗ (Madonna with Rosary; 1524) – the last Madonna created by Tilman Riemenschneider. She stands on a crescent moon hanging from the ceiling. One of the most famous works of art in Bavaria, it was stolen and held for ransom in 1962. The editor of *Stern* magazine paid DM100,000 for its return. From the church there is a panorama of Volkach, the vineyards and the Main river and valley. Volkach celebrates with a wine festival every weekend in October and November.

## Accommodation and food in Volkach

**Am Torturm** € *Hauptstrasse 41; tel: (09381) 80670; fax: (09381) 806 744; www.hotel-am-torturm.de.* A small hotel with a lovely courtyard and modern interior; it stands next to one of the city's old gatehouses.

**Zur Schwane** €€ *Hauptstrasse 12; tel: (09381) 80660; fax: (09381) 806 666; e-mail: schwane@romantik.de; www.romantikhotels.com/volkach.* This inn, one of the oldest in Franconia, has everything – romantic rooms upstairs, refined traditional cooking and its own wine estate. It's all *wunderbar.*

**Right**
The Rosenkranzmadonna

**Above**
Vineyards on the slopes below
Würzburg's Festung Marienberg

## Suggested tour

**Total distance:** 142km. Add 22km for the detour to Schwanberg.

**Time:** The driving time is only 2½ hours, but it is hard to do justice to a dozen wine towns in just 1 day. If your main purpose is to taste and buy wine, set your sights on Randsacker, Iphofen, Escherndorf and Volkach.

**Links:** From Würzburg, the *Romantische Strasse* continues 343km to Füssen (*see pages 54–71*).

Driving south out of **Würzburg** along the B13, prepare yourself for **RANDERSACKER ❶**, one of the most important wine towns in the

**◐ Romantik Hotel
Zehntkeller €€**
*Bahnhofstrasse 12, Iphofen,
tel: (09323) 8440; fax:
(09323) 844 123; e-mail:
zehntkeller@romantikhotels.
com; www.romantikhotels.com/
iphofen.* The former
residence of a prince-
bishop, tucked away in its
own park, has acquired
modern comforts thanks
to Herr Seufert, the
affable, English-speaking
owner. His wine pairs well
with tasty Franconian
specialities in the
restaurant.

region, which also has an attractive Altstadt (Old Town) up its sleeve. It is only 5km further south on the B13 to **SOMMERHAUSEN ❷**, where the heady combination of wine and history has attracted a colony of artists. You must cross the Main river to enter the Old Town of **OCHSENFURT ❸**. It occupies a walled quadrant at the southern tip of the *Maindreieck* ('Main Triangle') and prospers thanks to a nearby sugar factory and the fertile soil of its surrounding farms and, of course, vines. Cross back over the Main and turn right (east) on the *Landstrasse* on the north shore of the river. The weathered grey walls of **FRICKENHAUSEN ❹** will soon appear. At Segnitz, the river bends north.

**Detour:** Cross the bridge over the Main again to visit **Marktbreit**. On the way, you will pass an 18th-century wooden crane on the shore of the Main. Its **Rathaus** (1579) rivals the one in Ochsenfurt. It has the scenic advantage of a location on a bridge over the Breitbach stream. Marktbreit's baroque and Renaissance Altstadt was built in its most prosperous days (16th to 18th centuries) when it was the trading centre in the Earldom of Schwarzenberg.

**Sulzfeld am Main** is a cluster of grey stone houses behind a fortified wall. It is not picture-perfect but truly old and pastoral. Depending on the time of year, it smells of crushed grapes, fresh vegetables or dung. The local Zehnthof Winery impresses the palate with its Silvaner, Riesling and dessert wines. **Kitzingen**, the next major town, is famous for asparagus as well as wine. Its wobbly old tower, the **Falterturm**, overflows with masks, costumes and other clownish accessories – all part of the **Deutsches Fastnachtsmuseum** ('German Carnival Museum'; *open weekends only*). From Kitzingen, take the B8 south to **IPHOFEN ❺**, enter through one of four gates and look for the Market Square (no problem parking); try to find your way out through the quirky **Rödelseer Tor**.

**Detour:** North of Iphofen, take the *Landstrasse* going northwest that is signposted **Rödelsee**. The sleepy wine village, which stores its treasured vintages beneath the **Crailsheimer Schloss**, appears after 4km. The road turns northwest towards Wiesenbronn. Watch for the sign that says **Schloss Schwanberg** and veer right up the steep (11 per cent) road that twists and turns to get there. It passes through vineyards until halfway up and then dips into a mixed (evergreen and deciduous) forest. At the summit are meadows where rare wild flowers bloom exuberantly in spring. The view from the Schloss sweeps from the vineyards of the Main Valley across to the other peaks in the Steigerwald. The Schloss itself is most impressive for its huge park. Back at the foot of Schwanberg, carry on to **CASTELL ❻** by way of Wiesenbronn and Trautberg, or return to Iphofen.

From Iphofen, follow the signs for Birklingen. This road winds uphill through a corner of the Steigerwald and into a dense mass of beech trees before emerging on to a plateau beneath a mountain called Vogelgesang ('birdsong'). At the village of Birklingen, turn left (north) on the B286 and descend to Castell. Its Altstadt and wine estates are on a steep hillside of the Steigerwald. From Castell, continue on the B286 a short distance to Rüdenhausen where you will curve around a Gothic Wasserschloss ('Water Castle') wallowing in its little moat; watch for a sign on the left for Feuerbach and Atzhausen. A modest, pretty road passes under the *Autobahn*, through forest, farms and vineyards. At Düllstadt, turn left on the B22, which soon crosses the Main. Higgedly-piggedly **DETTELBACH** ❼ is so old and odd you might forget to drop a gear as the car climbs past its weathered grey walls, which seem to crisscross the town instead of encircling it. You have to pay for parking on many of the streets in the Altstadt. The road heads further uphill towards Neuses am Berg. After climbing a steep (10 per cent) incline, you will cross a plateau planted with vines and descend to the Main again and the riverside town of **ESCHERNDORF** ❽. Cruise around a long mellow bend in the river and follow the signs for **VOLKACH** ❾. The Altstadt funnels traffic in and out through its 16th-century Gaibacher and Sommeracher towers. Volkach's greatest artistic treasure, the **Maria im Weingarten Pilgerkirche (Pilgrimage Church)**, is on a hill outside the town – the same distance that separated Jerusalem from Golgotha based on medieval calculations. Go left just north of town on the *Landstrasse* that intersects the B286. An ancient road takes charge of the last 150m, lined in stone and punctuated by the Stations of the Cross. A Mercedes is too wide though an economy rental has been known to squeeze through. There is a viewpoint that allows you to study the landscape you have just driven through: the Main, its valley and hillsides blanketed in rows of vines, each one aligned to catch the sun. The road back to Würzburg is clearly signposted and uneventful.

## Franconian wine

The wines of Franconia are unlike anything you will drink on the Rhine. They are dry, earthy and rich in herbal aroma. The traditional grape is the Silvaner, but the humble Müller Thurgau, a workaday grape in other regions, develops more personality here. Though difficult to cultivate, the Riesling is unspeakably good. Franconia uses its own distinctive bottle: a flat, round-shouldered flask known as a *Bocksbeutel* ('goat's scrotum'). Wine connoisseurs, after studiously sniffing and parsing a glass of Franconian wine, will detect the perfume of hedge roses, scents of blackthorn and hints of peach. When Pope John Paul II visited Bavaria in 1980, he used Franconian wine at Mass and commented 'I knew already there was truth in wine but it is the first time I have found love there, too.' The novelist Kurt Tucholsky, after a bottle of Iphöfer Kronsberg, expressed his regret that he couldn't 'caress' it. Germany's greatest poet, Goethe, didn't bother with words. He simply drank it, in great quantities, purchasing 900 litres in one year alone.

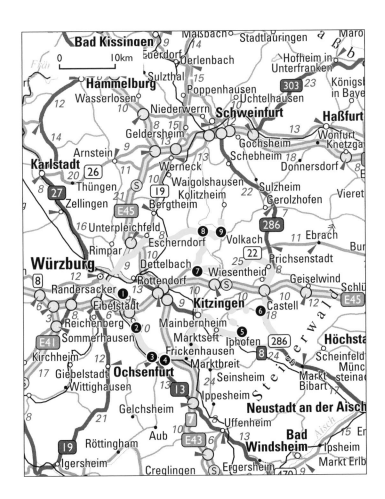

## Also worth exploring

While driving the suggested tour, turn right (east) at Düllstadt on to the B22 for a pastoral and occasionally forested stretch of road to **Ebrach Abbey** (25km). Two big-name baroque architects, J L Dientzenhofer and Balthasar Neumann, worked in succession on the interior. The abbey, alas, is now a prison for juveniles. Ebrach is intersected by the wild **Steigerwald-Höhenstrasse**. Take it going either south (shorter) or north (longer) and use the *Autobahn* (A3 or A70) to return to the Würzburg area. This lonely road follows a forested ridge once used by Celts and Romans; in their day, it was easier to walk on the mountain ridges and avoid the (then) swampy valleys.

# Bamberg

## Ratings

| | |
|---|---|
| Architecture | ●●●●● |
| Beer | ●●●●● |
| Churches | ●●●●● |
| History | ●●●●● |
| Entertainment | ●●●○○ |
| Food | ●●●○○ |
| Scenery | ●●●○○ |
| Nature | ●●○○○ |

In the Middle Ages, German monks referred to Bamberg as *caput orbis* – 'capital of the world' – and for many centuries a pillar stood on its cathedral square called the *Erdnabel* (earth's navel). Today, the navel is gone, but Bamberg has another claim to fame: it is simply the most beautiful city in Germany. Ironically, most foreign tourists seem never to have heard of it. The numerous wars in Germany's history left the unwalled town almost unscathed and, for over a thousand years, bishops, monks, merchants and townsfolk built on its seven hills and on the banks and islands of the Regnitz river. A walk through Bamberg is a tour of European architecture: medieval streets, cobblestone squares, baroque palaces, rococo pleasure gardens, walled monasteries and a cathedral graced by some of the country's finest sculpture. For all its artistic treasures, Bamberg is not a museum piece, rather it is a lively city, thanks to its university students, a renowned symphony orchestra and ten local breweries.

## Sights

**ⓘ Tourismus & Kongress Service**
*Geyerswörthstrasse 3; tel: (0951) 2976 200; www.stadt.bamberg.de. Open Mon–Fri 0900–1800, Sat 0900–1500; May–Oct also Sun 1000–1400.*

**Ⓛ Ludwig Porcelain and Faience**
*collection € Obere Brücke 1; tel: (0951) 871 871; fax: (0951) 871 464. Open Tue–Sun 0930–1630.*

### Altes Rathaus❖❖

The Town Hall is perhaps the oddest building in Bavaria. It owes its bizarre location to the bitter strife between the bishops and the *Bürger* of Bamberg (the bishops won more often than not and many merchants emigrated to Nürnberg). A sandbar in the middle of the Regnitz was the only neutral ground they could find for a Town Hall. It marked the boundary between religious and civil authority. This division is symbolised by the bishop's coat of arms on one side and the civil coat of arms on the other. It is a mostly Gothic building (1450–63) with baroque balconies. The 18th-century allegorical murals depict virtues that sovereigns are supposed to possess (but rarely did in the history of Bamberg). The **Ludwig Porcelain and Faience collection** is housed indoors.

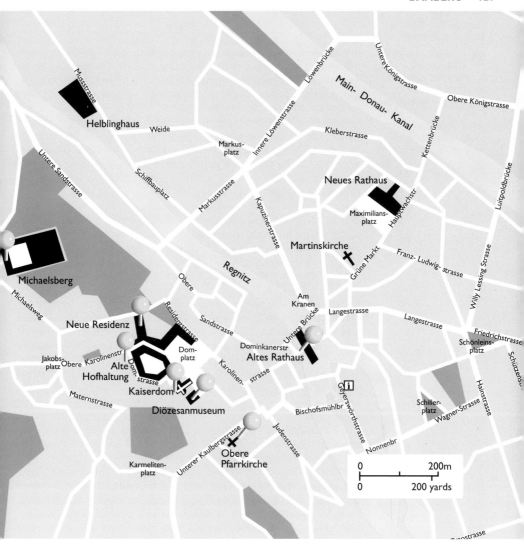

### Alte Hofhaltung*

Although it looks like an oversize medieval barnyard, the Old Court was, in its day, a palace. Heinrich II and the bishops of Bamberg lived there after it became a bishopric in 1007. Most of what you see today dates from the 15th and 16th centuries. The entrance to the 'Old Court' is through the **Reiche Tor**, a Renaissance gateway graced by a relief of the Virgin Mary. The other reliefs depict Heinrich and his queen, Kunigunde, with a model of the cathedral in their arms; and St Peter and St George accompanied by allegorical figures of the Main and Pegnitz rivers. Next to it stands the fine **Chancery Building**, built

**Diözesanmuseum**
€ *Domplatz 5;*
*tel: (0951) 502 325;*
*fax: (0951) 502 320.*
*Open Tue–Sun 1000–1700.*
There is also a delightful
collection of Nativity
scenes from all over the
world on the ground floor.

in the style of the German Renaissance by Bishop Veit II; the architect, Asmus Braun, is portrayed at the bishop's foot. The cobbled inner courtyard is surrounded by half-timbered buildings with wooden galleries and massive eaves that were used to store provisions. The complex was once linked to the cathedral. They are being restored and remodelled in order to provide more room for the modest **Historisches Museum**, now housed in the Ratstube. In the summer, *Life is a Dream*, the famous Spanish play by Calderón de la Barca, is performed in the open courtyard as part of the Calderón Festival.

### Diözesanmuseum*

The museum occupies the former chapterhouse, built between 1730 and 1733 by Balthasar Neumann, who succeeded in making his baroque style blend harmoniously with the much older cathedral. The collection offers what is left of the old cathedral treasury after many plunderings (including those by the ruling family of Bavaria, the Wittelsbachs) and the original figures from the **Adam's Portal** of the cathedral, moved indoors to protect them from further weathering. Its real glory, however, is the unique collection of fabrics displayed in the **Stone Chamber** on the first floor. The **Emperor Henry's Star Mantle** was a gift from an Italian prince in 1020; the **Choir Mantle of Kunigunde** and the **Shroud of Bishop Gunther** were both woven in Byzantium in the 11th century. The vestments of Pope Clement II (d 1047), taken from his tomb in 1942, constitute the oldest papal wardrobe in existence.

### Kaiserdom***

The cathedral of St Peter and St George is one of Germany's most important monuments from the Middle Ages. Construction began in 1215, on the site of two earlier cathedrals that burned down in 1081 and 1185. The builders intentionally worked in an old-fashioned, Romanesque style to recall the cathedral of Heinrich II, who had been canonised in 1146. However, the influence of modish Gothic made itself felt within a few years, hence the east chancel is Romanesque and the west early Gothic. Between them runs a nave with elements of both styles. The cathedral is extraordinary for the quality and variety of sculpture: *The Last Judgement* on the **Fürstenportal*** (Princes' Portal, 1228) on the north side of the nave is a masterpiece of Romanesque carving. The cathedral's most famous work of art is inside: the **Bamberger Reiter*** (c 1235) has been identified with the essence of chivalry though it depicts an unarmed man. He might represent Constantine the Great, one of the Three Magi, or King Stephen of Hungary; no one knows. There are many other notable sculptures in the east choir: a youthful, pregnant Virgin, and, next to her, the figure of Elizabeth – also called **The Bamberg Sibyl***. The female figures of **Synagogue*** and **Ecclesia*** personified Judaism and Christianity respectively in the medieval Christian mind: the former is blindfolded,

🏛 **Fränkisches Brauereimuseum**
€ *Michaelsberg 10f; tel: (0951) 53016. Open Apr–Oct Wed–Sun 1300–1600.* This small museum teaches the visitor about the methods of monastic brewing; you will see how they make *Benediktiner Dunkel* and sample it at the end of the tour.

looking undernourished and holding a broken staff; the buxom Ecclesia, the symbol of triumphant Christianity, wears a crown and a happy face. The sainted 11th-century rulers Emperor Heinrich II and Queen Kunigunde are buried in the marble **Imperial Tomb⁺⁺** in the centre of the nave. Scenes from their life cover the top and sides – one of the crowning achievements of Tilman Riemenschneider (*see page 105*) who worked on it for 14 years. On the left side of the west chancel is a late work by Veit Stoss, the **Weinachtsaltar⁺** (Nativity Altar, 1520). The western choir also holds the tomb of Pope Clement II (not accessible to the public) – the only pope buried north of the Alps.

### Michaelsberg⁺

A fortified monastery in the Middle Ages, Michaelsberg was rebuilt and expanded in the baroque style of Leonhard and Johann Dientzenhofer between 1696 and 1725. The vaulted ceiling of **Michaelskirche⁺**, called the 'Heavenly Garden', illustrates 600 plants with botanical precision. The last resting place of a famous Bishop, Otto the Holy, is behind the altar. Beneath his tomb there is a narrow gap. Crawling through the gap three times is supposed to be the definitive cure for backache. The **Holy Sepulchre Chapel⁺** (enter from the end of the right aisle) has to rank as one of the strangest chapels in Germany. Once used as a burial chamber, it has morbid, artistically refined scenes of death on the ceiling and in stucco relief. Death comes to take away the children and the elderly, rich and poor – all typical themes, but Death also blows soap bubbles and, assuming a Hamlet-like pose, seems to reflect on himself while looking at a skull. Outside, in the courtyard, the **Frankisches Brauereimuseum⁺** occupies a wing of the monastery. The terrace garden has wonderful views of Bamberg and a leafy *Biergarten*.

**Neue Residenz €**
*Domplatz 8; tel: (0951)
519 390; fax: (0951) 5193
9129. Open daily Apr–Sept
0900–1800, Thur until
2000; Oct–Mar
1000–1600. The palace has
a rococo rose garden and
café – a perfect place to
rest and study the city
rooftops and the Kloster
Michaelsberg.*

## Neue Residenz*

The huge L-shaped baroque palace facing the cathedral square was built for the Bamberg Prince-Bishop Lothar Franz von Schönborn (1693–1729), a talented and impulsive man. It was finished in 1703 as it stands today, the work of Leonhard Dientzenhofer. Inside, there are vivid frescoes in the **Kaisersaal** and richly furnished staterooms – only accessible by a guided tour. The small **Staatsgalerie** (State Gallery) is rather neglected although it does have a couple of notable paintings such as *Lucretia* by Lucas Cranach and *The Flood* by Hans Baldung Grien.

**Konzert- und Kongresshalle**
**Stadthallen** *Mussstrasse 1;*
*tel: (0951) 9647 200;*
*fax: (0951) 9647 222;*
*e-mail: info@konzerthalle-*
*bamberg.de;*
*www.konzerthalle-*
*bamberg.de*

**Obere Pfarrkirche**

Nicknamed 'Our Dear Lady', this church was the city's largest civil building project in the 14th century, privately financed by wealthy citizens who left their coats of arms (*Bäckerwappen*) on the ceiling of the tower. It was begun in 1338 and almost completed in 1420. The tower, built as a stopgap, has stood there ever since; indeed, it served as the city watch-tower from 1478 to 1926. The vast canvas by Tintoretto in the right aisle, showing the ascension of Mary to heaven, was a truly revolutionary work of art in its day (1500), particularly for a conservative city such as Bamberg.

# Entertainment

The Deutsches Orchester of Prague fled to Bamberg after the war and later changed their name to the Bamberger Symphoniker. Today, they enjoy an international reputation and and perform in a new riverside concert hall with striking acoustics. Some of its members have created the Bamberg Baroque Ensemble.

# Accommodation and food

**Barock-Hotel €€** *Vorderer Bach 4; tel: (0951) 54031; fax (0951) 54021.* A stately baroque building in a narrow street behind the cathedral. The rooms inside have solid, contemporary furnishings.

**Romantik Hotel Weinhaus Messerschmitt €€€** *Lange Strasse 41; tel: (0951) 297 800; fax: (0951) 297 8029; www.hotel-messerschmitt.de.* A quiet refuge of Persian rugs and polished antiques, this hotel has been in the same family for many generations. In the Hubertusstube restaurant, wild game, suckling pig cooked in beer, and freshwater fish are on the menu.

**Left**
Neue Residenz

**St Nepomuk €€** *Obere Mühlbrücke 9; tel: (0951) 98420; fax: (0951) 9842 100; www.hotel-nepomuk.de.* This hotel is a modern half-timbered building – a rare fake in Bamberg, but it has a dream location on an island in the middle of the river, and a welcoming staff.

Normally, you can eat well in a brewery. They tend to serve specialties such as *Blaue Zipfel* (small sausages stewed in vinegar and herbs), *Bier Hax'n* (pork knuckle with beer sauce), *Spanferkel* (suckling pig) and, in season, venison and wild boar.

The following breweries double as affordable hotels:

**Fässla €** *Obere Königsstrasse 19; tel: (0951) 22998; www.faessla.de*

**Braurei Spezial €** *Obere Königsstrasse 10; tel: (0951) 24304; www.bierstadt.de/spezial*

**Greifenklau €** *Laurenziplatz 20; tel: (0951) 59599; www.greifenklau.de*

## Suggested tour

**Total distance**: 2.5km walking, 5km with detours. Add 50km driving (return) to go to Schloss Weissenstein.

**Time**: Bamberg and its thousand years of history are worth at least a day. If you have less time than that, concentrate on the Dom (cathedral) and the Domplatz (cathedral square). It is futile to look for a parking place in the middle of the city. There are underground

**Above**
The Altes Rathaus

parking garages near Maximiliansplatz, the tourist office (Tiefgarage GeyersWörth), and in Schützenstrasse. P+R (Park and Ride, *see page 28*) car parks are located on Heinrichsdam along the Main-Donau-Kanal, and near Laurenziplatz.

Begin a walking tour in **Maximilliansplatz**, surrounded by the fruit and vegetables of its daily market and dominated by the **Neues Rathaus** ('New' Town Hall), of Balthasar Neumann. It leads into the **Grüne Markt**, a baroque avenue with department stores – the 17th-century bronze Neptune looks forlorn in his fountain. The Jesuit church of **Martinskirche** was built in only seven years (1686–93) by the Dientzenhofer brothers, who were responsible for much baroque splendour in Prague as well as Bamberg. Step inside for a moment to admire the *trompe l'œil* ceiling. Continue on to Lange Strasse, and turn right until you see the **ALTES RATHAUS** ❶ sitting on an island in the middle of the Regnitz river and straddling two bridges, the Obere Brücke and the Untere Brücke. Pause on the right-hand Untere Brücke for delightful views in both directions. **Klein-Venedig**, a row of medieval fisherfolk houses is to the right (downstream) and the ancient tanners' quarter is upstream. The hills on the far side of the river are thick with church spires belonging to the cathedral, churches and former monasteries atop Bamberg's main hills, the part of the city known as the Domstadt (Cathedral City), while the area at the bottom of the hill was called the Bürgerstadt (Citizens' City). Cross the river and make a U-turn into the Town Hall's stone gateway above the Obere Brücke. From here, retrace your steps to the river bank again.

**Detour:** Walk left a few paces and you will see yet another bridge, of iron this time. Walk out on to it for the best view (and picture) of the Rathaus and its half-timbered annexe that juts out over the water. If you continue on the footbridge and go right down Geyerswörthstrasse you will see the tourist information office to your left, as well as a large baroque palace, the **Schloss Geyerswörth**. Ask at the office for a key to the Schlossturm (Tower) to get an elevated view of the city from its tower.

**Beer Trail**

If you want to follow *Der Bierweg* ('beer trail'), ask the tourist office for their pamphlet about the city's breweries. It is in German but comes with a map.

Walk up Karolinenstrasse to the Domplatz. The square offers a thousand-year panorama of European architecture from the partly Romanesque **KAISERDOM** ❷ to Gothic, Renaissance and baroque styles in the surrounding buildings. The **DIÖZESANMUSEUM** ❸ is adjacent to the Dom. The **NEUE RESIDENZ** ❹ is on the opposite side of the square. Duck beneath the **Reiche Tor**, a magnificent gate, into the **ALTE HOFHALTUNG** ❺. The Domstrasse is at the rear of the uneven courtyard. It's uphill from here along Obere Karolinenstrasse to Jakobsplatz and right on Michaelsweg, then further uphill to the former Benedictine Abbey of **Michaelsberg**.

**Detour:** Retrace your steps to Jakobsplatz, cross the square and follow

**Schloss Weissenstein €**
Schlossplatz 1,
Pommersfelden; tel: (09548)
98180. Guided tours
Apr–Oct Tue–Sun
1000–1700. Young
musicians come from all
over the world in summer
to perform in the
Schlosskonzerte.

Maternstrasse down and uphill to the Karmeliten Kloster then down again via Unterer Kaulbergstrasse to the 14th-century **OBERE PFARRKIRCHE ❻**. Carry on down the same street to a small square and make a right on Judenstrasse. Bamberg had a signficant Jewish community in the Middle Ages that was forced to leave after about 1420; this was their neighbourhood. The street leads to a pair of baroque palaces built by a *nouveau riche* court official a couple of centuries later. The **Böttingerhaus** (No 14), probably the work of Johann Dientzenhofer, joyfully bulges out into the narrow street with an overbite of ostentatious stucco work just across from the **Klosterbräu** (entrance on *Obere Mühlbrücke*), one of Bamberg's most ancient breweries. The same Herr Böttinger also built a pleasure palace on the water, the **Wasserschloss Concordia**, located at the end of the Concordiastrasse. For the best view of it, retrace your steps to the beginning of Concordiastrasse, turn into the alleyway that leads to the river, cross the Obere Mühl Brücke on to Geyerswörth island and walk back in the same direction along the opposite shore. The Nonnenbrücke (Nuns Bridge) links the island with the northern bank of the Regnitz river and Schillerplatz where there is a small museum devoted to E T A Hoffmann, the Romantic writer whose stories inspired Tchaikovsky's *The Nutcracker* and *The Tales of Hoffmann* by Jacques Offenbach.

From the terrace of **Michaelsberg** there is a garden footpath – the Benediktinerweg – that leads through an orchard down to the lower city; it ends in a square. Cross to the left and carry on (right) down Obere Sandstrasse and follow its curves into Dominkanerstrasse, a narrow winding street crammed with medieval half-timbered residences. The **Schlenkerla** (No 6) is a brewery that occupies two late-Gothic vaulted rooms; it serves *Rauchbier* (smoked beer) and local dishes such as Bamberger onion – stuffed with beef and stewed in beer sauce and a thin variety of *Bratwurst*.

## Also worth exploring

It is a 25km drive south to **Schloss Weissenstein**, built about the same time as the Bamberg Residenz by the energetic Prince-Bishop Lothar Franz von Schönborn so that he could spend his summers here at the edge of the Steigerwald forest. The palace's three-storeyed staircase is an architectural wonder almost without precedent; to this day, art historians debate whether or not there existed a similar set of steps in Italy before its construction. It greatly influenced Balthasar Neumann's more famous staircase in Würzburg (*see page 106*). The summer palace also has a major picture gallery with works by Rubens, van Dyck, and other Old Masters; as well as the things no self-respecting baroque bishop could live without: a **Spiegelkabinett** ('Hall of Mirrors'), **Marmorsaal** ('Hall of Marble') and **English Garden**.

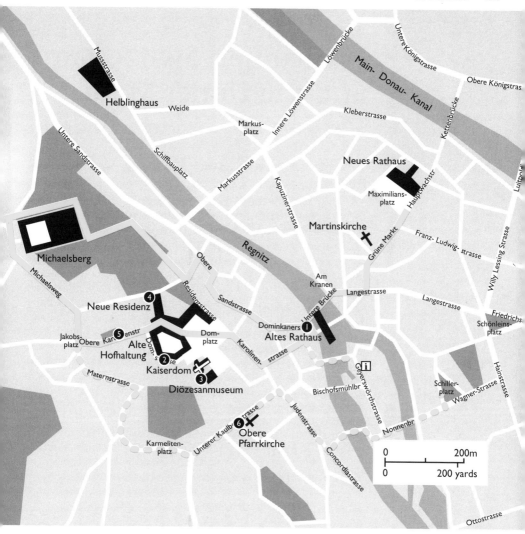

## Beer culture

Bamberg is a town where *Bierkultur* reigns supreme, in stark contrast to the Würzburg region (*see page 106*). It claims to have the highest per-capita beer consumption in the world. Ten Bamberg breweries produce something like 50 kinds of beers, including *Rauchbier*, made with smoked malt – it tastes a bit like liquid smoked ham. If you don't like it, remember that there are 49 other beers to sample, depending on the season. Most breweries put a special *Bockbier* on tap around Christmas, a *Starkbier* after Lent, and something special for the spring, too.

# Franconian Switzerland and the Upper Main Valley

## Ratings

| | |
|---|---|
| Architecture | ●●●●● |
| Castles | ●●●●● |
| Churches | ●●●●● |
| History | ●●●●● |
| Scenery | ●●●●○ |
| Geology | ●●●○○ |
| Nature | ●●●○○ |
| Food and drink | ●●○○○ |

The Fränkische Schweiz (Franconian 'Switzerland') is the over-the-top name given by German Romantics to the large stretch of land roughly bounded by the Regnitz, Pegnitz and Main rivers. It is a sparsely populated land of lush meadows and flowering apple groves lined with deep valleys such as the Weisental, and dotted with strange rock cliffs. The region's glory is a pair of baroque churches on opposite sides of the Main Valley – the Cistercian pilgrimage church of Vierzehnheligen and the Benedictine Kloster Banz. The rococo rock garden in Sanspareil evokes the whimsy of a Prussian princess and medieval mill houses still turn noiselessly in many streams. Coburger Land is further north, a corner of Bavaria famous for the 'royal stud farm' of Saxe-Coburg-Gotha – an amazing dynasty that provided a consort to Queen Victoria (among others). The region has also made a name for itself as a centre for toys and dolls. Bavaria's greatest castle, the 'Crown of Franconia', occupies a crag above the town of Coburg and jealously guards a horde of princely armour and paintings by Old German Masters.

## COBURG✦✦

**ⓘ Tourismus Information**
*Herrngasse 4; tel: (09561) 74180; fax: (09561) 741 829; www.coburg-tourist.de*

**ⓔ Ehrenburg €**
*Schlossplatz 1; tel: (09561) 80880; fax: (09561) 808 840; www.sgvcoburg.de. Open Tue–Sun Apr–Sept 0900–1700; Oct–Mar 1000–1500. Hourly guided tours.*

For many centuries, The Herzogtum ('Duchy') of Coburg was the seat of the Saxe-Coburg-Gotha, a family that married its way into monarchies all over Europe, creating dynastic ties with the courts at St Petersburg, London, Stockholm and Lisbon. It is astonishing to realise that, at one time, the ensemble of princes and princesses of this one little Duchy ruled approximately half of the planet. The lavish Renaissance palace of **Ehrenburg✦** – the city residence of the Saxe-Coburg-Gothas from 1547 onwards – was substantially renovated in the 19th century with neo-Gothic features and mod cons that included Germany's first water-closet (now on display) for Queen Victoria. But there is far more to Coburg than Victoriana. The well-preserved **Altstadt** is a potpourri of Renaissance and early baroque styles. The **Stadtplatz** is its heart, adorned by a late 16th-century **Rathaus** and **Stadthaus** (c 1600).

**Naturkundemuse-
um** € *Park 6; tel:
(09561) 808 120;
www.naturkunde-museum-
coburg.de. Open daily
0900–1200, 1330–1700.*

People who like the
porcelain figurines
designed by Franciscan nun
M I Hummel can watch
them being made and
purchase them direct at
the **Goebel factory**
*(Coburgstrasse 7;
tel: (09563) 920;
www.goebel.de. Open
Mon–Fri 0900–1700, Sat
0900–1200) in the small
town of Rödental, just
northeast of Coburg.*

Franconian
Switzerland has lots of
guesthouses, private rooms
and camping – all of it
affordable and delightfully
uncrowded, even in
summer. Contact the
**Tourismuszentrale
Fränkische Schweiz**
*(Postfach 1262, D-91317
Ebermannstadt; tel: (09194)
797 779; fax: (09194) 797
776; www.fraenkische-
schweiz.de).*

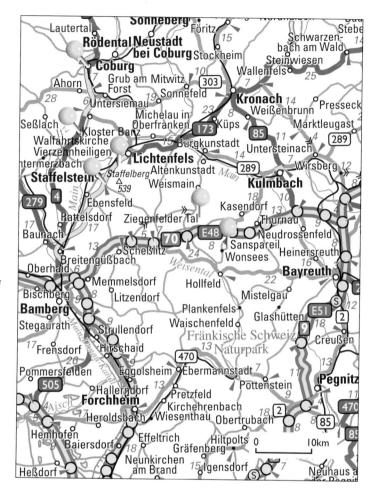

Just off the central square are two very fine examples of earlier half-
timbered architecture: the **Münzmeisterhaus** (1348) and the
**Hofapotheke** (c 1400), a pharmacy in the Middle Ages. If fossils,
bones and stuffed birds appeal, the **Naturkundemuseum**◆ is one of
the most important musuems of its kind in Bavaria.

Coburg's crowning glory (literally) is its fortress. Visible from afar on
its high dolomite crag between the Thuringian Forest and the upper
valley of the Main, the **Veste Coburg**◆◆◆ € *(tel: (09561) 8790;
www.kunstsammlungen-coburg.de. Open Apr–Oct Tue–Sun 1000–1700,
Nov–Mar 1300–1600)* is one of Bavaria's most impressive sights. Its
massive walls and triple set of ramparts overlook Coburger Land, the
Fränkische Schweiz, Kloster Banz, the pilgrimage church of

Vierzehnheiligen and, on a clear day, the Rhön mountains to the west and the Frankenwald in the east. Architecturally, its towers, parapets and gabled buildings are mostly late Gothic and Renaissance. You could easily spend a full day here. After the walls and inner garden, concentrate on the **Fürstenbau⁕⁕** (princes' hall) with its interiors from four different centuries. Don't miss the paintings by Lucas Cranach, whose eroticism is something of a revelation coming from the Middle Ages. The armour collection is full of sharp and blunt murder weapons, to say nothing of helmets, breastplates, chainmail and other paraphernalia. Europe's oldest functional coach is certainly worth a look. The greatest treasure of all is the priceless collection of engravings (300,000 sheets) dating from the Middle Ages to modern times.

## Accommodation and food in Coburg

**Coburger Tor €€** *Ketschendorfer Strasse 22; tel: (09561) 250 741; fax: (09561) 28874.* A small hotel with lots of individual touches. Its Schaller restaurant has a gourmet reputation for dishes such as oyster tempura and veal cutlet with two olive sauces.

**Festungshof €€** *Festungsberg 1; tel: (09561) 80290; fax: (09561) 802 933; www.hotel-festungshof.de.* There is much attention to detail here – the hotel only has 14 rooms. Strategically placed at the foot of the Veste Coburg, its *Biergarten* is the perfect place to recuperate from an overdose of *Kultur*.

**Goldene Traube Romantik-Hotel €€€** *Am Viktoriabrunnen 2; tel: (09561) 8760; fax: (09561) 867 222; www.romantikhotels.com/coburg.* The stately 19th-century building forms part of the Old Town profile just 100m from the historic Marktplatz. *Haute cuisine* and humbler Franconian fare are served with a flourish in the restaurant.

**Above right**
Veste Coburg

# KLOSTER BANZ*

This monumental ex-abbey is often called the *Heilige Berg* (Holy Mountain) of Franconia. The cult of St Denis was introduced in the early Middle Ages and the saint became the patron of the abbey that was founded by the Benedictine order in 1069; it was renovated in baroque style in 1695. Today, the complex is used as a training and conference centre of the Bavarian Christian Social Party. The **Klosterkirche*** (Abbey Church), by architect Johann Dientzenhofer, is notable for its oval-shaped nave and the fine woodcarving of the choir stalls. Its baroque towers look out over the Main Valley, counterbalanced by those of the Vierzehnheiligen church on the opposing mountain ridge. The **Prähistorisches Museum** has a fascinating collection of fossils including the 2m-long head of an ichthyosaurus.

# SANSPAREIL/BURG ZWERNITZ*

Margravine Wilhelmine (1709–58), the sister of Frederick the Great, was one of the most intelligent women of her age. She wrote plays, painted, composed music and acted for her court in Bayreuth, opposite her friend Voltaire. In Sanspareil, among its strange collection of cliffs and boulders, she found her dream 'wilderness'. She had some of the rocks moved around to create a baroque rock garden and constructed a 'ruined' theatre with a stone roof and a fanciful **Sommerschlösschen** ('little summer palace') made of pebbles and seashells. The grim castle up the hill, **Burg Zwernitz***, was not built for fun and seems strangely out of place with its clumsy bulk and gatehouse from which boiling oil was poured on troublesome neighbours.

# STAFFELSTEIN*

Staffelstein sits at the foot of Staffelberg, a mountain that is the subject of a famous song that German boy scouts sing on long hikes. Archaeologists have discovered Celtic walls on the summit. The town's most important native son was the medieval mathematician, Adam Riese (1492–1559), memorialised by a plaque on the richly decorated **Rathaus*** (1684) – one of the most beautiful in all Franconia. There are beautiful *Bürger* homes from the same period on the Marktplatz (Nos 3, 7 and 8). The **Friedhofslinde**, a linden tree in the town cemetery, is thought to be a thousand years old; it might also be the largest tree in Europe, with a girth of 16m. In 1985, Bavaria's hottest mineral springs (52°C) were discovered just to the north and, overnight, business boomed (*see Kurhotel*).

### Accommodation and food in Staffelstein

**Kurhotel €€** *Am Kurpark 7; tel: (09573) 3330; fax: (09573) 333 299; www.kurhotel-staffelstein.de.* The Obermain-Therme is a modern spa complex just outside of town. Contented middle-aged Germans paddle around in its naturally hot outdoor pool. It is most satisfying to swim there in winter. The adjoining hotel has a sauna, solarium and massage – in other words, it is a perfect place to take the *Kur*.

# WALLFAHRTSKIRCHE VIERZEHNHEILIGEN***

In 1445, and again in 1446, the 14 patron saints of Franconia appeared to a shepherd on a hill in the Upper Main Valley. A chapel was built on the spot in 1447 so that pilgrims could seek out the localised presence of these holy intercessors. Joan of Arc (born in 1412) had already heard the voices of two of them – St Catherine and St Margaret. Thanks to help given by the Cistercians, the spot became the focal point of a pious cult. The church that replaced the chapel was erected centuries later, between 1743 and 1772. It is regarded as the most mature work of Balthasar Neumann (*see page 107*) and there is certainly nothing else like it in Franconia. The gold-yellow sandstone façade radiates warmth in the afternoon sun. Inside, the multiple altars and pulpits seem lighter than air and a mysterious source of light illuminates the central choir and ceiling fresco – both dedicated to the 14 saints, said to help people in trouble. Students wishing for good grades pray to St Catherine; farmers pray to St George; and St Christopher, of course, is the patron saint of travellers. It is the most popular pilgrimage church in northern Bavaria. A vast procession of pilgrims enters the church on the fourth Sunday after Easter. There is an inn and souvenir shops just as there was, no doubt, in the Middle Ages.

# ZIEGENFELDER TAL***

The Weisser Main ('White Main'), flowing north, has created the microcosm of a deep, haunting valley. The strange rock cliffs bear fairytale names reflecting the need to humanise it: 'Monk', 'Blacksmith Tower', 'Stone Virgin'. A baroque pilgrimage church by Balthasar Neumann bristles from the cliffside hamlet of Arnstein. Behind the walled cemetery of Modschiedel squats a fortress-like *Pfarrkirche* ('parish church'). The only real town, **Weismain**, is a jumble of historic buildings at the foot of Kordigast (535m), a summit with panoramic views. Just east of it, a forgotten road leads east 4km to a ruined castle – **Niestener Schlossberg** – where the last king of the Meranian dynasty died in 1248.

# Suggested tour

**Total distance:** 146km; the detour to Neustadt bei Coburg adds 27km in each direction.

**Time:** Without detours, this drive can be done comfortably in a day, but if you dawdle too long *en route* you might miss the Veste Coburg, which closes at 1700. If you are pressed for time, skip Kloster Banz and drive directly to Coburg from Vierzehnheiligen church (via the B173, B289 and B4).

**Below**
Bamberg's Neue Residenz

**The House of Saxe-Coburg in Great Britain**

Queen Victoria of Britain was the daughter of Coburg's Princess Victoria. When she married her cousin Albert in 1840, the 'marriage offensive' of the House of Coburg scored its ultimate victory. A woman of Coburg descent was sitting on the throne of the most powerful Empire in the world and her consort was a Saxe-Coburg prince. The British royal family was now the House of Saxe-Coburg in Britain (changed to 'House of Windsor' when German names went out of fashion during World War I). Prince Albert was born northeast of Coburg at Schloss Rosenau. Queen Victoria visited Coburg six times and once wrote in her diary: 'If I weren't the person who I am this would be my true home'.

Drive east from **Bamberg** and take the *Landstrasse* (avoid the *Autobahn*) towards Memmelsdorf and carry on through farmland to Schesslitz. Signs for the *Autobahn* will again compete for your attention; watch out instead for the B22 (Würgau). It trails through pastoral scenery, sweeps uphill to Würgau and meets the Wiesent river at Steinfeld. Slow down and enjoy the fabulous stretch of road between here and **Hollfeld**. From Hollfeld take the *Landstrasse* in the direction of the town of Kainach; the road beyond it skirts the Kainach river, passes Wonsees, climbs a rise and runs almost right into **Burg Zwernitz** in SANSPAREIL ❶. The 18th-century rock garden begins a few metres further on and is perfect picnic territory. Next, retrace the route to Kainach; at the fork in the road, drive in the opposite direction from Hollfeld, towards Stadelhofen. After 5km, the road passes under the *Autobahn*; 2km further on, Weismain is signposted and requires a right turn and an immediate left. You will now follow the Weismain river, which has its source in the nearby village of Kleinziegenfeld. The first town you come to in ZIEGENFELDER TAL ❷ is Weiden. Drive deeper into the valley; at one of its lower points sits a wonky old mill, the **Weihersmühle**, in an enchanted corner formed by a side valley. **Weismain** is the main town in the valley; from there, continue 4km on the same road in the direction of Burgkunstadt. Go left at the fork in the road (signposted Roth and Kloster Langheim) and cruise past isolated farms, the hamlet of Roth and surviving baroque ruins of ex-monastery Langheim. Lichtenfels is the centre of basket-making in Germany, with a Korbmuseum (Basket Museum) in the neighbouring village of Michaelau. If you don't need a basket, get on the B173 heading south; after 2km there is a sign for the pilgrimage church of VIERZEHNHEILIGEN ❸, which lies on a hill to the east. On crowded days, you can only go as far as the lower car park and will have to walk up the last 100m. It looks close enough but the drive to reach the opposite side of the Upper Main Valley is roundabout. Start by returning to the B173 and turning left (south) towards STAFFELSTEIN ❹. Drive into Staffelstein, watching carefully for a sign (Kloster Banz or Unnersdorf) to get on the *Landstrasse* that crosses the Main river. On the further side, turn right on the second *Landstrasse* heading north – signposted KLOSTER BANZ ❺. After the abbey, continue further north on the same *Landstrasse* until you reach B289 (in the neighbourhood of Lichtenfels again). Going northwest, the B289 leads to the B4 and then north to COBURG ❻. If you are returning to Bamberg, it is just a quick 37km south on the B4.

**Detour: Neustadt bei Coburg**, the Mecca for lovers of toys and dolls, is 27km northeast of Coburg. **The Museum der Deutschen Spielzeugindustrie €** (*Hindenburgplatz 1; tel: (09568) 5600; www.spielzeugmuseum-neustadt.de, open daily 1000–1700*) has a huge collection of dolls dressed in regional costumes. For people who want to play with toys rather than to look at them, **Rolly Toys Franz Schneider** (*Siemensstrasse 13–19; tel: (09568) 8560; www.rollytoys.com;*

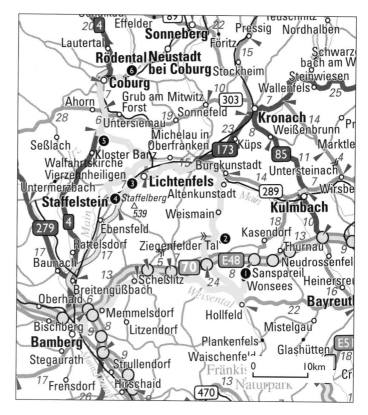

*open Mon–Thur 0800–1200, 1300–1600, Fri 0800–1200)* is a general toy factory right next door; you can buy your sand toys and teddy bear direct and save about 25 per cent. **Lissi Bätz Puppen** (*Hutstrasse 31, Wildenheid district; tel: (09568) 216 667; open Mon–Fri 1000–1200, 1300–1700, Sat 1000–1300*) specialises in dolls for all ages (with savings of 25–50 per cent).

## Also worth exploring

Turn right at Hollfeld (instead of left as above) in the direction of Plankenfels/Waischenfeld for a drive through the scenic heart of the Fränkische Schweiz along the Wiesent river. At Gössweinstein, you are spoiled for choice between two winding, idyllic stretches of the B470: either continue further along the Wiesent river west (and back to Bamberg via the A73) or east towards Pottenstein and Pegnitz (23km south of Bayreuth).

# Regensburg

## Ratings

| | |
|---|---|
| Architecture | ●●●●● |
| Art | ●●●●● |
| Churches | ●●●●● |
| History | ●●●●● |
| Beer | ●●●●○ |
| Food | ●●●○○ |
| Children | ●●○○○ |
| Nature | ●●○○○ |

Regensburg is one of Bavaria's best-kept secrets – a city with 2000 years of history that was never destroyed in a war. Built by the Romans as an outpost on the Donau, it became a bishopric in the early Middle Ages. By the 13th century, it was fabulously rich and received the all-important status of 'Free Imperial City' in 1245, allowing for self-rule. The influence of its largest trading partner in the Middle Ages – Italy – is striking. Regensburg has been called the San Gimignano of southern Germany because of the castle-like towers that loom over its ancient palaces. Having no military value, they were a medieval status symbol used by merchants to put themselves on an equal footing with princes. Today, ordinary people live in the ancient buildings and there is a refreshing absence of tourist kitsch. Locals dominate the beer festivals though visitors are welcome. Regensburg is a university town with first-rate breweries and the voices of its *Domspatzen* ('cathedral sparrows', an internationally famous boys' choir) can be heard in the cathedral every Sunday.

## Sights

ℹ **Tourismus Information** *Altes Rathaus, Rathausplatz 4; tel: (0941) 5074 410; www.regensburg.de. Open Mon–Fri 0915–1800, Sat 0930–1600, Sun 0930–1600 (Nov–Mar 0930–1430).*

🏛 **Altes Rathaus €** *Rathausplatz; tel: (0941) 5074 412. Guided tours in German (and English in summer) Mon–Sat 0930–1200, 1400–1600, Sun 1000–1200.*

### Alte Kapelle❖

The Carolinian chapel is one of the oldest churches in Bavaria (AD 967). The lower part of the freestanding clock tower was built with Roman stones. Its austere exterior does nothing to prepare the visitor for the psychedelic rococo interior by Anton Landes. The vivid ceiling frescoes relate episodes from the lives of Heinrich and Kunigunde, the sainted Holy Roman Emperor and his Queen.

### Altes Rathaus❖❖❖

The Old Town Hall is also known as the **Reichstagsmuseum❖❖** (Imperial Diet Museum). It is really an ensemble of buildings: the eight-storey Gothic tower in the middle; to the left the 1360 Reichsaal building with its beautiful oriel; the Renaissance staircase that was

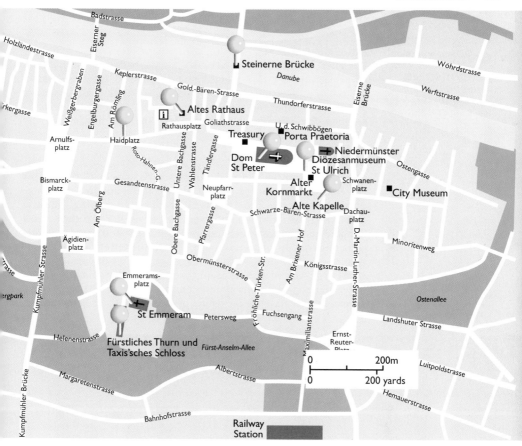

Badstrasse
Holzländestrasse
Eiserner Steg
Keplerstrasse
Weißbergergraben
Engelburgergasse
Am Römling
rkergasse
Arnulfs-platz
Haidplatz
Rathausplatz
Gold.-Bären-Strasse
**Steinerne Brücke**
Danube
Wöhrdstrasse
Werftstrasse
**Altes Rathaus**
Goliathstrasse
Thundorferstrasse
Eiserne Brücke
U. d. Schwibbögen
**Treasury**
**Porta Praetoria**
**Niedermünster**
**Diözesanmuseum**
**St Ulrich**
Ostengasse
Roco-Hahnen-G.
**Dom St Peter**
Untere Bachgasse
Wahlenstrasse
Tändlergasse
Bismarck-platz
Gesandtenstrasse
Neupfarr-platz
**Alter Kornmarkt**
Schwanen-platz
**City Museum**
Am Ölberg
Obere Bachgasse
Pfarrergasse
**Alte Kapelle**
Schwarze-Bären-Strasse
Dachau-platz
Ägidien-platz
Minoritenweg
D.-Martin-Luther-Strasse
Kumpfmühler Strasse
Emmerams-platz
Obermünsterstrasse
Fröhliche-Türken-Str.
Am Brixener Hof
Königsstrasse
ergpark
**St Emmeram**
Petersweg
Fuchsengang
Maximilianstrasse
Ostenallee
Helenenstrasse
**Fürstliches Thurn und Taxis'sches Schloss**
Fürst-Anselm-Allee
Ernst-Reuter-Platz
Landshuter Strasse
Luitpoldstrasse
Kumpfmühler Brücke
Margaretenstrasse
Albertstrasse
Hemauerstrasse
Bahnhofstrasse
**Railway Station**
0                200m
0            200 yards

added in 1564; and, to the right, 17th- and 18th-century buildings with the Ratskeller (town dining room). The **Reichsaal** is famous as the meeting place for the Holy Roman Emperor's Diet (beginning in the 14th century) but it was originally built as somewhere to dance by the city's pleasure-loving patrician families. The Diet, a form of parliament, moved from city to city within the German-speaking lands until 1663, when Regensburg became its permanent home. Napoleon abolished it in 1806. The two figures above the entrance of the Town Hall, **Schutz** and **Trutz** (Defence and Defiance), sum up the politics of medieval Regensburg. It was a free, independent city where the citizens proudly elected their own *Bürgermeister* and city councillors – as close as anyone would get to democracy in the Middle Ages. Downstairs is the somewhat less democratic **Fragestatt** (Interrogation Room) and its adjoining dungeon. The judges would sit behind a screen and wait for a confession to be forced from the accused by torture. Although such places were common in the Middle Ages, few of them still exist in their original state.

**Diözesanmuseum St Ulrich** *Domplatz 2; tel: (0941) 322 530; www.bistumsmuseen-regensburg.de. Open Tue–Sun 1000–1700.*

### Diözesanmuseum St Ulrich✦

The church of St Ulrich mixes Romanesque bulk with Gothic flair, particularly the odd nave that is only partly vaulted. It makes a perfect setting for a collection of medieval sculpture, painting, gold jewellery and tapestries from the 11th to 20th centuries. Look for the *Beautiful Madonna* by Albrecht Altdorfer (1480–1538), a masterpiece by Regensburg's greatest painter.

### Dom St Peter✦✦✦

The most imposing Gothic monument in southern Germany, the cathedral of Regensburg took 600 years to finish and the spires were only completed in the 19th century. The odd-looking Eselturm (donkey's tower) on the north side is a leftover from an even earlier Romanesque cathedral and was used as a crane and elevator during the construction of its successor. The 14th-century stained-glass windows in the choir invite prolonged craning of the neck. On the western pillars of the transept, the famous 'laughing angel' of Regensburg blithely grins at an astonished Madonna. At the western entrance to the nave are the figures of the Devil and his grandmother.

**Below**
Alter Kornmarkt

**Dom St Peter and Domschatzmuseum**
Krauterermarkt 3;
tel: (0595) 322 530;
www.bistumsmuseen-
regensburg.de. Guided tours
of the cathedral in German.
Open Tue–Sat 1000–1700;
Sun and holidays
1200–1700.

**Fürstliches Thurn und Taxis'sches Schloss**
€€€ Emmeramsplatz 5;
tel: (0941) 5048 133;
www.thurnundtaxis.de.
Guided tours of the palace
and cloisters (every half
hour) Apr–Oct Mon–Fri
1100–1600, Sat–Sun
1000–1600; Nov–Mar
Sat–Sun 1000–1700.

On the north side, the tomb of Father Maier always has fresh flowers and burning candles. Determined to save the city during the last days of World War II, Father Maier tried to mediate the surrender of Regensburg to approaching American forces. The Nazis hanged him and an associate on a public square. The **Domschatz** (Treasury), a former bishop's residence on the south side of the museum, is filled with vestments, reliquaries and other sacred items. Also on the south side are two of the cathedral's finest monuments (accessible only by guided tour): the Gothic cloister, full of finely carved tombstones; and the **Allerheiligenkapelle**, a Byzantine-style chapel built by Italian craftsmen that is reminiscent of Ravenna.

### Fürstliches Thurn und Taxis'sches Schloss*

The enormous complex – it has more rooms than Buckingham Palace – belongs to the Thurn and Taxis, one of Europe's richest families. Franz von Taxis (1459–1517) was the founder of the international postal system in western Europe. The Taxis also exercised a monopoly of German postal services until 1867. Thurn und Taxis *Pilsener* beer is a staple in many Regensburg pubs. The family gift for maximising profit is reflected in four separate prices for a complete tour of the premises: two for guided tours of the **Schloss** (when the countess is not at home) and the Gothic **Kreuzgang** (cloister) that leads to St Emmeram (*see below*); and admission to two museums: the **Marstall** museum – noted for its collection of carriages and vintage cars – and the **Thurn und Taxis Museum**, which houses a magnificent collection of furniture, porcelain and *objets d'art* from the 17th to 19th centuries.

### Haidplatz*

Haidplatz was the city's largest open space during the Middle Ages and the city's No 1 address. The richest patrician families built palaces on it, and the square was also the ground for tournaments and jousting. A famous Regensburg ballad tells the story of how local hero Dollinger vanquished Krako the Hun here. In August and September, a local festival – the *Dollingerspiel* – re-enacts the medieval dual. The **Haus zum Goldenen Kreuz** (on the north side) provided luxurious accommodation to princes attending sessions of the Imperial Diet. On one such visit, the Emperor Charles V seduced a local girl named Barbara Blomberg (the affair is the subject of a play performed each year in the annual Altstadt Festival, *see page 143*). Their illegitimate son, Juan of Austria, was born in 1547. He became a great soldier, the hero of the 1571 battle against the Turks at Lepant, and later an unpopular governor of the rebellious Netherlands. His statue dominates tiny Zieroldsplatz. The neo-classical **Thon-Dittmer Palace**, built out of several earlier Gothic houses, has a wood-panelled concert hall inside and an arcaded Renaissance courtyard where outdoor concerts are held during the summer.

**Above**
The Steinerne Brücke

### St Emmeram✦✦

Founded on the site of a late Roman structure in the 7th century, the Benedictine monastery is among the oldest in Germany, as are the figures sculpted in the porch above the double doors. The baroque décor inside is by the Asam brothers from Munich. There are three crypts where you will find the tomb of St Emmeram, a melancholy tombstone of Queen Hemma (1280) and graves of early Wittelsbach dukes such as Heinrich the 'Quarrelsome' (d 995). The church has a famous Gothic cloister that can only be seen as part of a tour of the Thurn und Taxis'sches Schloss (*see page 141*).

### Steinerne Brücke✦✦

The **Steinerne Brücke** (Stone Bridge), constructed in only 11 years between 1135 and 1146, was an engineering feat unsurpassed in the Middle Ages. At the time it was built, it was the only permanent bridge spanning the Donau between Ulm and Vienna and of incalculable importance to Regensburg's economy. Legend has it that it was not the 2000 workers but a pact between the devil and the bridge's builder that brought it to such swift completion. The architect promised Satan the first eight legs to cross the bridge (who was more interested, one assumes, in the souls attached to them). To fulfil his part of the bargain, he sent two chickens and a dog over the newly completed bridge. One of the city's landmarks is the **Brückemandl** – a funny little man sitting on a pillar and staring at the cathedral to see if it is finished. For centuries boats unloaded their cargo of salt in the covered wharves of the **Salzstadel** (salt warehouse) on the northeast side, now a restaurant.

# Entertainment and festivals

**Golf Museum: Insam Antiques**
€€ *Tändlergasse 3; tel: (0941) 51074; www.golfmuseum.de.* Open Mon–Sat 1000–1800. If historic golf clubs are your thing, head for the Golf museum in the stone cellar. Golf clubs from 1550 to 1930 are exhibited, as well as art and posters depicting the sport.

Regensburg is a city of music and home to the boys' choir, the *Domspatzen* ('cathedral sparrows'). The tourist office publishes a free *Monatsprogramm* (monthly programme) of what's on, and offers a ticket reservation service. The main theatre, the **Städtische Bühnen**, *Bismarckplatz 7; tel: (0941) 59156*, stages opera and dance as well as drama and comedy. The **Thon-Dittmer-Palais**, *Haidplatz 8*, offers jazz, classical music and theatre. In summer, it holds open-air performances in its Renaissance courtyard. Nightlife in Regensburg centres mainly on cafés and beer gardens. The **Südhaus**, *Untere Bachgasse 8*, is a cellar disco.

The **Altstadt Festival** (held in the summer) has jugglers and street theatre, a morality play about Emperor Charles V and Barbara Blomberg, folk music and lots of food and drink. There are two big beer festivals – the **Frühjahrsdult** (two weeks in May) and **Herbstdult** (two weeks in August/September). There are also several annual music festivals, including the **Bach-Woche** (Bach week, June or July) and the **Bayerisches Jazz-Weekend** (July), when up to 50 jazz bands take over the city's cafés, squares and hidden courtyards. A traditional **Christmas Market** is held on Neupfarrplatz and a **Crafts Market** on Haidplatz; both have hand-made gifts for sale.

# Accommodation and food

If you visit Regensburg, make a point of sleeping in the historic centre of the city. Hotel guests have the right to drive into the pedestrianised city centre to unload luggage. Most hotels have no parking, but there are overnight parking garages at Arnulfplatz and Bismarckplatz.

**Medieval fast-food**

The **Würstküche** was built 800 years ago to feed the workers building the bridge. It still serves the same medieval fast-food – pork sausages grilled over beechwood with sweet mustard. Boat tours of the Donau leave from here.

**Bischofshof am Dom** €€€ *Kräutermarkt 3; tel: (0941) 58460; fax: (0941) 5846 146; www.hotel-bischofshof.de.* The bishops held court here for many centuries, with emperors and kings as guests. The rooms are all different, reflecting eight centuries of architecture. Many have views of the cathedral and all are within earshot of its bells. The restaurant and courtyard *Biergarten* are Old Regensburg at its best.

**Hotel Arch** €€ *Haidplatz 4; tel: (0941) 58660; fax: (0941) 586 6168.* This ancient patrician house – named 'ark' because it resembles an overladen bulky ship – is found on the city's most beautiful square, Haidplatz. Most rooms have views. Those in the attic bulge with medieval beams.

**Hôtel d'Orphée** € *Untere Bachgasse 8; tel: (0941) 596 020; fax: (0941) 5960 2222; www.hotel-orphee.de; reception in the* **Restaurant Orphée**; *tel: (0941) 52977.* An exquisite hotel in the city's oldest street. 'Shelter for individualists' is its motto. Instead of a lift and minibar you get breakfast served all day and free bottles of mineral water and wine on the nightstand. Rooms are individual too; most have wrought-iron beds. Number 2 has a balcony and view.

**Brauerei-Gaststätte Kneitinger €** *Kreuzgasse 7; tel: (0941) 593 020.* A brewery-tavern with primeval Bavarian atmosphere that serves great beer and a lot of calories for little money. If you are not in the mood for grilled pig's heart, there's venison ragout or baked carp. Service can be slow.

**Dampfnudel-Uli €** *Watmarkt 4; tel: (0941) 53297.* Sit down in the ground floor of a medieval tower for the speciality of the house: huge dumplings served in a pool of vanilla or fruit sauce – delicious, filling and cheap.

**Vitus €** *Hinter der Grieb 8; tel: (0941) 52646.* A popular French restaurant-café in an ex-Gothic chapel in a tiny back-street. Mussels are the house speciality. Some evenings there are *chansons*.

**Zauberturm €** *Wahlenstrasse 14.* This ancient tower overlooks the city's oldest street and has a pub at the top.

## Suggested tour

**Distance:** 1.7km or 2.4km with detours. Walhalla is 11km from Regensburg.

**Time:** The Old Town is confined to the north side of the Donau and is relatively compact. If time is an issue, the walk can be done in half a day, but adding the guided tours of historic buildings, wandering into detours, museum visits and a cruise on the Donau make for a more lasting impression. Don't look for parking in the Altstadt. The closest parking is at the Donaumarkt, just east of the Eiserne Brücke. There are overnight underground parking garages at Arnulfsplatz and Bismarckplatz.

From the Donaumarkt, the narrow street, Unter den Schwibbögen, goes past the **Porta Praetoria**. The arched gate was the main entrance to the Roman city. The Romans built Regensburg in AD 179 to defend the empire against the wild Celtic and Teutonic tribes living beyond the Donau. Its military purpose was reflected in the city's original Latin name, Castra Regina – 'Fort on the Regen river' (the Regen flows into the Donau nearby). This gate is particularly impressive when you realise that it is only a fragment of a much larger gatehouse (the **Historisches Museum** has a model of the entire structure). Walk beneath the arch and up Niedermünsterstrasse, and then turn right. The **Niedermünster** is on your left. Watch your step as you walk into this ancient church, which originally belonged to a convent. Like many of Regensburg's churches, it is outwardly Romanesque but done up inside in baroque style. St Erhard lies beneath the altar and stone baldachin in the north aisle. Just a few paces in the opposite direction is the Domgarten (cathedral garden), with a pile of stones in the middle. When the Dom's builders fell on hard times, they began using cheaper green stone. A team of stone-masons are kept busy today replacing it with better quality stones left here to weather. Walk around the **DOM ST PETER** ❶ to have a look at its west front. Enter beneath the triangular porch, which contains some of the best carving in its niches. You leave the Dom on the south porch. You will immediately run into the **DIÖZESANMUSEUM ST ULRICH** ❷ on the south side. Duck under the archway that joins two very old structures – the **Römerturm** and the **Herzogshof** – to reach the **Alter Kornmarkt**. The Karmelitenkloster (monastery) is at No 7. You can buy little bottles of *Regensburger Karmelitengeist* from the father on duty at a small glass window inside; first distilled from herbs and roots in 1718 by father Ulrich, it is a potent (75 per cent alcohol) cure for indigestion, flatulence, the common cold and a host of other ailments. The **ALTE KAPELLE** ❸ is on the north side of the square. A

**Below**
Fürstliches Thurn und Taxis'sches Schloss

**Walhalla ferry excursion.**
The first departure from Regensburg is at 1030, April to mid-October. The excursion takes 2½ hours. The landing stage of the **Steinerne Brücke** is at Regensburger Personenschiffahrt Klinger; *tel: (0941) 55359; fax: (0941) 565 668; www.schifffahrtklinger.de*

narrow alley leads to Schwarze-Bären-Strasse. Go right (east) to **Neupfarrplatz**. A Jewish Quarter in the Middle Ages, it was demolished in a 1519 pogrom and the construction of a new church, the Neupfarrkirche, began just 2 days later.

**Detour:** Going north on Speichergasse and taking the first right (Drei-Kronen-Gasse) leads to Dachauplatz; the **Historisches Museum der Stadt Regensburg** (*tel: (0941) 5071443; open Tue–Sun 1000–1600, Thur until 2000*) is on the far side. The museum's 100-plus rooms (in a former monastery) explore the history and culture of eastern Bavaria from the Stone Age to the present.

Cross Neupfarrplatz going west and enter Gesandten Strasse. Go left on Obere Bachgasse. The carved stone portal of No 15 was once part of a 12th-century private chapel belonging to a wealthy merchant. Number 7 was the house of painter Albrecht Altdorfer, one of the most important German painters after Dürer. Going left at the end of the street, you will find **ST EMMERAM** ❹ across the square. The **FÜRSTLICHES THURN UND TAXIS'SCHES SCHLOSS** ❺ is around the corner.

**Detour:** Return to Gesandten Strasse and go left five blocks to Bismarkplatz. Jakobstrasse enters the square on the opposite side and the **Schottenkirche St Jakob** (St James Church) is to the left on the first block. Monks from Ireland were energetic missionaries in the early Middle Ages, although they were mistakenly described as 'Schotte' when they arrived in 10th-century Regensburg. Oddly enough, the monastery really did become Scottish in the 16th century; the father confessor of Mary, Queen of Scots, lies buried inside. The Romanesque **portal** is one of Germany's most important early Christian works of art, but no one has adequately explained its tableau of mermaids, sea monsters, farm animals, hangmen and prostitutes, juxtaposed with Christian icons. It might be *The Last Judgement* or, then again, the story of the sea voyages made by Irish monks on their way to convert pagans on the Continent.

Retrace your steps to Obere-Bachgasse, which becomes Untere-Bachgasse after it crosses Gesandten Strasse. Watch out on your left for a small alley and the chance to step back in time on **Hinter der Grieb**, a stone alleyway which still contains most of its original *Bürger* homes from six centuries ago. Turn right on the next street, **Rote-Hahnen-Gasse**, walk 100m, and you will be on **HAIDPLATZ** ❻. Walk past its Justitiabrunnen ('Justice fountain') and bear left. The **ALTES RATHAUS** ❼ is along on your right. Look for the statue of Juan of Austria and follow the alleyway (behind) to the riverside Fischmarkt – the market operates every morning. A right turn on Kepplerstrasse soon leads to Goldene-Bären-Strasse and the gatehouse of the **STEINERNE BRÜCKE** ❽. Walk to the middle of Germany's oldest bridge for the best view of Regensburg.

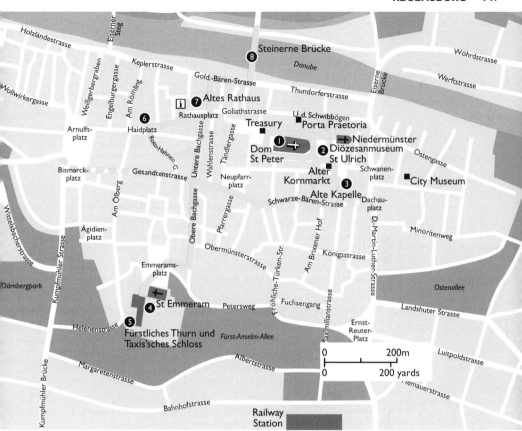

## Also worth exploring

**Walhalla**✦ lies on a hill overlooking the Donau east of Regensburg (*Douaustauf bei Regensburg; Walhallastrasse 48, tel: (09403) 961 680; Open Apr–Sept: 0900–1745, Oct 0900–1645, Nov–Mar 1000–1145 and 1300–1545*). It is a copy of the Parthenon in Athens (the interior measurements are almost exactly the same), built by King Ludwig I in 1842 to immortalise 'great Germans'. In Norse mythology, Walhalla was the place where the god Odin received the souls of fallen heroes. Inside this version, busts and plaques portray around 200 'immortals' – generals, artists, scientists and German royals such as Kaiser Wilhelm I. Visitors who find it too pompous can console themselves with spectacular views of the Donau, the ruins of Donaustauf castle and the spires of Regensburg. The controversy over the definition of a German hero never quite dies down because this is a 'living' monument, bequeathed to the State of Bavaria with the condition that the authorities add to its collection of marble busts. Gregor Mendel, the priest who pioneered genetic science, was so honoured on the 100th anniversary of his death in 1984.

# Around Regensburg (the Donau, Altmühl and Laaber valleys)

## Ratings

| | |
|---|---|
| Castles | ●●●●● |
| Scenery | ●●●●● |
| History | ●●●●○ |
| Nature | ●●●●○ |
| Outdoor activities | ●●●●○ |
| Walking | ●●●●○ |
| Children | ●●●○○ |
| History | ●●●○○ |

The scenery around Regensburg inspired a group of German artists in the late Middle Ages (the 'Donau School') to paint landscapes instead of portraits. Many rivers flow through the region: the Donau, Europe's longest waterway, reaches its northernmost point; the lower stretch of the Atlmühl river (*see page 90*) courses through a Jurassic valley; and both are fed by idyllic tributaries such as the Schambach and Schwarze Laaber. The force of the water has created a variety of landscapes: riverside meadows alternate with stands of forest, deciduous and evergreen, and sheer sandstone cliffs. The valleys' first inhabitants were Stone Age cave dwellers and local museums exhibit their stone tools, along with dinosaur fossils and Celtic ornaments. The terrain is dotted with historical landmarks: Bavaria's best preserved Roman fortress, its oldest monastery and dozens of castles, most dating from the turbulent 12th century.

## BURG PRUNN❖❖

**Burg Prunn €**
*Riedenburg; tel: (09442) 3323; fax: (09442) 3335; www.schloesser.bayern.de. Guided tours daily Apr–Sept 0900–1800, Oct–Mar Tue–Sun 1000–1600.*

This formidable castle sits atop a high cliff with the Altmühl Valley at its feet, in an excellent state of preservation from its moat to the 31m-high *Bergfried* (keep). Wernherus de Prunne is the first recorded knight to occupy it. The castle belonged to the Frauenberger family from 1338 until the line died out in 1567, and their arms, containing a leaping white stallion, are still painted on the walls. The most famous Frauenberger was a warring knight named Hans 'the Joyful'; his red-marble tomb is located in the village church of Prunn. A famous manuscript of the great German medieval epic *Nibelungenlied* (*The Prunner Codex*) was discovered in the castle but is now in the Munich Staatsbibliothek.

## BURG ROSENBURG❖❖

Rosenburg was once the centre-piece of a massive complex of fortifications that included the ruined castles of **Tachenstein** and

**Burgkeller €**
*tel: (09442) 2597.*
The castle cellar serves
*Weisswurst* and the local
*Weizenbier.*

**Rabenstein** and the city walls and gatehouses of Riedenburg. Its *Bergfried* (keep) is 13th century but much of it dates from between 1556 and 1558, including the extraordinary two-storey oriel in the northeast wing. The **Jagdfalkenhof**✦ keeps the tradition of falconry alive as it was practised in the Middle Ages in Rosenburg and other German castles. The falconers and falcons put on a show every day between March and November (1100 and 1500). Many of the birds in the collection, such as falcons, eagles, buzzards and other birds of prey, are now extinct in the Altmühl Valley.

# ESSING✦

The tiny town of Essing sits at the foot of the ruins of **Burg Randeck**, known for its footbridges. The **Alte Brücke** (bridge) and its **Bruckturm** (gate tower) span the old basin of the Altmühl river. A modern wooden bridge – the longest in Europe at 193m – snakes across the canalised Altmühl (Main-Donau-Kanal) to join Altessing to Neuessing. On the Neuessing side, the attractions include the nearby **Grosse Schulerlochhöhle** – a cave once inhabited by Neanderthalers and Ice-Age animals. Today, there are also New Agers, who meditate to live

**Right**
Essing's Alte Brücke

Didgeridoo music and CDs of music by Hildegard von Bingen, a medieval abbess and composer of spiritual hymns (*guided tours only, Easter–Oct daily 1000–1600, until 1700 in summer*). The disused 19th-century **Ludwig-Main-Donau-Kanal** now seems more whimsical than industrial. Part of it was designed by Leo von Klenze, the man responsible for Munich's Alte Pinakothek and the Walhalla near Regensburg (*see page 147*). Its locks and wharves are overgrown with grass and moss, and the towpaths are lined with maple trees.

# KELHEIM*

**ℹ Tourismus Information**
*Ludwigplatz 16; tel: (09441) 7010; www.kelheim.de. Open Apr–Nov Tue–Sun 1000–1600.*

**⛏ Archäologisches Museum der Stadt Kelheim** € *Lederergasse 11; tel: (09441) 10492. Open Apr–Oct Tue–Sun 1000–1600.*

**Befreiungshalle** €
*Befreiungshallestrasse 3; tel: (09441) 682 070; fax: (09441) 682 077. Open daily Apr–Sept 0900–1800; Oct–Mar 1000–1600.*

**⚑ Keldorado** €
*Rennweg 60; tel: (09441) 2267; www.keldorado-kelheim.de. This 'water Eldorado' is a vast complex for indoor and outdoor swimming with a two-storey waterslide, Jacuzzis and water-jet massage.*

Kelheim lies at the point where the Atmühl and Donau rivers meet. In summer, it gets very busy with coachloads of day-trippers and dozens of tour boats moored on the shore. The Wittelsbach Herzöge (dukes) lived here long ago. Following the assassination of Ludwig I in 1231, they moved away, first to Landshut and, ultimately, Munich. In places, the **Altstadt** (Old Town), wedged between two rivers, still looks like the capital of a medieval duchy, with a **Herzogsschloss**, stretches of moat and fortified wall, and its original towers and gatehouses. There is also a late-Gothic **Pfarrkirche**, a **Herzogskasten** with an **archaeological museum** inside, containing an intriguing hoard of Celtic art and artefacts, and an ancient *Weissbier* brewery (*see Klosterbrauerei below*). The **Befreiungshalle** (Liberation Hall), on Michelsberg, can be reached by walking uphill from the Altstadt or by car. Begun in 1842 and completed in 1863, it was the second monument of Ludwig I to German nationalism (*see Walhalla, page 147*), commemorating the German victories against Napoleon in 1813–15. Just for the record, Bavaria actually fought on the same side as Napoleon in many battles before switching sides. The exterior of the three-storey rotunda – sometimes compared to a gasworks, sometimes to a coffeepot – is graced with 18 oversized German virgins, symbolic of the 18 tribes of Germany. Inside, it is a fantasy in cold marble. The circle of 34 9m-tall Victory Goddesses holding hands in pairs and propping up bronze shields stand for the people who fought Napoleon. The marble floor inscription could have been incised for a later century: 'May the Germans never forget what made the struggle for freedom necessary and how it was won'.

## Accommodation and food in Kelheim

**Brauerei Hotel Aukofer** €€ *Alleestrasse 27; tel: (09441) 2020; fax: (09441) 21437*. The hotel offers perfectly clean and comfortable rooms in the Old Town, close to the Befreihungshalle.

**Klosterbrauerei** € *Klosterstrasse 5; tel: (09441) 50150; fax: (09441) 501555*. This 17th-century hotel-brewery has fine views and uniformly modern rooms. It serves its famous *Weissbier* on a terrace.

# RIEDENBURG✢

**ⓘ Fremdenverkehr-samt** *Marktplatz 1;* tel: *(09442) 905 000;* fax: *(09442) 905 002;* *www.riedenburg.de*

The romantic town of Riedenburg straddles the Altmühl river. It is often full of tourists, due to the boat traffic from the Main-Donau-Kanal. Immediately obvious are its three castles (*see Burg Rosenburg, page 148*) on the hills above it. The **Kristalmuseum €** (*Bergkristallstrasse 1. Open daily 0900–1800*) has an impressive collection of crystals, including what claims to be the world's largest, an 8-tonne wonder from Arkansas.

# SCHLOSS EGGERSBERG✢

**🏛 Hofmarkmuseum** **€** tel: *(09442) 1374.* Open Apr–Oct Wed–Sun 1400–1700.

A former hunting lodge for the local nobility, this Renaissance manor (1600) hides its manicured Schlossgarten behind thick walls. It has a panoramic view of the Altmühl Valley from its terrace and a *Biergarten*. The small **Hofmarkmuseum✢** displays a model of the smallest dinosaur ever discovered (near Eggersberg), Celtic ornaments and other exhibits of local archaeology.

### Accommodation and food in Schloss Eggersburg

**Schlosshotel Eggersberg €€€** *Obereggersberg; tel: (09442) 91870; fax: (09442) 918 787; www.schloss-eggersburg.com.* Every room has a story to tell at this castle-hotel, yet it is surprisingly intimate for all its antiques and history. You can order a *Rittermahl* (Knight's Dinner) in one of its two restaurants. For recreation, there is hiking, horse riding (you are allowed to bring your own horse!) and, in winter, cross-country skiing.

# WELTENBURG BENEDIKTINERABTEI✢✢

The Benedictine Abbey lies at the downstream mouth of the **Donaudurchbruch✢✢✢** (Danube Gorge) – perhaps the most scenic stretch on the Donau. The Donau has cut a narrow path through the sheer walls of dolomite, eroding it into strange shapes; riverboat captains have given them nicknames such as 'Bavarian Lion', 'Bishop's Mitre', 'Kissing Couple' and 'Man with No Shame'. The cliffs above are heavily forested.

The abbey claims to be the oldest monastery in Bavaria (AD 620). Its stately baroque **Klosterkirche✢✢** houses a stunning interior by the Asam brothers. The swirls of paint and stucco transport you, along with a technicolour horde of cherubs, patriarchs and saints, into the sky-blue heights of its oval nave. The real showstopper is St George – illuminated by a hidden source of light – plunging his spear into a gilt dragon. Next to him, a beautiful maiden is frozen in a shriek. The monastery has brewed its own very dark beer since 1050, which you can taste in the **Klosterschenke** (Abbey Inn) or beneath the trees of its *Biergarten*.

**Opposite**
Weltenburg Benediktinerabtei

**Above**
Burg Prunn

# Suggested tour

**Total distance:** 135km.

**Time:** All day.

**Links:** Regensburg is the capital of Eastern Bavaria, which includes the Bavarian Forest. It marks the end of the Bavarian Forest tour (*pages 164–7*). This drive takes in the lower Altmühl Valley, the upper part of which is covered on *pages 97–9*.

From **Regensburg** take the B16 which follows the Donau south to **Bad Abbach**, the site of mineral springs used since Roman times and modern facilities effective in the treatment of rheumatism. Heinrich II – Holy Roman Emperor and saint (*see Bamberg, page 120*) – was born in 973 in the keep of its ruined castle, Heinrichsburg. (Ignore the turn-off for Kelheim; the route returns to it later). Get off the B16 in **Abensberg**, a town famous for white asparagus (the feeding frenzy

**Gasthof Hotel Schwan €€**
*Marktplatz 5, Riedenburg;
tel: (09442) 1272; fax:
(09442) 2807.* A former
brewery that opened its
doors in 1683, the Schwan
has been completely
renovated. Its tavern
serves legendary *Riemhofer*
beer and Bavarian
specialities.

**Fuchs-Bräu €**
*Hauptstrasse 23,
Beilngries; tel: (08461)
6520; fax: (08461) 8357;
e-mail: fuchs-braeu@
landidyll.de.* This 16-century
building (formerly a
brewery), in the historic
heart of the town, has
modern but tastefully
decorated rooms.

**Gewürzmühle €**
*Gredinger Strasse 2,
Berching; tel: (08462)
20050; fax: (08462) 200
051; www.hotel-
gewuerzmuehle.de.* You can
contemplate the gatehouse
of the Old Town from the
terrace-café of this hotel,
which is near the town
walls. It is an attractive,
modern conversion of an
historic building.

begins in mid-April and lasts through June) where a *Landstrasse* will
lead through farmland to Eining. The Römerkastell in **Eining** is the
best preserved Roman fortress in Bavaria. Nevertheless, it still takes
some imagination to appreciate it. Turn north on the *Landstrasse* that
runs parallel to the Donau (with no view most of the way) alternating
between fields and the woods; a pleasant, curving descent leads to the
town of Weltenburg. Just before the town, you will see the
**WELTENBURG BENEDIKTINERABTEI ❶** clearly signposted. The
narrow road scrapes past a sheer dolomite cliff to the abbey on a sandy
peninsula at the mouth of the Donau Gorge. Back on the road to
Kelheim, you will loop through woods above the gorge and pass a
smoke-belching factory before crossing the Donau. The **Altstadt** of
**KELHEIM ❷** and the **Befreiungshalle** are 4km upriver at the
confluence of the Donau and the Altmühl rivers.

**Getting out of the car:** From 1 May to 10 October, it is possible to
cruise the rivers by boat. The most scenic stretch is on the Donau,
between Kelheim and Kloster Weltenburg (40 minutes). You can also
cruise from Kelheim as far as Berching (*see below*) with seven stops in
between (a total of 6 hours one way).

The road now follows the scenic lower Altmühl Valley. It is still one of
Bavaria's most romantic landscapes even though this stretch of the
Altmühl river forms part of the Main-Donau-Kanal, which accounts
for it being so wide in places and the occasional concrete sluice.
**ESSING ❸**, the next town, occupies both sides of the river. Further
on, turn off at the village of Nusshausen and watch for a sign for
**BURG PRUNN ❹**. The road to it climbs steeply through woods for
2km and turns right on to the plateau above the river. **RIEDENBURG
❺** occupies a wide basin in the valley and its **BURG ROSENBURG ❻**
overlooks the town. The wide bend in the river that comes next is one
of the most charming in the valley, overlooked by the Teufelsfelsen
('devil's cliff') and hang-gliders floating above it. You will soon see
signs for **SCHLOSS EGGERSBERG ❼**, which is on the left bank of the
river.

**Detour:** Continue along the Altmühl river to **Dietfurt**, geologically
interesting as a point where seven small valleys meet in a basin
squeezed by a wooded ridge. The town still has a medieval profile.
**Beilngries** marks the spot where the Altmühl meets the River Sulz. Its
pride and joy is the baroque residence of **Schloss Hirschberg**, once
the summer residence of the powerful prince-bishops of Eichstätt.
Drive 11km north into the Sulz Valley (on the B286) to investigate the
town of **Berching**, which comes right out of the 15th century. Like
Rothenburg ob der Tauber, it is an almost perfectly preserved medieval
town. Only the church interiors were redecorated in the later baroque
style. You can experience its narrow streets of half-timbered houses,
cobblestone squares, 12 towers and fortified walls much as they were
500 years ago.

Turn right (northeast) on the *Landstrasse* for Beratzhausen, 1.5km before the town of Dietfurt. It is a tranquil country road that climbs a couple of hundred metres up to a partly wooded plateau and curves in and out of small villages on the way. After 10km, the baroque **Wallfahrtskirche Eichlberg** is visible on a hill above the hamlet of Einöd. **Beratzhausen** is on the Schwarze Laaber river and, from here on the route follows the Laaber Valley east. The first historical mention of the town was in 866. In the 13th century, it belonged to a Herr von Ehrenfels. The ruins of his castle occupy a hill above the town (off the road to Parsberg); the defensive wall and moat have survived. The road meets the river again just before **Laaber**; its ruined castle is from a century later and was home to the Minnesänger Hadamar III – a poet-musician from the 14th century. The road and river become inseparable for the next 6.5km as they squeeze through the **Felsental** ('Cliff Valley'). Above Eichhofen, the **Burgruine Loch** is one of only two Bavarian castles constructed in a cave. The Schwarze Laaber flows into the Donau at Sinzing. From there it is only 7km back to Regensburg.

## Also worth exploring

The **Schambachtal** is like the Altmühl Valley in miniature – an enchanted river landscape with its own ensemble of creaky water-mills, cliffs, castles and holy places. You can follow it first to **Schloss Hexenagger**, a castle where light-hearted baroque trappings reveal a grim Romanesque core; **Altmannstein**, the birthplace of the great rococo sculptor, Ignaz Günther, with an enormous crucifix by him as the centre-piece of its modern church; and **Bettbrunn**, one of the oldest pilgrimage churches in Bavaria.

## The Main-Donau-Kanal

The Main-Donau-Kanal, built between 1960 and 1992, was one of the largest civil engineering projects in history and – measured in terms of its economic usefulness – one of its biggest follies. Thanks to the canal, a barge can float 2500 tonnes of cargo 3500km from the North Sea to the Black Sea, passing through 18 countries *en route*. But shipping the goods by rail is less expensive and ten times faster. The 171-km canal begins near Bamberg and travels via the Altmühl river to Kelheim. The modern canal had two predecessors: Emperor Charlemagne set an army of men to work digging a canal in the 8th century until it flooded and 'Charlemagne's Ditch', the Fossa Carolina, is now a popular fishing hole near the town of Treuchtlingen. The Ludwig-Donau-Main-Kanal was constructed in nine years (1837–46) along virtually the same route as the modern canal. It never paid for itself though it remained open until World War II. Today, the abandoned canal is a romantic spot and functions, unintentionally, as an open-air museum of 19th-century industry.

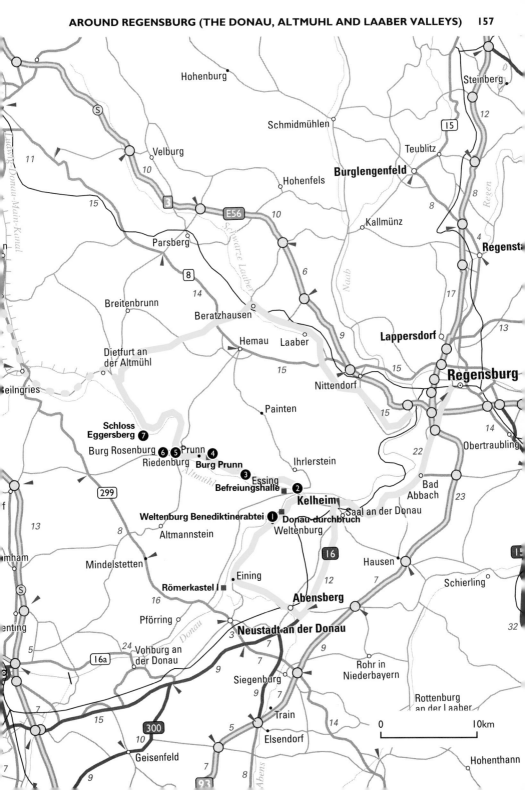

Nationalpark
Bayerischer Wald

# The Bavarian Forest and Passau-on-the-Danube

## Ratings

| | |
|---|---|
| Nature | ●●●●● |
| Scenery | ●●●●● |
| Walking | ●●●●● |
| Architecture | ●●●○○ |
| Children | ●●●○○ |
| Wildlife | ●●●○○ |
| Food and drink | ●●○○○ |
| History | ●●○○○ |

Elegant Passau revels in its command of rivers – the Donau, the Inn and the Ilz – and bears a strong resemblance to Salzburg (*see page 168*). By contrast, Bavaria's wildest region – the Bavarian Forest – begins at a point just a little further north on the highlands above the Donau river valley. The Bavarian Forest also shares an international border and wilderness (the Bohemian Forest) with the neighbouring Czech Republic. Partly because of Cold War neglect, these European borderlands still harbour ancient trees, rare wild flowers and infinite shades of green. The art of blowing glass has been practised here since the early 14th century thanks to the region's silica-rich soil and seemingly endless supply of firewood. Apart from one or two large factories, glass is still produced by individual craftsmen using traditional methods. Colourful local festivals include the *Drachenstich*, Bavaria's second-most important folk event after the *Octoberfest*. Food and accommodation are the least expensive in Germany and there are very few foreign tourists.

## BAVARIAN FOREST NATIONAL PARK✦✦✦

ⓘ **Bavarian Forest National Park Visitor Centre**
(Nationalpark Bayerischer Wald) *Hans-Eisenmann Haus, Böhmstrasse 35, Neuschönau (near Grafenau); tel: (08558) 96150. Open daily 0900–1700. The centre offers tours of the park, maps and advice on hiking.*

The Bavarian Forest is one of the last wilderness areas in Europe and the largest protected area outside Scandinavia, a region of forest meadows, high-lying moorland, mountain lakes and rare plants such as the insect-eating *Sonnentau*. There are 200km of trails and many opportunities to cross over into the Narodni Park Sumava – 'Bohemian National Forest' – in the Czech Republic (if you plan to do this, be sure to take your passport).

Bavaria almost doubled the amount of land designated as Nationalpark in 1997. Germany and the Czech Republic are now making a collective effort to save the area for future generations as a vast 'park without borders', which will be called **Intersilva**. The best towns to use as a base for exploring the park are **Grafenau**, **Finsterau**, **Neuschönau** and **Zwiesel**, and the best views of the region are from the peaks of the **Grosser Arber**, **Lusen** and **Rachel**.

Pfreimd Teunz Schönsee 193 DomaÅlice "vihov Mjøin

Nabburg Oberviechtach Signalberg Klenøi pod Öerchovem 22 10 Klatovy

E50 Schwarzenfeld Winklarn Tiefenbach 15 Öerchov Mrákov Kdynj 21 191 22 12 Plánice NalAovské Hory 21

Neunburg vorm Wald Waldmünchen 1042 26 Schönthal Fürth im Wald 22 18 Schwarzriegel 1079 Lam Janovice nad Uhlavou 40 Borek 859 Hradeóice Kolinec 18

Wackersdorf Rötz Neukirchen-Balbini Pemfling Eschlkam Neukirchen beim Heiligen Blut 27 Großer Osser 1293 Lohberg E53 Suóice 187

Steinberg Bodenwöhr 85 Pösing Weiding Rimbach Hohenwarth Grosse Arbersee 145 Hartmanice

urglengenfeld Nittenau Roding Cham 85 Kötzting Grosser Arber Bayerisch Eisenstein ελezná Ruda Kaóperské Hory

Walderbach Wald 17 Traitsching Miltach Blaibach Arnbruck Drachselsried 11 Lindberg

Regenstauf 16 13 Schorndorf 20 Prackenbach Rißlochfälle Bodenmais Glass Museum 1453 Černá Hora 1315

ersdorf Falkenstein Konzell Viechtach Teisnach Zwiesel Großer Rachel

gensburg Bernhardswald Stallwang Wiesenfelden Patersdorf Langdorf Regen Frauenau

Wenzenbach Wiesent Haibach Ruhmannsfelden Gotteszell Rinchnach Kirchdorf im Wald Bavarian Forest National Park

Neutraubling E56 Steinach Hundersdorf Schwarzach Bischofsmais Mauth Neuschöna

raubling Mintraching Kirchroth Bogen Offenberg Kirchberg Hohenau

Alteglofsheim Rain Aiterhofen Irlbach E53 Deggendorf Innernzell Grafenau 533

Aufhausen Straubing Straßkirchen Plattling Hengersberg Aschenstein 942 Saldenburg Röhrnbach Museumsdorf Bayerischer Wald 12

15 Schierling Geiselhöring Salching Oberschneiding 92 Otzing Moos Schöllnacht Iggensbach Tittling Neukirchen vorm Wald

Pfaffenberg Laberweinting Leiblfing 20 Wallersdorf Winzer E56 Eging am See Büchlberg

Mallersdorf Pilsting Wallerfing Osterhofen Künzing 3 Tiefenbach

Neufahrn in Niederbayern Bayerbach bei Ergoldsbach Landau an der Isar Eichendorf Vilshofen Windorf Salzweg

ttenburg der Laaber Postau 11 E53 Gottfrieding Roßbach Aldersbach Passau S

Essenbach 11 Dingolfing Niederviehbach Simbach Arnstorf Aidenbach Ortenburg

Landshut Niederaichbach Frontenhausen Reisbach Johanniskirchen Egglham Fürstenzell Neuhaus am Inn 137b

dorf Adlkofen Aham Malgersdorf Dietersburg Haarbach Griesbach im Rottal Schärding

hing Kumhausen Gerzen Schönau Bad Birnbach 388 Ruhstorf an der Rott Suben 137

Geisenhausen Gangkofen Falkenberg Pfarrkirchen Triftern Bayerbach Pocking Bad Füssing Mitterding Obernberg am Inn

Altfraunhofen 388 Vilsbiburg Eggenfelden Hebertsfelden 388 12

tenberg 388 299 Bodenkirchen Massing Mitterskirchen Rotthalmünster Wittibreut Ering 12

berg 15 Velden Buchbach Taufkirchen (Vils) Neumarkt-St Veit 588 Tann Reut 143 E56

khorn Mettenheim Erharting Reischach Zeilarn Simbach am Inn Braunau am Inn

Dorfen Schwindegg Ampfing 94 Marktl Haiming Mauerki

Volfgang Isen E552 Mühldorf am Inn 12 Tüßling Altötting Neuötting Schalchen nauβer Wald

Waldkraiburg Garching an der Alz Burgkirchen an der Alz Burghausen 156 Neukirchen an der Enknach Uttendorf

Reichertsheim Gars am Inn Ach St Radegund Geretsberg

Haag in Oberbayern Engelsberg

0 10 20km

# FRAUENAU*

**ⓘ Tourismus Information**
Hauptstrasse 12;
tel: (09926) 94100;
fax: (09926) 1799;
www.frauenau.de.

**ⓖ Glasmuseum €**
Am Museumpark 1; tel:
(09926) 940 035; fax:
(09926) 940 036;
www.glasmuseum-
frauenau.de. Closed until end
May 2005.

**Glashütte Valentin
Eisch** Am Steg 7; tel:
(09926) 1890; fax: (09926)
189 250. Open Mon–Fri
0900–1800, Sat 0900–1600;
May–Oct 1000–1600.

Frauenau prides itself on being 'the glass heart of the Bavarian Forest'. It is home to the **Glashütte Freiherr von Poschinger** (*Moosauhütte 12; tel: (09926) 94010; fax: (09926) 1711. Open Mon–Fri 0930–1800, Sat 0900–1200*), the region's oldest glass factory (1420), which became famous centuries later for its *Jugendstil* pieces. Contemporary artists such as Erwin Eisch – his motto is 'poetry in glass' – are working in styles that are more avant-garde. The **Glasmuseum***  displays two and a half millennia of glass history from ancient Egypt to art deco.

# GRAFENAU*

**ⓘ Tourismus Information**
Rathausgasse 1; tel: (08552)
962343; fax: (08552) 4690;
e-mail: tourismus@
grafenau.de. Open Mon–Fri
0830–1630, Sat 1000–
1130, Sun 1000–1100.

Grafenau was once an important station on the *Goldener Steig*, the medieval salt road between southern Germany and Bohemia, but lost most of its historic buildings in repeated fires. It was also a major producer of snuff tobacco, which is still sold in an open market on Saturdays (as well as delicious local smoked ham). Today, Grafenau makes its living from tourism, serving as a convenient gateway to the Bavarian Forest and a base for a forest vacation. An 8km trail that starts from the Nationalparkhaus in nearby Neuschönau (*see Bavarian Forest, National Park, page 158*) leads through the **Tier-Freigelände***, a reserve for animals that used to roam wild in the forest such as bears, wolves, lynx and buffalo.

### Accommodation and food in Grafenau

**Sporthotel Sonnenhof €€€** *Sonnenstrasse 12; tel: (08552) 4480; fax: (08552) 4680.* A hotel for people who want to get fit, with an archery range, tennis courts, sauna, swimming pool, ski instructors in winter and massage all year round. All rooms have balconies with views of the Bavarian Forest.

**Säumerhof €€** *Steinberg 32; tel: (08552) 408 990; fax: (08552) 408 9950; www.saeumerhof.de.* This family-run inn is a hilltop idyll with inspiring views and modern, comfortable rooms. People come from far and wide to eat from the *Bayrische Menü* in the restaurant.

## GROSSER ARBER***

The Grosser Arber (1456m) is 'King' of the Bavarian Forest. It can be reached by *Sesselbahn* (chair lift) from the road above the Grosser Arbersee. On a clear day, you can see the shiny glaciers of the Alps from its summit. It is the most popular peak in the region and, on Sundays and holidays, feels like one big *Volksfest*. Walkers who want more solitude should continue on to the **Kleiner Arber** (1384m).

## GROSSER ARBERSEE**

The lake was created in the last Ice Age at the foot of the **Grosser Arber**, the highest peak in the Bavarian Forest; it is an easy 6km walk to its cousin, the **Kleiner Arbersee**. There is a *Märchenwald* (fairytale forest) for children and a *Biergarten* for their parents. A footpath along the **Arber river** leads past a brace of waterfalls and cascades in the **Rieslochschlucht***(gorge).

**Below**
The snowy banks of the Arber river

# MUSEUMSDORF BAYERISCHER WALD*

**Museumsdorf €** Am
*Dreiburgensee, 3km
northwest of Tittling.
Herrenstrasse 11; tel:
(08504) 40461;
www.museumsdorf.com*

This is a walk through a bygone way of life, spread out under the open sky. A whole village of farmhouses from all over the Bavarian Forest, some with all of their outbuildings, has been brought together, including a 15th-century mill, a 17th-century schoolhouse, a smithy and an 18th-century tavern where you can drink beer.

# PASSAU***

**Passau Tourismus**
*Rathausplatz 3;
tel: (0851) 955 980;
fax: (0851) 35107;
www.passau.de/tourist. Open
Easter–mid-Oct Mon–Fri
0830–1800, Sat–Sun
1000–1400; mid-Oct–Easter
Mon–Thur 0830–1700, Fri
0830–1600.*

A romantic Donau cruise is the best way to see Passau. The
**Dreiflüsse Rundhfahrt**
**€€** ('Three Rivers Round Trip') is a city tour lasting 45 minutes. Contact Donauschiffahrt **Wurm & Köck,** *Höllgasse 26; tel: (0851) 929 292; fax: (0851) 35518; www.wurm-koeck.de.* Boats leave from the Luitpold-Brücke.

**Veste Oberhaus €**
*Veste Oberhaus 125;
tel: (0851) 49335;
www.oberhausmuseum.de.
Open Tue–Fri 0900–1700,
Sat–Sun 1000–1800.
Closed in Feb.*

**Glasmuseum €** Am
*Rathausplatz; tel: (0851)
35071; fax: (0851) 31712;
www.glasmuseum.de. Open
Mar–Sep daily 1000–1600;
shorter hours in winter.*

Passau has one of the most beautiful settings of any city in Europe, on the confluence of three rivers, crossed by 15 bridges. Although it is one of the oldest cities north of the Alps, it lost most of its medieval features to the fires of 1662 and 1680. Italian architects gave it a new baroque identity and, at times, you might think you are in Italy. For most of its history, Passau was ruled by prince-bishops, who built the medieval fortress of **Veste Oberhaus**, high above the town on a cliff across the Donau. Its grandiose panorama elicited praise from people as diverse as Napoleon and Richard Wagner, who wanted to build his opera house there instead of in Bayreuth. The **Dom** is the largest baroque church north of the Alps, with the world's largest church organ – 17,388 pipes (*there are weekday concerts at noon, and 1930 on Thursday*). The play of light and water along the **Dreiflusseckspaziergang** ('Three Rivers Walk') seems almost Mediterranean. It is equally impressive indoors, reflected in the 20,000 exhibits of the **Glasmuseum**, whose highlights are the exquisite Bohemian glass and the *Jugendstil* and art deco pieces.

## Accommodation and food in Passau

**Rotel Inn €** *Tel: (0851) 95160; fax: (0851) 9516 100; e-mail: info@rotel.de; www.rotel-inn.de.* Built in the shape of a sleeping man on the bank of the Donau, this 'rotel' is, to say the least, an unusual place to stay. The rooms are the width of a double bed. It is friendly, very cheap and popular with backpackers and people on bicycle tours.

**Schloss Ort €€** *Ort 11; tel: (0851) 34072-73; fax: (0851) 31817; www.schlosshotel-passau.de.* Located right near the romantic Dreiflusseck ('three-river-corner'), this 13th-century castle has 21st-century hotel rooms.

**Wilder Mann €€€** *Am Rathausplatz; tel: (0851) 35071; fax: (0851) 31712; www.wilder-mann.com.* A converted patrician house on the waterfront across from the Rathaus. It has the city's best restaurant, a rooftop café and the Glass Museum.

**Heilig-Geist-Stiftschenke** €€ *Heilig-Geist-Gasse 4; tel: (0851) 2607; fax (0851) 35387; www.stiftskeller-passau.de.* A wine bar with a thousand-year-old cellar, trellised garden and regional cooking.

# SCHLOSS FALKENSTEIN*

The castle of Falkenstein rises abruptly from a cliff above the town of the same name and is surrounded by a delightful Naturpark. Once inside the arcaded inner courtyard, you can mount the narrow steps and enter the *Bergfried* (keep) through a coin-operated gate. Enjoy the view at the top and try to imagine the most famous incident in the castle's history when a group of women in the 15th century saved the castle by fighting off warring Hussites from this stone tower. Medieval festivities are held in the courtyard in summer (*June–August*). The **Naturpark Falkenstein***, between the castle and the Perlbach river, is a maze of gnarled oak, beech and pine trees, dotted with moss-draped cliffs. The soil is rich in ferns and a variety of Alpine flowers.

**Below**
Schloss Falkenstein

# ZWIESEL*

**ⓘ Kurverwaltung**
*Stadtplatz 27; tel:
(09922) 84050; fax: (09922)
840 545; www.zwiesel.de*

**ⓜ Waldmuseum €**
*Stadtplatz 29;
tel: (09922) 60888;
www.waldmuseum-zwiesel.de.
Open mid-May to mid-Oct
Mon–Fri 0900–1700, Sat–Sun
1000–1200, 1400–1600;
closed Nov, limited hours in
winter.*

**Dampfbier-brauerei €**
*Regener Strasse 9–11; tel:
(09922) 84660. A brewery
tour is followed by
a sampling of local ales.*

**🍴 Bayerwald-
Bärwurzerei** *2km out
of Zwiesel on Frauenauer
Strasse 80–82; tel: (09922)
84330; www.baerwurzerei.de.
The Hieke family distils over
20 types of Schnaps.*

The glass-blowing centre of the region sits in a basin surrounded by three peaks – **Arber**, **Falkenstein** and **Rachel**. More than 1500 of its residents are employed in blowing, engraving or painting glass. Most of them welcome visitors, and its **Waldmuseum***  is one of the most popular of Germany's provincial museums, thanks to its creative exhibits about forestry, the traditions and crafts of the Bavarian Forest and the history of glass-making. The town is the venue for the *Volksgesangswettbewerb* ('Folk Song Competition'), Bavaria's most authentic folk music festival, held in June and September.

## Accommodation and food in Zwiesel

**Hotel zur Waldbahn €€** *Bahnhofsplatz 2; tel: (09922) 8570; fax: (09922) 857 222; www.zurwaldbahn.de.* An elegant hotel originally opened to serve passengers arriving by train on their way to or from the Czech Republic.

**Deutscher Rhein €** *Stadtplatz 42; tel: (09922) 50096-0; fax: (09922) 5009639.* Sit down in the Jankabräu with the locals and order a *Böhmische Bohème Bier*.

# Suggested tour

**Total distance:** 215km. The detour to Furth im Wald adds 46km if you return to the main itinerary, but only 6km if you use it as an alternate route.

**Time:** One long day of driving with short stops, or 2 to 3 leisurely days with forest walks and visits to glass blowers and museums.

**Glasbläserei Schmid** *Stadtplatz 36; tel/fax: (09922) 609 509; www.glasblaserei-schmid.de. Open Mon–Fri 1000–1800; Sat 1000–1600; Sun 1100–1600.* Watch glass being blown by virtuoso craftsmen and women.

The 'Waldbahn' or 'forest route' (*tel: (09942) 905 504; www.bayerwald-ticket.com*), narrow-gauge railway travels through the forest between Grafenau and Bodenmais.

**PASSAU ❶** is on the Austrian border, 179km east of Munich. Often described as a smaller version of Salzburg, it is best seen on foot. There is a large car park (beneath the Holiday Inn) on the Donau side of town near the train station. The B85 follows the Ilz river north to Tittling. One of the largest open-air museums in Europe, the **MUSEUMSDORF BAYERISCHER WALD ❷** is on the Dreiburgensee, 3km northwest of Tittling (20km), in the direction of Thurmansdorf. The B85 continues north; before it reaches Schönberg, turn east on the B533 and carry on up a deep gorge that winds its way up to **GRAFENAU ❸**, the gateway to the **BAVARIAN FOREST NATIONAL PARK (Nationalpark Bayerwald) ❹**. A *Landstrasse* heads north through dark stands of forest along the edge of the park to the glass-making towns of **FRAUENAU ❺** and, 3km further along the banks of the Kleine Regen, **ZWIESEL ❻**. In the village of Ludwigsthal, the road rubs shoulders with a Byzantine-style church. Inside, it is covered from top to bottom with luminous *Jugendstil* (German art nouveau) painting and mosaics.

**Getting out of the car**: Between Ludwigsthal and Regenhütte, watch for signs to the **Zwiesler Waldhaus**, once an inn on the Bohemian *Salzstrasse* ('Salt Road') and now a well-appointed hotel. A path from the car park leads into the **Mittelsteighütte**, a primeval forest of 500-year-old trees, which can be reached in 30 minutes. For people who have time and stamina, a strenuous 2-hour climb scales the summit of the **Grosser Falkenstein** (1315m).

Several hairpin turns climb up to the **GROSSER ARBERSEE ❼**. The chair lift to the **GROSSER ARBER ❽** is further up the road. Turn on the car radio and you are more likely to hear Czech than German as the road runs parallel to the Czech border for the next 46km. From a high ridge it executes sweeping turns on its way down to the Weisser Regen river, which it follows through the **Lamer Winkel** ('corner') an idyllic triangle bounded by the mountain ranges of the Osser, Arber and Kaitersberg. The main town is **Lam**.

**Left**
The Bavarian Forest National Park

**Detour**: Continue northwest to **Neukirchen beim Heligen Blut**. In the 15th century, this town was called 'Neukirchen vor dem Böhmerwald'. During one of the region's frequent religious brawls, Hussites (Bohemian Knights) were pillaging the town and one of them carelessly struck a wooden statue of the Virgin Mary. Blood flowed from the crack, soaking the splinters. The church that was built on the spot became one of the largest pilgrimage churches in Europe. Further north (11km) lies **Furth im Wald**, famous among Bavarians for the **Drachenstich** in August (the second biggest folk festival after *Oktoberfest*). Based on a medieval mystery play about St George and the Dragon, the play stars a local young man and woman as the *Ritterpaar* ('knightly couple'). When the hero spears the 19m mechanical monster, its spews real fire and squirts a fountain of fake blood.

## Forest-dying and forest prophecy

The Bavarian Forest appears healthy – only a trained eye can detect the symptoms – but *Waldsterben* ('forest-dying') is a problem on both sides of the border. The mysterious disease can kill a mature, healthy-seeming tree in a matter of weeks. There appears to be many causes for it, including farm fertilisation and acid rain that drenches trees with factory pollution. However, the latest research indicates that the principal cause is the emission from the millions of cars travelling German *Autobahns*. The phenomenon of *Waldsterben* recalls the alarming prophecies of *Der Mühlhiasl*, a Nostradamus of the common people who lived in the 18th century. The 'forest-prophet' said that he could see 'what is coming as if it were happening'. According to him, 'wood will become as expensive as bread' and 'the Bavarian Forest will be ravaged and devoured, the Bohemian Forest swept with a broom; the forest will be desolate, its people sick'.

Continue through the Weisser Regen Valley towards Kötzting. The road climbs up and down a shoulder of the Kaitersberg. **Kötzting** ❾ is a pretty town, wedged between mountain and river. The local **Pfingstritt** is an ancient Whit Monday festival going back to 1421: a procession of several hundred horses and men, both in regional costume, sets off at 0800 for the pilgrimage church of Steinbühl. Their return triggers a mass celebration on the market square. The Schwarzer Regen joins the Weisser Regen east of town and the two rivers become one Regen flowing towards the Donau. Turn right on the B85 at Miltach. Cham, the next major town, has few monuments from its long history but knows how to brew beer as well as anyone in the Bavarian Forest. If do you stop there, stock up on the Hofmark brewery's *Würzig-Mild* and *Würzig-Herb* (a bitter). The town's main surviving landmark, appropriately, is the **Biertor** ('beer tower'). The *Landstrasse* from Cham to **SCHLOSS FALKENSTEIN** ❿ curves and dips through relatively empty country passing isolated farms and stands of woods. When you enter the town of Falkenstein, head straight for its castle – 150m up a sheer hill that begins behind the church. If there is time, walk through the **Naturpark Falkenstein**. On leaving the town, follow the signs north (signposted Zell or Roding) towards the B16. The *Landstrasse* follows the Perlbach river downstream through a dreamy valley of woods, cliffs and meadows where you will be frequently tempted to stop and get out. There is a tottering castle ruin – **Sengersberg** – on a hill before the hamlet of Au. When you reach the B16, go left (west) to drive to Regensburg.

**Detour:** Drive south from Falkenstein on the country road 15km to **Wörth an der Donau**. From there you can reach **Regensburg** ⓫ (*see pages 138–147*) by way of the road that skirts the north shore of the Donau (signposted Kruckenberg, Bach, Sulzbach) with a scenic stop at the **Walhalla** (*see page 147*), particularly beautiful at sunset, or simply zip down the *Autobahn* (A3).

## Also worth exploring

From Passau, drive on the B12 to Philippsreut (46km from Passau), a border town that suffers from crossborder traffic jams. The *Landstrasse* going south (signposts for Bischofsreut, Haidmühle) will plunge you into the depths of the borderland forest. Leopoldsreut is a village right out of Grimm's Fairy Tales. Best of all, you can drive almost to the top of **Dreissessel** – 'Three Armchairs' (67km from Passau). The summit is an easy 20-minute walk from the car park. Locals claim you could always cross the border by way of this lonely mountain even at the height of the Cold War.

# Salzburg

### Ratings

Architecture ●●●●●

Music ●●●●●

Scenery ●●●●●

Shopping ●●●●○

Children ●●●○○

Museums ●●●○○

Food and drink ●●○○○

Nature ●●○○○

The legendary traveller, Alexander von Humboldt, called Salzburg one of the seven most beautiful places on earth. Although it was a Celtic and Roman settlement, its glory days began in the Middle Ages when it became a bishopric and fabulously rich from trade in salt. At its height, Salzburg was the capital of a powerful clerical state that included parts of the Tyrol and Italy. The ruling prince-archbishops, inspired by Italian models, built a 'German Rome' at the foot of the Alps, a quintessentially baroque city of fountains, domes and church spires, crowned by an impregnable fortress, the Festung Hohensalzburg. The clerical realm only became part of Austria in 1816. 'Happiness lives here, nothing evil enters', according to a Roman inscription dug up in the 19th century in a city square. No tourist brochure could put it better. Today, 'all Salzburg is a stage' that honours (and crassly exploits) its native son, Mozart. In summer, it is the setting for Europe's most élite music festival, the *Salzburger Festspiele*.

## Sights

**ℹ Salzburg Information**

*Mozartplatz 5; tel: (0662) 889 870; fax: (0662) 8898 732; www.salzburg.info. Open daily 0900–1900.* The **Salzburg Card** is a kind of single-price admission to the whole city (24, 48 or 72 hours for €21, €28 or €34, children half price), which includes public transport, the castle and castle funicular, museums and palaces, etc.

### Dom✦✦

The Cathedral is the most impressive early baroque church north of the Alps. St Virgil built the first church on the spot in 774, but it, and many successors, burned down. Their floorplans are inlaid in the crypt beneath the central rotunda. Santino Solari designed the present cathedral, which was begun in 1614 under prince-archbishop Markus Sittikus and consecrated in 1628 by archbishop Paris Lodron. The magnificent dome was largely destroyed in one of 19 attacks by Allied bombers in World War II, but was later painstakingly restored.

The bronze doors symbolise (from left to right) faith, hope and charity. Mozart was baptised in 1756 in the huge bronze baptismal font that stands to the left as you enter. The **Dommuseum** (cathedral museum and treasury, entrance in the vestibule) holds holy treasures collected by the archbishops from the Middle Ages to the 19th century and the secular **Kunst- und Wunderkammer** (art and rarities collection) is from the 17th and 18th centuries.

Innsbrucker Bundestrasse

Aiglhofstrasse

Warfelsteinstr

Lindhofstrasse

Müllner Hauptstrasse

Schwarzstrasse

Franz Josef Strasse

Schrannengasse

Rainerstrasse

P. Lodron Str

Linzer Gasse

Bayerhamerstrasse

Schallmooser Hauptstrasse

**Mirabell Palace and Gardens**

■ **Natural History Museum**

■ **Salzburg Barockmuseum**

*Kapuzinerberg*

**Mozarts Wohnhaus**

Ganshofstrasse

Ed. Baumgartner Str

Bayernstrasse

Schwedenstrasse

Maxglaner Hauptstrasse

*Mönchsberg*

Reichenhaller Strasse

Neutorstrasse

Griesgasse

Staats-brücke

Steingasse

Imbergstrasse

Salzach

Getreidegasse

Hofstallgasse

**Mozart's Birthplace**

**Residenz**

Moz...platz

ℹ️

**Franziskanerkirche**

✝ **Dom**

**Stiftskirche St Peter**

**Petersfriedhof**

**Nonnberg Convent**

Hellbrunner Strass

Moosstrasse

Leopoldskronstrasse

Gorianstrasse

Nussdorfer Strasse

*Rainberg*

Sinnhubstrasse

Oskar Kokoschka W.

**Hohensalzburg Fortress**

*Mönchsberg*

Brunnhausgasse

Nonnberggasse

Petersbrunnstrasse

Erzabt Klotz Strasse

Bräuhausstrasse

Dürlingerstrasse

Haslbergerweg

Leopoldskronstrasse

Leopoldskroner Allee

Sinnhubstrasse

Fürstenallee

Nonntaler Hauptstrasse

Firmianstrasse

König Ludwig Strasse

*Leopoldskroner Weiher*

Gotschenweg

Thumeggerstrasse

Fürstenallee

Hofhaymer Allee

Moosstrasse

Zwieselweg

Berchtesgadener Strasse

Gneiser Strasse

Morzger Strasse

Georg. Nikolaus von Nissen Strasse

Santnergasse

Jakob Hacksteiner Weg

Konstanze Weber Gasse

**St Peter's Churchyard, Cemetery & Catacombs**

Höglwörthweg

0     400m

0     400 yards

**Festung**
**Hohensalzburg** €€
*Mönchsberg 34; tel: (0662)*
*8424 3011; fax: (0662)*
*8424 3020; e-mail:*
*salzburger.burgen.schloesser*
*@salzburg.gv.at. Open mid-*
*Mar to mid-Jun 0900–1800;*
*mid-Jun to mid-Sept*
*0900–1900; mid-Sept to*
*mid-Mar 0900–1700. You*
*can take a tour either with*
*a guide or with an*
*audiophone; the guide will*
*let you see the castle loo*
*but the recording is*
*actually more informative.*

**Mozarts Geburtshaus**
€€ *Getreidegasse 9; tel:*
*(0662) 844 313; fax:*
*(0662) 840 693; e-mail:*
*archiv@mozarteum.at.*
*Open daily 0900–1800;*
*Jul–Aug until 1900.*

### Festung Hohensalzburg***

Hohensalzburg Fortress is the largest fully preserved fortress in central Europe (c 1077). It was built to protect Salzburg's ruling prince-archbishops from their enemies and, on occasions, from their own parishioners. Prince-archbishop Leonhard von Keutschach greatly expanded the fortress in 1500 (his symbol was a turnip, and you will see turnips carved all over the castle). The fortress grounds are open to the public and you are free to wander around its courtyards, narrow lanes and ramparts. The fortress was a city unto itself with its own bakery, blacksmith, armoury, granary and stables. A tour inside begins with a look at seven historic models of the castle from its crude beginnings as a wooden structure to the mighty stone edifice of today. It continues on to the torture chamber, the prison tower, the staterooms and the **Golden Chamber**, with a pillar damaged by a cannonball during the Peasants' Revolt of 1525. There are two small museums: the **Rainer Regimental Museum** follows one regiment through centuries of military history; and a small **Castle Museum** contains historic odds and ends, the most interesting relating to the all-powerful prince-archbishop Wolf Dietrich von Raitenau, whose career ended in the castle dungeon.

### Franziskanerkirche**

The Franciscan Church, architecturally speaking, is an interminable lesson in art history in which many styles have been given equal time. Surprisingly, the end effect is one of deep harmony. The first church was founded during the 8th century and destroyed by fire in 1167. The dark Romanesque nave, built in 1223, gives way to a brilliantly illuminated late-Gothic choir (1408–60); the baroque high altar by Fischer von Erlach (1709) was created to hold a Madonna carved centuries earlier.

### Getreidegasse*

Walking down this narrow street will remind you that the medieval city, wedged between Mönchsberg and the Salzach river, could only expand in one direction. The heavy flow of tourists is subject to the same restrictions. The elaborately ornamented signs (one of the largest belongs to McDonald's), finely carved portals and arcaded courtyards add a decorative touch to the main business of shopping. Wolfgang Amadeus, one of seven children, was born to Leopold and Anna Mozart in 1756 in a third-floor apartment at No 9. The family lived there until 1773, then moved across the river. Mozart's birthplace is now a museum, **Mozarts Geburtshaus***, where visitors can see family portraits, his childhood violin and clavichord, and the rooms where he lived and wrote music – Mozart composed his first piece when he was just four years old.

**Right**
Karajansplatz (formerly
Sigmundsplatz)

### Mozarts Wohnhaus*

World War II bombing raids all but destroyed the house that was

**Mozarts Wohnhaus**
€€€ *Makartplatz 8; tel: (0662) 8742 2740; fax: (0662) 872 924; e-mail: archiv@mozarteum.at. Open daily 0900–1800; Jul–Aug until 1900.*

**Katakomben €** *Tel: (0662) 8445 760; fax: (0662) 844 576 80; www.stift-stpeter.at. Open May–Sept Tue–Sun 1030–1700; Oct–Apr Wed–Thur 1030–1530, Fri–Sun 1030–1600.*

**Below**
The Mirabell Garden

Mozart's second home, and the present building is largely a reconstruction. The exhibits do not justify the price of admission but an audiophone recording and film provide a moving account of Mozart's family life.

### Petersfriedhof✦✦✦

There is no better place to contemplate the particularly Austrian fascination with death than St Peter's, one of the oldest and most beautiful cemeteries in the world. Its origins go back at least as far as the days of the Roman settlement, Juvavum. 'Sealed in dreams' is how Salzburg poet Georg Trakl described it. Early Christians carved out the first tombs and cells – the **Katakomben✦** – in the cliff of Mönchsberg. The elegant arcades that now line the cliff were built over a thousand years later. Many generations of Salzburgers lie buried beneath them, including Santino Solari (the Dom's architect), Nannerl Mozart (Mozart's sister) and Michael Haydn (younger brother of Joseph Haydn). In the middle of the graveyard, the Gothic **Margarethenkapelle✦** is all but draped in delicately carved tombstones.

**ⓘ Residenz €€**
*Residenzplatz 1; tel:*
*(0662) 8042 2690; fax:*
*(0662) 8042 2978; e-mail:*
*salzburger.burgen.schloesser*
*@salzburg.gv.at. Open daily*
*1000–1700. Art Gallery*
*closed Oct–Mar.*

## Residenz*

Prince-archbishop Wolf Dietrich von Raitenau had this palace built in 1595 on the site of an earlier one. Its modest exterior hides magnificent chambers and vast swathes of pomp and circumstance – ornate chairs beneath frescoed ceilings, Gobelin tapestries and curiosities such as a brass balustrade that has been 'tuned'. The northwest wing was added in the 18th century. The **Residenz Gallery***
(art gallery) has an interesting but not unmissable collection of European paintings from the 16th to 19th centuries, with a couple of Dutch masters (Rembrandt, Rubens) and Italian, French and Austrian works from the 19th century (Amerling, Ender, Waldmüller). Paintings to look out for are Rembrandt's *Rembrandts Mutter, betend*; Paulus Potter's *Viehaustrieb*; Gaspard Dughet's *Heroische Landschaft mit Figuren*; Ferdinand Georg Waldmüller's *Kinder im Fenster*; and Hans Makart's *Gesellschaftsszene*.

## Stiftskirche St Peter*

This Benedictine abbey church (c 800) belongs to one of the oldest monasteries north of the Alps. Two major baroque face-lifts and the addition of a dome fail to completely obscure the massiveness and geometry of the original Romanesque, triple-aisled basilica. Look out for the Roman tombstones used as building blocks in the walls of the main portal. Inside, there are no fewer than 15 side altars. One of them, in the south aisle, is said to contain the tomb of St Rupert. The decoration of the central nave with so many works on canvas is something of an anomaly. They tell the life stories of Saints Rupert and Benedict, while frescoes on the ceiling of the nave depict scenes from the life of St Peter. The grille between the porch and nave is a famous example of wrought-iron artistry.

# Entertainment and festivals

 **Salzburger Festspiele**
*Hofstallgasse 1; tel: (0662)*
*8045 500; fax: (0662)*
*8045 555; e-mail:*
*info@salzburgfestival.at*

**Marionettentheater**
*Schwarzstrasse 24; tel:*
*(0662) 8724 060; fax:*
*(0662) 882 141;*
*www.marionetten.at. Open*
*Apr–Sep, also at Christmas,*
*Easter and during Mozart*
*Week (Jan).*

The **Festspiele** (Festival Hall), crouching beneath the cliff of Mönchsberg, is the main venue for operas and operettas, and the world-class **Salzburger Festspiele** ('Salzburg international festival'; *late July to the end of August*). The **Osterfestspiele** at Easter, and **Mozart Week** in late January, are other high points of a prodigious musical calendar. Concerts are performed in leafy **Schloss Hellbrunn** from early May until mid-September. The delightful **Marionettentheater** employs marionettes that gesticulate and dance in the air to recordings of operas and ballets. Other important venues are: the **International Mozarteum Foundation** (*Schwarzstrasse 26; tel: (0662) 873 154; fax: (0662) 874 454; www.mozarteum.at*); the **Landestheater** (*Schwarzstrasse 22; tel: (0662) 8715 120; www.theater.co.at*) for classical music, ballets and plays; the **Jazzclub Urban-Keller** (*Schallmooser Hauptstrasse 50; tel: (0662) 870 894; www.urbankeller.at*) for live jazz;

and **Rockhouse** (*Schallmooser Hauptstrasse 46; tel: (0662) 8849 140; www.rockhouse.at*) for rock and pop bands.

## Accommodation and food

The **Salzburg Information** office will help with reservations for a small fee, but remember, the city is hopelessly overbooked during the Festspiele in early summer.

**Goldener Hirsch €€€** *Getreidegasse 37; tel: (0662) 80840; fax: (0662) 843 349; www.goldenerhirsch.com*. This inn has has been coddling its well-heeled guests since 1465. The lobby and bathrooms are modernised; otherwise it is still traditional. The rooms have deep windows with views, hand-painted farm furniture and fluffy feather beds.

**Haus Wartenberg €** *Riedenburger Strasse 2; tel: (0662) 848 400; fax: (0662) 8484 005*. It is a pleasant 10-minute walk from this small, rustic hotel (20 rooms) to the Altstadt (Old Town). The restaurant serves refined variations on Austrian fare.

**Schloss Mönchstein €€€** *Mönchstein-Park 26; tel: (0662) 8485 550; fax: (0662) 848 559; www.monchstein.com*. One of the top hotels in the city, set in a castle with its own park. The exquisite chapel is popular for weddings. Although the restaurant is essentially French, it displays a sense of imagination in the use of Alpine ingredients – try their *Blutwurst* ravioli.

**Café Tomaselli €€** *Alter Markt 9; tel: (0662) 8444 880*. This is the local bastion of *Kaffeehauskultur*, old ladies in hats and *Jeunesse Doré*. Mozart loved their pastries and so will you.

## Shopping

**Grünmarkt** *Universitätsplatz. Open Mon–Fri 0600–1900, Sat 0600–1300*. The market is the best place for a quick snack or to gather provisions for a picnic – bread, fruit, vegetables and sausage, either smoked, grilled or steamed.

**Stranz & Scio** *Sigmund-Haffner-Gasse 16; tel: (0662) 841638*. The shop regales you with pastries based on recipes popular in Mozart's day – try the ineffable *Capezzoli di Venere* (once you get over the name, which means 'warts of Venus'). Each one packs a punch of nougat, white and dark chocolate and marinated cherries.

**Salzburger Heimatwerk** *Residenzplatz 9; tel: (0662) 884 110; fax: (0662) 844 110 44; www.sbg.heimatwerk.at*. This is the first address for investigating Salzburg crafts, from fabrics to ceramics.

# Suggested tour

The Altstadt of Salzburg is a mostly pedestrian zone. The enclosed parking garage is the 24-hour **Altstadt-Garage** at Mönschsberg.

**Distance:** 2km.

**Time:** The Salzach river divides the city in two with the Altstadt on the left bank. If time is short, a half day is enough visit the fortress and cathedral first and spend the rest of the time walking around the Altstadt. It is densely packed with churches, palaces, museums, fountains and shops. However, a long weekend is a more reasonable allotment of time

Start at the **DOM** ❶. Walk out into the Domplatz and then left around the cathedral into **Kapitelplatz**. The elegant fountain in the

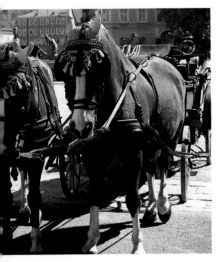

corner, **Kapitelschwemme**, was used to water the horses of the prince-archbishops. The funicular that ascends to the fortress of **HOHENSALZBURG** ❷, more than a century old but still well oiled, is across the square in a bend in the Festungsgasse (Fortress Lane). It delivers its passengers to the lower ramparts, where stone steps lead up into the fortress itself. At the end of a tour of the fortress follow signs into the castle courtyard. Walk past the vast linden tree to the octagonal cistern in the middle and duck under the unmarked portal beyond it. It leads down steep steps through 'hell's gate' and over a tiny drawbridge into the upper end of Festungsgasse that links castle and city.

**Detour:** On the way down, the road forks. The right-hand path will take you to the **Stift Nonnberg** (Nonnberg Convent). This Benedictine convent, founded by St Rupert around 700, is the oldest continuously inhabited nunnery in the German-speaking world. The late-Gothic church has intriguing but faded Romanesque frescoes (c 1150) of saints in Byzantine dress, and an old crypt. It has a view of Salzburg that is as charming as the one from the Festung, but in the contemplative setting of a small terrace shaded by ancient trees. You might come across a Sound of Music tour. The character of Maria (played by Julie Andrews) was a novice nun in the Nonnberg abbey.

Near the end of the Festungsgasse, the **Stiegl-Keller** appears on the right. This is the city's oldest *Bierkeller*, founded in 1492, though part of the interior was redecorated in the 1920s. Best of all is its *Biergarten*. Around a bend, the Festungsgasse runs right into a narrow entrance to **PETERSFRIEDHOF** ❸, which is squeezed next to Mönchsberg. After walking around the cemetery, continue on to the **STIFTSKIRCHE ST PETER** ❹, passing, on your left, the **Peterskeller**. Originally the wine cellar of the Salzburg prince-archbishops, it has been welcoming guests for over a thousand years. Cross the square and go straight through the passageway to the **FRANZISKANERKIRCHE** ❺; the entrance is around the corner to the left in Sigmund-Haffner-Gasse. Exit by the same way and walk down Sigmund-Haffner-Gasse, ducking left under the covered passageway to Universitätsplatz. There is a daily market – the **Grünmarkt** – here, and it is an excellent place for a quick lunch. The **Kollegiankirche** (1696–1707), by Fischer von Erlach, dominates the square. Architecturally, it is a masterpiece that influenced many other baroque churches in Austria, southern Germany and Prague with its geometric forms and undulating, convex façade that rises dynamically to its towers. Enter the portal of **Universitätsplatz.** You will find yourself in an inner courtyard surrounded by Romanesque arcades with one of Salzburg's best sweet shops, **Schatz**, at your elbow. It doubles as a small café. Buy your

*Mozartkuglen* (Mozart 'chocolate balls') here; they are the best in town. The opposite end of the passage leads into **GETREIDEGASSE ⑥** and you will emerge at No 3. **Mozarts Geburthaus** (Mozart's Birthplace) is a couple of doors to the left at No 9. Carry on down the street as far as Sterngasse, going right through it and right again on Griesgasse. There is a **Trachtenmuseum** (Museum of Folk Dress) at No 23 which will give you an idea of what traditional folk dress looks like and to what extent the many *Trachten* shops in Salzburg follow or depart from it.

**Detour:** Cross the footbridge – Makartsteg – to Makartplatz, a busy square where tourists and taxis compete for space. The **Landestheater**, **Marionettentheater** and **Mozarteum** are to the left, in Schwarzstrasse (Nos 22, 24 and 26). **MOZARTS WOHNHAUS ⑦** is on the right-hand side, across the square; **Mirabell Palace and Gardens** are to the left. The prince-archbishops who ruled Salzburg, for all their power, were not allowed to marry. Most of them kept several *Schlafweiber* ('bed wenches') who discreetly used the servants' back door. Wolf Dietrich von Raitenau broke with this 'tradition' by loving a woman openly and faithfully – Salome Alt, a merchant's daughter – and acknowledging the 16 children he had with her. He went so far as to build a palace and gardens for her in 1606, the 'Altenau', later renamed Mirabell. It was substantially remodelled between 1721 and 1727, and again in 1818 after a disastrous town fire. The symmetrical **Mirabell Gardens** are adorned with figures from Greek mythology and huge marble vases. The **Zwerglgarten**, an 18th-century collection of grotesque garden gnomes, provides comic relief. Somewhat more highbrow, the **Salzburg Barockmuseum** has a small but rewarding 17th- and 18th-century collection of European art (*open Tue–Sat 0900–1200, 1400–1700*). The palace itself, now the Town Hall, is most interesting for its **monumental staircase***. The figures – larger-than-life Roman goddesses with perky breasts, and proud heroes with bulging thighs – are by Georg Raphael Donner. He also carved a dozen chubby *putti* for the staircase banisters. The **Marble Hall**, on the second floor, is used for weddings and concerts.

Go right into Hagenauerplatz and return to Getreidegasse, turning left to reach the **Rathausplatz**. The modest **Rathaus** (Town Hall) pales in comparison to the grand monuments of the prince-bishops. Getreidegasse now becomes **Judengasse**. It was, as the name suggests, once the heart of a Jewish community, first mentioned in 1284. The synagogue, now the Gasthof Höllbräu, was at No 15 until 1415. Large numbers of Jews were executed in 1349 and 1404. In 1498, prince-archbishop Leonhard von Keutschach banned Jews from his realm 'forever and eternally'. The commercial nexus of medieval Salzburg was the **Waagplatz**, where goods were weighed for taxation and grain hoarded in the attic. Number 4 has a Roman cellar used for art exhibitions. A memorial plaque and small museum in the courtyard of No 1a honour Georg Trakl (1887–1914) who was born in the house. Trakl, the city's most famous literary son, remains something of an

🅗 **Haus der Natur €**
*Museumplatz 5; tel:
(0662) 842 653; fax:
(0662) 847 905;
www.hausdernatur.at. Open
daily 0900–1700.*

**Hellbrunn Palace €€**
*Fürstenweg 37 (5km south
of Altstadt); tel: (0662) 820
3720; www.hellbruhn.at..
Guided tours of castle and
fountains, Apr and Oct daily
0900–1630, May–Sep daily
0900–1730, Jul–Aug until
2200.*

embarrassment. One of the finest modern poets writing in German, he was a trained pharmacist who became a drug addict. His love for his sister is an obsessive theme of his writing. He died of an overdose of cocaine at the age of 27. **Mozartplatz** is dominated by a solemn 19th-century monument to the great composer. Wolf Dietrich von Raitenau was determined to make Salzburg look like Rome, and had a couple of hundred medieval houses knocked down to make room for five city squares. The **Residenzplatz** is the most magnificent of them and makes a suitable setting for the **RESIDENZ** ❽. Its spectacular baroque fountain, the **Residenzbrunnen**, was added later (1658–61). It is the largest fountain of its type north of the Alps. If you are in the square at 0700, 1100 or 1800, the **Glockenspiel** will play for you as it has done without fail since 1702.

## Also worth exploring

The **Haus der Natur** (Natural History Museum) makes a great first impression with its ground-floor exhibit of a 10m-long squid. The vast collection takes up another 79 rooms. There is an aquarium, a reptile house with snakes and alligators, and flora, fauna and mineral collections. Interactive exhibits deal with physics and astronomy, and there are a few bizarre displays as well, such as a collection of deformed human embryos.

The **Hellbrunn Palace**, an early baroque pleasure palace, was built by Santino Solari (1612–15) for the hedonistic prince-archbishop and ladies' man, Markus Sittikus, who loved all things Italian and, seemingly, all things pagan, too. His extensive baroque gardens are full of surprises, from naughty stone satyrs to the famous trick fountains that spray water on unsuspecting visitors. It is also water that moves 113 figures in the **Mechanical Theatre**.

## The Sound of Music

Most Austrians have never seen *The Sound of Music*, which was filmed in and around Salzburg. By contrast, an estimated 90 per cent of Americans who visit the city go on a 'Sound of Music' tour. They are joined by Japanese, Canadians, Australians and South Americans. Many of the foreign tourists break out in song when they see Leopoldskron, the lakeside baroque palace used in the film as the von Trapp mansion. For the record, the musically gifted von Trapp family fled Austria in 1938, but the Nazis were not in hot pursuit, nor did nuns sabotage their car. The von Trapps never profited from the film starring Julie Andrews and Christopher Plummer, the most successful musical in the history of Hollywood. They had already sold the rights to their story (for $10,000) to a German company, which had made an earlier German-language film, *die Trappe-Familie*. The descendants of the von Trapp family run a hotel in Vermont.

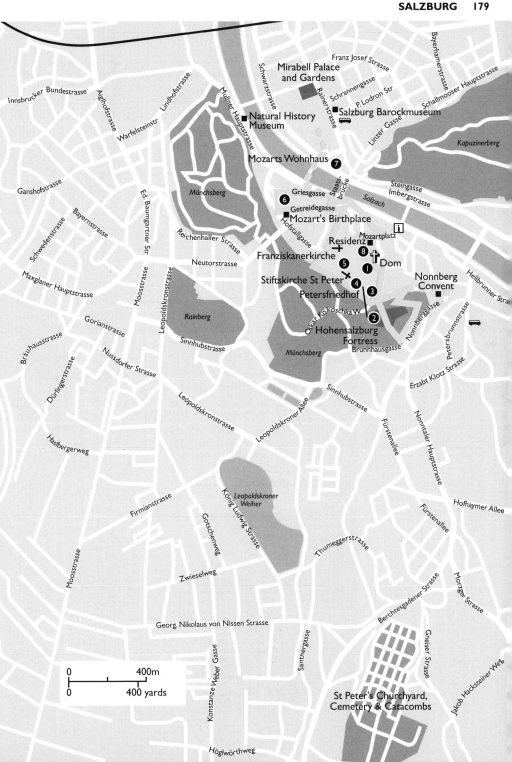

Innsbrucker Bundesstrasse

Aiglhofstrasse

Lindhofstrasse

Warfelsteinstr

Müllner Hauptstrasse

Schwarzstrasse

Rainerstrasse

Franz Josef Strasse

Schrannengasse

P. Lodron Str

Bayerhamerstrasse

Schallmooser Hauptstrasse

Mirabell Palace
and Gardens

Natural History
Museum

Salzburg Barockmuseum

Linzer Gasse

Kapuzinerberg

Ganshofstrasse

Bayernstrasse

Schwedenstrasse

Ed. Baumgartner Str

Mönchsberg

Mozarts Wohnhaus **7**

Staats-brücke

Steingasse

Imbergstrasse

Griesgasse

**6**  Getreidegasse

Salzach

Reichenhaller Strasse

Hofstallgasse

Mozart's Birthplace

Maxglaner Hauptstrasse

Moosstrasse

Leopoldskronstrasse

Neutorstrasse

Mozartplatz

**i**

Residenz

Franziskanerkirche

**8**  Dom

**5**

Stiftskirche St Peter

**4**  **1**

**3**

Nonnberg
Convent

Hellbrunner Stra

Gorianstrasse

Nussdorfer Strasse

Rainberg

Sinnhubstrasse

Petersfriedhof

Oskar Kokoschka W.

**2**

Hohensalzburg
Fortress

Nonnberggasse

Erzabt Klotz Strasse

Petersbrunnstrasse

Bräuhausstrasse

Dürlingerstrasse

Mönchsberg

Brunnhausgasse

Fürstenallee

Nonntaler Hauptstrasse

Häslbergerweg

Leopoldskronstrasse

Sinnhubstrasse

Fürstenallee

Hofhaymer Allee

Firmianstrasse

Gotschenweg

König Ludwig Strasse

Leopoldskroner
Weiher

Thumeggerstrasse

Zwieselweg

Berchtesgadener Strasse

Morzger Strasse

Gneiser Strasse

Moosstrasse

Georg. Nikolaus von Nissen Strasse

Konstanze Weber Gasse

Santnergasse

St Peter's Churchyard,
Cemetery & Catacombs

Jakob Hacksteiner Weg

Höglwörthweg

0 — 400m
0 — 400 yards

# The Kaiser Mountains

## Ratings

| | |
|---|---|
| Hiking | ●●●●● |
| Nature | ●●●●● |
| Scenery | ●●●●● |
| Skiing | ●●●●● |
| Architecture | ●●●○○ |
| Children | ●●●○○ |
| History | ●●●○○ |
| Shopping | ●●○○○ |

The Kaisergebirge roughly forms the northeast boundary of the Tyrol, beginning just outside Kufstein. It is not the highest mountain range in the province, but still offers awesome scenery thanks to a chain of deep valleys that encircle it. There are two main ridges: the northern Zahmer ('tame') Kaiser; and the southern ('wild') Kaiser, which rises abruptly out of a landscape of meadows and gentle hills up to an elevation of almost 2400m. This region is one of the places where mountaineering got its start in the 19th century when climbers first braved peaks with such names as Totenkirchl ('death's church'), Totensessel ('death's armchair') and Predigtstuhl ('pulpit').

## FIEBERBRUNN✦

ℹ️ **Tourismusverband**
*Dorfplatz 1;*
tel: (05354) 56304;
fax: (05354) 52606;
www.fieberbrunn-tirol.at

One of Fieberbrunn's claims to fame is its sulphur springs that have an amazing salutary effect on royals: they saved a Tyrolean princess, Margarethe Maultasch, in 1354, from a terrible fever; and did the same for Claudia von Medici in 1632 – hence the name ('fever spring'). Aside from being a health spa, Fieberbrunn is also an excellent point of departure for many hikes and mountain climbing tours, including a combination cable car ride and hike to the **Wildalpsee✦** mountain lake.

# KUFSTEIN❖

ℹ **Tourismusverband**
*Unterer Stadtplatz 8;
tel: (05372) 62207; fax:
(05372) 61455;
www.kufstein.at. Open
Mon–Fri 0830–1700; Sat
0900–1200.*

Kufstein lies on the Inn river almost on the border of Bavaria between the Kaiser Mountains and the Bavarian Alps. It was strategically important to Bavaria until 1504 when it was ceded to the Austrians and became equally important to them. To get a clear idea of the historical relationship between Bavaria and the Tyrol all you have to do is examine the **Festung Kufstein❖❖**. The area it covers is larger than the entire historic town centre; in places, the walls are almost 5m thick. The bulky tower of the **Kaiserturm❖** is the castle's highest point and interesting architecturally; it is built around a massive central pillar with a vaulted gallery. The prison cells on the third floor were in use between 1814 and 1867. The fortress also houses a **Heimatmuseum**. The **Burgturm** contains the mighty 1931 **Heldenorgel** ('Heroes Organ'), built as a memorial to German and

**Festung Kufstein**
€€ *Tel: (05372) 602 360, (05372) 71060; www.festung. kufstein.at. Open daily mid-Mar to Oct 0900–1700; Nov to mid-Mar 1000–1600. Museum open same hours.*

Austrian soldiers who died in World War I. Two songs are played on it every day at noon (also at 1800 in summer); the second song is always *Ich hatt' einen Kameraden* ('I had a comrade'). When the weather is calm, the music can be heard from miles away. The town below the fortress was destroyed many times during its history, and most of its buildings are modern.

## Accommodation and food in Kufstein

**Batzenhäusl** €€ *Römergasse 1; tel: (05372) 62433.* This historic inn – one of the oldest in the Tyrol – is guaranteed kitsch-free, despite its location at the foot of Kustein castle. The Empress Maria Theresia slept here and probably dined on rabbit (the house speciality).

**Weinhaus Auracher Löchl** €€ *Römerhofgasse 3; tel/fax: (05372) 62138; e-mail: hotel-weinhaus@auracher-loechl.at; www.auracher-loechl.at.* You can soak in the Gothic atmosphere while drinking wine – or beer – in this establishment, which was founded as a brewery centuries ago.

# ST JOHANN IN TIROL❖

 **Tourismusverband**
*Poststrasse 2;*
*tel: (05352) 633 350;*
*fax: (05352) 65200;*
*www.st.johann.tirol.at. Open*
*Mon–Fri 0830–1200 and*
*1400–1800, Sat*
*0900–1200.*

**Left**
Festung Kufstein

**Right**
St Johann in Tirol

St Johann dates back at least to the year 738, and made its living from copper mining in the Middle Ages. In recent times, it has enjoyed a meteoric career as a ski resort thanks to its sunny location in a wide valley with the Kitzbüheler Horn to the south and the Ackerlspitze and the Kaiser range to the northwest. Its charming baroque houses and stately parish church – the **Pfarrkirche Mariä Himmelfahrt** – have been given one coat of paint too many and look impossibly perfect. The winter skiing includes many of the same slopes as Kitzbühel. Downhill skiing is concentrated on the North Slope of the Kitzbüheler Horn, where the runs are challenging despite the low elevation (1700m). Ballooning, winter and summer, is very popular (*Ballooning Tirol: Speckbacher Strasse 33a; tel: (05352) 65666; fax: (05352) 65644; www.ballooningtyrol.com*).

# ST ULRICH AM PILLERSEE✧

**ⓘ Tourismusverband** *Dorfstrasse 17;*
*tel: (05354) 88192;*
*fax: (05354) 88727;*
*www.tiscover.at/st.ulrich.*
*Open Mon–Sat 0900–1900;*
*Sun 1300–1900, shorter*
*hours in winter. In summer,*
*Jun–Sept daily at 1000 and*
*1100, there are guided*
*tours of the high mountain*
*meadows of the Upper Söll*
*region that go from one*
*cheese hut to the next, to*
*watch cheese being made*
*and to taste it.*

**ⓐ Tracht- und Heimatwerk** *Strass*
*74; tel: (05354) 88554.*
*Frau Ritsch is highly skilled*
*in the age-old craft of*
*sewing leather (normally*
*practised by men). She*
*sews traditional Lederhosen*
*for men and sexier*
*versions for women. They*
*are not cheap, but they*
*never wear out or go out*
*of fashion.*

**ⓗ Latschenöl-Brennerei** *Gries 27;*
*tel: (05354) 88108;*
*www.mack-natur.de. Guided*
*tours May–Oct Mon–Fri*
*0800–1700, Sat–Sun*
*1000–1200, 1300–1700.*

The town on the lake of the same name is the starting point for many excursions. The lake itself, 2km long and 300m wide, is famous for trout fishing. The late-Gothic **Ulrichskirche** has notable ceiling frescoes by the baroque Tyrolean artist, Simon Faistenberger. The **International Pillersee Dog-Sleigh Races** are held here every January. Mushers descend on the town with four different dog breeds in tow – malamutes from Alaska, Greenland dogs, Siberian huskies and samoyeds. Dwarf pine oil has been used since time immemorial in the Alps for the treatment of various illnesses. You can tour the premises (**Latschenöl-Brennerei**) where the oils are extracted for medicinal purposes from dwarf pine, silver fir, arnica and Alpine flowers.

## Accommodation and food in St Ulrich am Pillersee

**Gasthof St Adolari €** *Neidersee 8; tel: (05353) 20003; fax: (05353) 20004.* A simple inn with a magnificent setting on Piller Lake. It serves beer and ubiquitous Tyrolean standards such as *Schweinsbraten* (roast pork) and *Knödel* (dumplings).

### Ski Welt Wilder Kaiser-Brixental

It is possible to travel through 'Ski World' – 250km of ski-runs joined by 90 lifts – without ever removing your skis (well almost, you have to take them off for the Hartkaser Gondola). One ski pass covers the entire area and the facilities of nine resorts. Most of the runs are intermediate, many of them through forests at a medium elevation. The best points of access are the resorts of **Scheffau**, **Söll** and **Brixen**. The most difficult runs are on **Hohe Salve**.

# SÖLL✧

Söll is the largest of the nine resorts that make up the **Ski Welt✧✧**. For all its popularity, it has managed to maintain some Tyrolean charm and tradition. The baroque **Peter and Paulkirche** (don't miss the sadistic Crucifixion scene on the ceiling) and its romantic graveyard still form the core. At the bottom of the hill the church occupies is the quirky, onion-domed **Gasthof Post** with an 18th-century, frescoed façade.

A cable car leads to **Hohe Salve**++. The sweeping views from its summit stretch from the Wilder Kaiser in the north to the Grosser Rettenstein (Kitzbüheler Alps) in the south, the far-away Grossvenediger (in the Hohe Tauern Nationalpark) and the Zillertaler Alps. Celtic weapons have been found near the summit and it is likely that the mountain had some kind of ancient cult status. By Christian times, it was the site of the **Marien- und Wallfahrtskapelle Stampfganger** (chapel for pilgrims) whose wood-shingled roof rises from a sharp outcrop. The present building dates from 1670. Most people who visit the peak today aren't there to pray. A long ski-run back to Söll, popular among experienced skiers, begins at the top of its North Face.

# WAIDRING+

**ⓘ** **Tourismusverband** *Dorfstrasse 9; tel: (05353) 5242; fax: (05353) 52424; e-mail: www.waidring.at*

**ⓝ** **Glockengiesserei Lugmair** *Dorfstrasse 43; tel: (05353) 5530; fax: (05353) 5378; www.glockengiesser.com. Open 0800–1200 and 1300–1730.*

The town of Waidring lies in a broad valley near the corner where the Tyrol intersects the Bundesland of Salzburg and the German province of Bavaria. The town square is flanked by classic Tyrol wooden houses with shingle roofs and cobwebbed belfries. The rococo church lies in an old churchyard bristling with iron-wrought grave-markers. Its pleasantly untrendy and uncrowded ski area, the **Steinplatte**+, lies on a cliff above town, which you can reach directly from town by means of a new cable car or via the **Höhenstrasse** road that climbs up 4km to the lower station of the chair-lifts. From there, you can ski into Bavaria – the vast Winklmoosalm ski resort is only a couple of pistes and lifts away. The mountain is well known for fossilised mussels, snails and various other ammonites and a 'learning trail' explains its geological history with illustrations and German-language captions.

Waidring has one of the last cowbell foundries in the Tyrol – the **Glockengiesserei Lugmair**. Tours take place on Wednesday mornings and you can have a bell of your own poured out of molten copper and zinc; contact the tourist board for details.

# WALCHSEE+

The lake of Walchsee, at the foot of the Kaisergebirge, is the second largest lake in the Tyrolean lowlands (after Achensee, *see page 198*) and very popular for swimming and windsurfing. The western and southern sides of the lake are full of caravans; the east side is full of reeds. The village of Walchsee is touristy but still low key. North of Walchsee, the moorland – **Die Schwemm**+, a remnant of the last Ice Age – is the largest landscape of its kind in northern Tyrol and a magnet for birds and bird-watchers. In spring and early summer it is a haven for wild flowers and large species of butterfly.

# Suggested tour

**Total distance:** 102 km.

**Time:** The driving time, not counting detours, is about half a day.

**Links:** This route overlaps briefly with the Chiemgau route when it passes by Kössen (*see Klobensteinpass on page 75*).

From **KUFSTEIN** ❶ drive southwest on the B173 along the Weissache river through a steep gorge. Turn right on to the B312 to drive into **SÖLL** ❷ – just right (1.5km) of the intersection with B312 – if you intend to ride the cable car to **Höhe Salve**. Otherwise, turn left and carry on towards Ellmau. You will now be driving parallel with the Wilder Kaiser Mountains.

**Detour:** Turn left on to the Scheffau road to **Hintersteinersee**. The pristine water of the mountain lake mirrors the rugged peaks of the Wilder Kaiser, best seen from the footpath that leads around the lake. There is a small beach for swimming and a couple of inns to eat lunch at, such as the Seestüberl, situated right on the lake.

A small chapel with an onion-dome spire is the main landmark of the little town of **Ellmau**.

**Getting out of the car:** Drive from Ellmau on the toll road to the Wochenbrunner Alm. From there, you can walk to Hintere Goinger Halt (2192m), one of the highest peaks of the Wilder Kaiser mountain range. It is a fairly difficult hike that requires sure-footedness; one steep stretch is belayed with steel cable.

**Going am Wilden Kaiser** is the next town in the valley. Its rococo

○ **Stanglwirt €€€**
*Sonnseite 50, Going;*
*tel: (05356) 2000;*
*fax: (05356) 200 031;*
*www.stanglwirt.com.*
Admittedly, this place
resembles a posh Tyrolean
theme park with Tyrolean
music on the loud-speakers
and Lipizzaner in the
stables, but it is still a lot of
fun. One of the dining
rooms is separated from a
cow-shed by a glass wall so
diners and cows can watch
each other eat. The owner
has been accused of
creating a 'Lederhosen-
Disneyland'. As if to
apologise, he holds an
indisputably authentic
festival of Volksmusik twice
a year (*April and November*),
with leading folk musicians
from all over the Tyrol.

village church is considered one of the most beautiful in the Tyrol, but
it is far better known for the hotel-restaurant-cum-leisure centre
**Stanglwirt** that rightly describes itself as an 'experience'. Going plays
host to a traditional Tyrolean Handicraft Fair during the summer (*third
Friday of June, July, August and September*). The village of **Spital** is
interesting for the **Spitalkirche zu heligen Nikolaus**, which has the
oldest stained-glass window in the Tyrol (behind the altar) and Gothic
frescoes by Tyrolean artist Simon Benedikt Faistenberger. The ski resort
of **ST JOHANN IN TIROL** ❸ lies at a crossroads in the region and
valleys fan out in several directions. From **FEIBERBRUNN** take the
*Landstrasse* north to the village of **St Jakob in Haus**. The **Pillerseetal**,
the valley between Waidring and Fieberbrunn, is one of the most
idyllic in the Tyrol. The first hamlet, **Flecken**, has a lovely collection
of sun-bleached Tyrolean farmhouses, including one that looks like a
fortress. **ST ULRICH AM PILLERSEE** ❹ occupies the middle of the
valley, surrounded by the peaks of the Loferer range. Drive north
along the lake shore to the pilgrimage church of **St Adolari**, set
between mountains and the lake. The first historical mention of it is
in 1073. Its polygonal choir is a landmark in the history of Tyrolean
art because of its cycle of 34 paintings, the most complete Gothic
iconography of the Virgin Mary in North Tyrol. Sadly, they have only

**Above left**
Hintersteinersee

**Right**
St Johann in Tirol

survived in fragments. A local (absurd) legend claims that they were painted by Leonardo da Vinci! If it is closed, ask for the key from the **Gasthof St Adolari**, next to the church.

**Getting out of the car**: From the **Gasthof St Adolari**, a relatively steep 40-minute hike explores the **Teufelsklamm**＊ ('devil's gorge'), rich in Alpine flora. After the first 20 minutes, you reach a waterfall. Here, you really do meet the devil – at the end of the gorge – carved in wood and nailed to a cliff.

The road now leads through a narrow gorge nicknamed the 'Waidringer oven'. The town of **WAIDRING** ❺ itself has a brace of wonky Tyrolean houses whose balconies overflow with geraniums in spring and summer. Turn west on the A312. After 6km, you will reach **Erpendorf** ❻ . The village church is a regarded as a modern architectural masterpiece, the work of Clemens Holzmeister, who designed the concert hall of Salzburg's International Festival. The village also has cable cars, ski-lifts and an ice rink. From there, take the *Landstrasse* that is clearly signposted for Kössen. It skirts the Grossache river for 12km through a magnificent, almost empty valley (it doesn't even have a tourist board).

Upon arriving in **Kössen** (*see page 77*), turn left (west) again, this time on the B172. The road parallels the Zahmer ('tame') range of the Kaiser mountains to the north, in concert with the lovely Kohlenbach stream on its way to the lake of **WALCHSEE**.

**Detour**: Drive through the picturesque village of Nierendorf and follow the *Landstrasse* along the Inn river to **Erl**. The town, like Oberammergau in Bavaria (*see page 54*), maintains the medieval tradition of the *Passionspiel* – the re-enactment of Christ's Passion – in which villagers themselves play all the roles. They have performed the Passion every six years since 1619 (the next one is in 2009). In off years, the Passionspiel stage is used for mystery plays and oratorios.

**Ebbs** is the next village. Its Halfinger horses are almost as famous as Vienna's Lipizzaner. They are a cross between Tyrolean and Arabian breeds and are used for mountain trekking and as mounts by the Austrian army. At the **Fohlenhof Ebbs** you can look at the sturdy horses and go for a carriage or sleigh ride drawn by them (*tel: (05373) 42210; fax: (05373) 42150; www.haflinger-tirol.com*). Ebbs also has another claim to fame – the exquisite acoustics inside its large baroque church.

**Getting out of the car**: Just before Kufstein, the B175 passes a gorge – **Sparchenbach**. From here, follow the footpath into the **Kaisertal** for one of the most famous walks in the Tyrol. A short uphill stretch – with striking over-the-shoulder views of Kufstein – leads through stands of fir and beech to a narrow valley between the peaks of the

'tame' and 'wild' Kaiser Mountains. On the way, the trail passes just above a cave, the **Tischoferhöhle**, that was inhabited in the Bronze Age. The skeletons of 30,000-year-old wolves, bears, foxes and reindeer were found there and are now on exhibit in Kufstein's Heimatmuseum (*see page 181*). The austere and solitary **Antoniuskapelle⁺** is 7km up the valley. This is a convenient point to turn around. A lodge, the Kaisertalhütte, waits at the end of the valley. From there, the going gets tougher and the path climbs 640m via switchbacks past the Totenkirchl massif to the Stripsenjoch mountain pass.

Return to Kufstein.

## Also worth exploring

**Detour:** Drive north on the B176, first through a broad clearing and then up a lovely ascent through the Leukental. At Griesenau, turn left (west) on the toll road that leads up to the Stripsenjoch pass. From here, there is a path that climbs up to **Stripsenkopf** (1807m), with views of the north walls of the Wilder Kaiser (4 hours return).

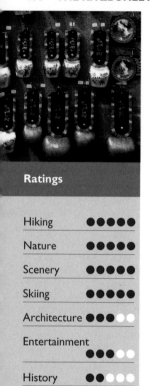

# The Kitzbühel and Ziller valleys

**Ratings**

| | |
|---|---|
| Hiking | ●●●●● |
| Nature | ●●●●● |
| Scenery | ●●●●● |
| Skiing | ●●●●● |
| Architecture | ●●●○○ |
| Entertainment | ●●● |
| History | ●●○○○ |
| Museums | ●●○○○ |

The Kitzbühel and Ziller valleys sum up all the extremes of the Tyrol, from Alpine grandeur to tourist tackiness, folklore to kitsch, wilderness to trendiness. Kitzbühel is one of the richest and most fashionable towns in the Alps and the Ziller is Tyrol's most famous valley where 'the guest is king'. The Kitzbühel and Ziller Alps have every conceivable facility for every imaginable winter and summer sport. They are the stage for events that reflect the old and new Tyrol: the medieval Gauderfest and the Hahnenkamm downhill ski race. The Krimml Waterfall – one of the world's highest – is a memorable excursion in the neighbouring province of Salzburg.

## GERLOS✧

Gerlos was once an important stop on the traditional route between the Ziller Valley and Salzburg. In winter, it becomes a sprawling 'ski circus' as the Austrians call it; in summer, it serves as gateway to the **Wilde Krimml✧✧**, a haunting valley of miniature lakes and wild flowers. New six-person chair lifts have compromised its otherwise wildly beautiful landscape.

## KITZBÜHEL✧✧

The origins of Kitzbühel go back to the Bronze Age. In the Middle Ages, it benefited from its position on a trade route between Munich and Venice. By the turn of the 19th century, it was just another mining town, with a medieval centre. Then a delivery of skis arrived from Norway. It has since become one of the world centres of skiing,

ⓘ **Tourismusverband**
**Kitzbühel**

*Hinterstadt 18;*
*tel: (05356) 777;*
*fax: (05356) 77777;*
*www.kitzbuhel.at*

particularly during the annual **Hahnenkamm** downhill race – the most exciting event in the World Cup calendar. It is also an important stop on the international tennis circuit and a major venue for golf.

Kitzbühel is a place where the rich and famous buy second homes and hordes of tourists arrive on package deals to test its famous slopes and the supposedly raucous reputation of its nightlife. Its historic centre, crammed with chic boutiques, has two interesting monuments – the graceful, late-Gothic **Pfarrkirche St Andreas** (the interior is baroque), and its hilltop companion, the **Liebfrauenkirche**, which groans under the weight of an oversized tower. As a ski resort, Kitzbühel's first-rate infrastructure and pistes are offset by its low altitude (760m rising to only 2000m) making it an uncertain prospect for early- and late-season visits. As far as driving is concerned, traffic congestion makes downtown Kitzbühel the Bermuda Triangle of the Tyrol.

**Above**
Krimmler Wasserfälle

## Accommodation and food in or near Kitzbühel

The tourist office (except during the winter high season) can arrange for a room either in a private home or in a pension. Most of the pubs and discos are concentrated in the Hinterstadt area.

**Hotel Jagerwirt €€** *Jochberger Strasse 12; tel: (05356) 4281.* A family-run hotel close to the town centre with lots of British guests.

**Romantik Hotel Tennerhof €€€** *Griesenauweg 26; tel: (05356) 63181; fax: (05356) 6318 170; e-mail: tennerhof@romantikhotels.com.* This is a self-described 'rendezvous for golfers and gourmets' who no doubt also appreciate the view of Hahnenkamm and the swimming pool with frescoes of Tuscany. It manages a delicate balance between cosiness and luxury with farmstyle furniture and rooms that are quaint rather than grand.

**Camping Schwarzsee €** *Off the B170, 2km outside Kitzbühel in the direction of Wörgl, tel: (05356) 628 060, fax: (05356) 6447 930.* Located on a hilly meadow at the edge of a forest. The money saved on a hotel room can be spent at the nearby 18-hole golf course.

# KRIMMLER WASSERFÄLLE***

The Krimml Waterfalls are among the most impressive in Europe (and the sixth highest in the world). The Krimml river plummets in three stages into the valley. The entire elevation difference is almost 400m. The water drops 140m over the upper river fall to the 'Schönangerl'. The middle river fall drops around 100m and the lower river falls another 140m. A power station was being planned for the area when the falls were saved by legislation in 1961. The water in the falls comes from the glaciers of the Dreiherrenspitze in the Venediger mountain range to the south. The quantity varies considerably depending on the season and time of day and is at its greatest on early afternoons in July and August, when the sun is hottest on the glaciers above. At the top of the falls, there is an inn, the **Krimmler Tauernhaus**, that first opened its doors in 1437. Its wood panelled walls are full of inscriptions from over the centuries. There is a road up to the top of the falls but it is closed to private vehicles. If you don't want to walk, a national park taxi can take you there (*tel: (06564) 228*). The official walking time on the footpath is 30 minutes to the mid level of the falls and an hour to the upper level but it can take twice as long if you stop at many of the frequent viewpoints. Don't expect to have the waterfall to yourself; unless you get there at dawn or dusk, you will share it with coachloads of tourists. Wear waterproof clothing in spring or early summer when walking to the foot of the falls is like walking into the rain.

# ZELL AM ZILLER*

The name 'Zell am Ziller' ('cell on the Ziller') probably refers to monks who lived in the area in the 9th century – missionaries sent by Salzburg's sainted bishops Rupert and Virgil. Empress Maria Theresia helped the town after a severe flood by building the baroque

## Gauderfest

The **Gauderfest** is to the Tyrol what the **Oktoberfest** is to Bavaria. First celebrated over 400 years ago, the spring festival in Zell am Ziller re-enacts, on 1 and 2 May, medieval events that once took place on the **Gauderlehen** (a meadow belonging to the local brewery). Would-be local heroes engage in Tyrolean-style wrestling and rams are paired off for the *Widderstossen*, or 'butting of heads'. The rams are from the local breed, Zillertaler Steinschafe, that provides grey wool for traditional *loden* jackets. There is lots of brass music, food (spicy beef sausages called *Gauderwürsten*) and the strong *Gauderbock*, a brew that makes even strong men faint. The high point is the **Gauderfestzug** – a parade of hundreds of villagers and local militia wearing *Tracht* (traditional costume), accompanied by local lads running back and forth and shaking bells of different sizes to 'wake up' the natural world from its winter sleep.

Pfarrkirche St Veit, which has the largest dome in the Tyrol and a Greek-cross floorplan, surrounded by chapels. The most famous Tyrolean festival takes place in Zell each May (*see Gauderfest, page 193*). Zell has been a regular venue for a round of the Paragliding World Cup in late May.

# ZILLERTAL✢✢

**ⓘ Tourismusverband Zillertal-Mitte**
*Bahnhof, Hnr. 40, Kaltenbach; tel: (5283) 2218; fax: (5283) 2885; www.zillertal-mitte.at. Open Mon–Fri 0830–1200, 1400–1800 and Sat 0900–1200.*

**Ⓡ Zillertalbahn railway** The Zillertal railway has been in operation since 1902. Diesel trains run on the hour in summer between Mayrhofen and Achensee (*see page 198*) and steam trains puff back and forth twice a day. For a fee, passengers are allowed to operate the train. A train ride can be combined with a lake cruise on Achensee or a hike. (*Information: Zillertaler Verkehrsbetriebe, Jenbach; tel: (05244) 6060; fax: (05244) 60639; www.zillertalbahn.at*)

The Ziller Valley, created by a glacier in the last Ice Age, is the broadest, flattest and greenest of the Inn's tributary valleys. History has divided the valley in curious ways. It was the border between two Roman provinces and, from the Middle Ages until 1815, both a political and religious fault-line between the clerical state of Salzburg and the Habsburg Empire. To this day, there are two dioceses and hence the colour scheme of church towers: those east of the Ziller river have green steeples (for Salzburg), while those west of the river have red ones, to show they belong to Innsbruck. Though fertile, the Ziller Valley is only 32km long and its inhabitants were never able to live from farming alone; they sank into poverty after the decline of mining in the 1600s. During the 18th century, many of them wandered across Europe peddling lotions, tinctures, extracts and dubious folk remedies with ingredients such as powdered lavender, pine cone, frogs and worms. Eventually, they hit upon another export – their folk music. Music groups from the Ziller Valley sang and yodelled their way all over Europe in the 19th century, appearing before the British Royal family and the Russian Czar. We have one of these groups, the Rainer Truppe, to thank for the popularity of 'Silent Night'.

## Accommodation and food in the Ziller Valley

**Jägerklause** € *Gattererberg 1a, Stumm; tel: (05283) 2793; fax: (05283) 27937*. The family that owns the inn are passionate folk musicians (they perform some evenings) and hunters. Wild game is always on the menu.

**Landgasthof Linde** € *Dorf 2, Stumm; tel: (05283) 2277; fax: (05283) 2277 50; www.landgasthof-linde.at. Closed Mon–Tue*. The owners of this inn, one of the oldest in the Tyrol, cook with produce from their own vegetable garden and farm. They organise 'cultural evenings', too, with authentic Tyrolean music and dance.

# Suggested tour

**Total distance:** The circuit of Kitzbühel and the Ziller valleys, with the excursion into Salzburg province, is 163km. The detours to Mayrhofen and Spertental add 12km and 14km respectively (there and back).

**Time:** 1 day (without detours) is enough to complete this route, while

**Above**
Zillertal railway

still leaving time to stretch your legs beneath the Krimml waterfall. It would make an ideal long weekend. Taking into account the remoter corners of this region, you could easily spend weeks exploring it.

**Links:** This route meets the Kufstein to Innsbruck route (*see pages 202–7*) and follows the same route for 31km along the B171, from St Gertraudi to Wörgl.

From **KITZBÜHEL** ❶ take the 161 south to **Jochberg**, a town where copper was mined for 3000 years, until 1926. It is possible to tour the old copper mine – the **Schaubergwerk Kupferplatte** – on diminutive trains once used by miners (€ *Bergwerksweg 10, Jochberg; tel: (5355) 5779; fax: (5355) 5459; www.schaubergwerk.kupferplatte.at. Open mid-May–mid-Oct daily, hourly tours 0900–1600*). The mountain pass of Thurn marks the border with the province of Salzburg. There are fine views of **Mittersill** and the Gross Venediger mountains during half a dozen downward curves. Get on the B165 going west and cruise the pastoral scenery of the broad Salzach Valley to the **KRIMMLER WASSERFÄLLE** ❷. The falls are only a couple of minutes from the road. There are also a number of opportunities to park and look back at the waterfall while navigating the hairpin turns of the dramatic toll road – the **Gerlosstrasse** – that takes you over Gerlos Pass to **GERLOS** ❸ and past **Durlassboden See**. The road follows the course of the Gerlosbach until the Gerlos Valley becomes wilder – almost a chasm. The B165 executes a well-engineered downward spiral with fine views of the **ZILLER VALLEY** ❹ before bringing you to **ZELL AM ZILLER** ❺.

**Detour:** Turn left (south) on B169. From **Hippach**, it's possible to drive up to the **Zillertaler Höhenstrasse**, a vertiginous mountain toll road (*open from early May until 31 October*) on the west side of the valley that leads from 550m to an altitude of 2020m. It is only recommended for people with plenty of experience in mountain driving. To relax here is strictly *verboten*. You have to concentrate on every bend in the road because there are no guard-rails, no hard shoulders and no margin for error. It is a one-lane road for much of its length and passing another car on the outer edge of a turn-off can be scary. The reward for all this stress is an unmatched view of the Kitzbühel and Zillertal Alps and the adrenalin rush of being *on the edge*. It is also a starting point for many rewarding hikes. **Atlas Sportalm** and **Hirschbichlalm** both have inns where you can eat lunch or drink a glass of fresh milk. Either return to Hippach or use the access road that descends to **Aschau** further north.

The town of **Mayrhofen**, one of the most popular ski resorts in the Alps, lies at the end of the valley where four side valleys branch off into the Zillertal Alps – the **Zemmgrund**, **Zillergrund**, **Stilluptal** and **Tux** valleys.

**Getting out of the car:** Mountain lifts, including the spectacular Penkenbahn gondola, are open in the summer to make the ascent easier for the less energetic. Peter Habeler who, along with Reinhold

Messner, was the first man to climb Mount Everest without oxygen, has a mountaineering school that accepts beginners (*Ski- und Alpinschule Mount Everest, Hauptstrasse 458; tel: (05285) 62829; www.habeler.com*). Mayrhofen is the point of departure for one of the longest (intermediate) wild river runs in the Tyrol. It is also a Mecca for hang- and paragliders who come to ride the thermal air currents in the sky above.

Take the flat *Landstrasse* that runs between meadow and forest edge from Zell am Ziller to **Aschau** and **Kaltenbach**, a peaceful country road that reveals more about life in the valley than the busy B169. The last major town is touristy **Fügen**. Its Gothic church, **Pfarrkirche Mariä Himmelfahrt** (14th- to 15th-century), has a remarkable pair of carved wooden doors and early frescoes; otherwise, the interior is standard baroque. More interesting is the **St Pankraz Kirche** (1497) – on a hill outside the town. The region was important for the mining of iron ore and the miners erected this church and proudly decorated it with sculpture and frescoes. When the B169 passes through the village of **Schlitters**, turn right and drive on the *Landstrasse* east through **Imming** and north to **Bruck am Ziller** – both traditional villages with Tyrolean atmosphere and affordable pensions. Carry on to the intersection with the B171 at St Gertraudi. It will take you through the Inn Valley to Wörgl (with a possible stop in the medieval town of Rattenberg, *see page 201*) and to the entrance of Brixental, a wide valley that fans out between the Kaiser mountain range in the north and the Kitzbühel Alps to the south. Watch out for **Schloss Itter** on a high outcrop to the left, a 13th-century castle that was made to look more like a 'fairytale' in the 19th century. **Hopfgarten** lies at the foot of Hohe Salve. It is possible to ski from here to Ellmau on the other side of the mountain (*see World, page 184*). Hairpin turns wind through the town past its dignified church, **St Jakob und Leonhard**. The curves become more intense further up the valley and threaten to drop you into the torrent of the Windauer Ache. The road levels out before reaching **Kirchberg**, a town that was already popular with tourists in the 1920s but has always remained in the shadow of Kitzbühel.

**Detour:** The valley of Spertental is so tranquil you will wonder how it can be just 9km from Kitzbühel. The short (7km) and steep road through it ends in the *cul-de-sac* of **Aschau** (not to be confused with Aschau in the Ziller Valley). The town used to supply 18th-century mines with provisions.

**Getting out of the car:** Starting from a point just past the town of Aschau, is the **Aschauer Hohenweg** (6 hours return), a trail that leads through unspoiled high Alpine meadows, along the **Schwarzkogel** and the **Kleine Rettenstein** up to the **Stangenjoch**.

After Kirchberg, the road through Brixental passes almost imperceptibly into the Kitzbüheler Valley and follows the Kitzbüheler Ache on its way to Kitzbühel.

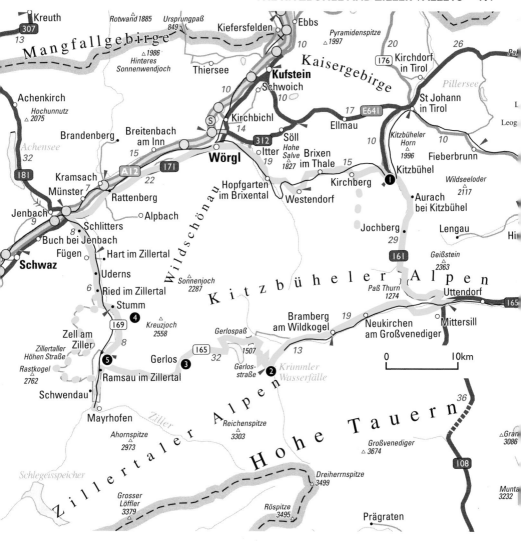

## Also worth exploring

The high mountain valley of **Wildschönau** (turn off near Wörgl or Hopfgarten) in the heart of the Kitzbüheler Alps is a fine place to escape from the tourist masses of the larger ski resorts and the snootiness of Kitzbühel. In winter, there are beautiful ski-runs, never crowded, down **Schatzberg** (take the funicular at **Auffach**). In early summer, the valley meadows bloom with primroses, crocuses and wild marigolds. At higher elevations, there are heaths of rosemary and Alpine azaleas.

# Kufstein to Innsbruck

## Ratings

| | |
|---|---|
| Castles | ●●●●● |
| Nature | ●●●●● |
| Scenery | ●●●●● |
| Architecture | ●●●●○ |
| History | ●●●●○ |
| Villages | ●●●●○ |
| Children | ●●●○○ |
| Shopping | ●●●○○ |

The lower valley of the Inn river forms a flat, green trough across the Tyrol. The province's mountainous geography has dictated the concentration of commerce and population here. Except for a couple of battles fought in mountain passes, the history of northern Tyrol has been played out between Kufstein and Innsbruck. Until the 19th century, the Inn was the main form of transport between the two cities: the downstream voyage took five hours and the horse-powered trip upstream, five days. The Inn Valley *Autobahn* – one of central Europe's main traffic arteries – now covers the distance in 40 minutes, unless it is clogged by lorries and tourists. People who prefer travel to transit, however, will find that the valley's byways lead to scenery as beautiful as any in the Alps, dotted with castles and castle ruins, medieval towns, monasteries and idyllic villages.

## Achensee✦✦

**🚂 Train ride €€**
The *Dampf-Zahnradbahn* (steam cog-railway) is the oldest train of its kind in the world that is still in operation. For more than a hundred years it has linked **Jenbach** with the shore of **Achensee**. The 7km ride is an impressive trip into the mountains of Tyrol with a maximum gradient of 16 per cent; it takes you directly to a ship landing pier in **Seespitz** *(for information, tel: (05244) 62243; fax: (05244) 622 435; www.achenseebahn.at).*

The fiord-like Achensee, wedged between the Karwendel and Rofan mountain ranges, was born in the last Ice Age and is nicknamed Tyrol's 'blue eye'. It is far too cold to swim in, but people sail and windsurf here. Ferryboats cross the lake from **Seespitz** to **Skolastika** and back (about an hour each way). The best view of the region around the lake requires a cable car trip from the village of **Maurach** up to 1800m, then a moderate hike (2½ hours return) to the alpine meadow of **Dalfaz Alm**. In winter, **Pertisau** is the starting point for 85km of cross-country ski trails that penetrate deep into the Karwendel mountain range or a classic panorama route between Pertisau and Maurach.

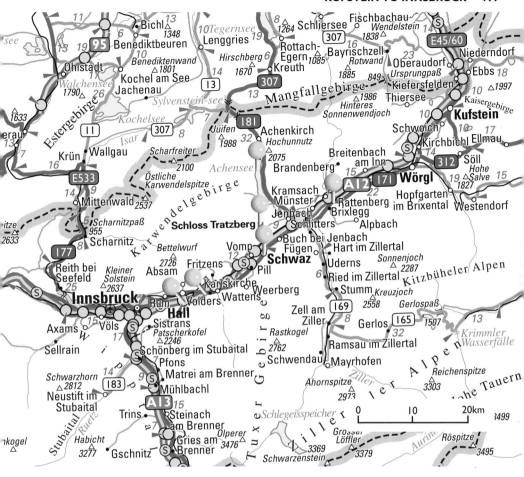

# HALL✦✦

**ⓘ Tourismusverband Hall** Wallpachgasse 5; tel: (05223) 56269; fax: (05223) 5626 920; e-mail hall.tirol@netway.at; www.tiscover.at/hall and www.regionhall.at. Open Mon–Fri 0830–1230, 1400–1800; Sat 0900–1200.

Hall is the Tyrol's best-preserved medieval city. The original source of its wealth was salt, which was already being mined by Celts when the Romans arrived. It was the most important city in the northern Tyrol until the 15th century when it was eclipsed by rival Innsbruck. Today, it has the same beautiful natural setting as its more famous neighbour, but without the hordes of backpackers and day-trippers. Its **Altstadt**✦✦(Old Town) is the largest and most harmonious ensemble of historic buildings in the Tyrol. The **Burg Hasegg**✦ once guarded the river's trade in salt. Its polygonal tower, the **Münzerturm**✦, is the city's most famous landmark and climbing it is the best way to get to know the lay of the surrounding land. The **Pfarrkirche St Nikolaus**✦ is another impressive reminder of the city's former wealth and importance, and is one of the strangest churches in Austria. The choir

**Gasthof Badl €**
*Huller Innbrücke 4; tel:
(05223) 56784; fax:
(05223) 567 843; e-mail:
badl@tirol.com; www.hotel-
badl-tirol.com.* The Steiner
family are good-natured
hosts at this solid, cosy
pension located right on
the Inn river near the
*Autobahn* exit; its *Biergarten*
fills up in the evening with
cyclists pedalling up and
downstream. You can
reach Hall on foot via a
charming covered wooden
bridge.

**Ritterkuchl €€**
*Salvatorgasse 6, Hall; tel:
(05223) 53120; fax:
(05223) 531 204;
e-mail: m.klausner@
ritterkuchl.at;
www.ritterkuchl.at.* Reserve
ahead for a place at a
medieval banquet in a
ancient Gothic residence.
Be prepared for countless
courses.

**Arnold Posch**
*Schlossergasse 11;
tel: (05223) 54290.* Herr
Posch is a talented young
violinmaker happy to
explain the mysteries of his
craft from his small shop in
the Old Town.

**Bauernmarkt** *Oberen
Stadtplatz.* This farmers'
market is held on Saturday
mornings and is the best
source of local produce,
*Wurst*, smoked ham and
*Schnaps*.

is crooked because the church rests on a cliff and could not be
enlarged equally in both directions. Florian Waldauf, a widely
travelled diplomat and friend of Emperor Maximilian I, built the
**Waldauf Kapelle⁕** on the north wall (to thank the Virgin Mary for
saving them in a storm off the coast of Holland) and stocked it with a
floor-to-ceiling assortment of holy bones. Its screen is (for the Alps) a
rare example of Gothic wrought-iron work. The city's oldest church,
the diminutive Romanesque **Magdalenenkapelle⁕**, lurks behind St
Nikolaus. It has a not-to-be-missed fresco of the **Last Judgement⁕** with
a motley cast of medieval characters, and does double duty as a war
memorial. The **Bergbaumuseum** is a reconstructed salt-mine with an
intriguing series of pits and shafts and a long, slippery wooden slide. It
is not as impressive as the one in Schwaz (*see page 202*) but there are
no queues to get in, either.

**Right**
Hall's Müntzerturm

# KARLSKIRCHE✧

One of the most fanciful baroque buildings in the Tyrol, Karlskirche was designed by a 17th-century doctor and biologist, Hippolytus Guarinoni (1571–1654), a resident of nearby Hall. He dedicated it to Karl Borromäus, a religious zealot and headstrong leader of the Counter-Reformation. Later generations added side chapels and the noted baroque artist Martin Knoller painted the cupolas and the high altar in 1765. Unfortunately, the engineers of the *Autobahn* placed their speedway next to the church, which is in the town of Volders. For the best view of its quirky ensemble of onion-domed clock tower and helmeted roofs, walk out on to the nearby bridge over the Inn.

# RATTENBERG✧✧

Crushed against a cliff on the south shore of the Inn, Rattenberg seems to be clinging to the Middle Ages as well as the rock face. The city missed out on any form of industrial development because there was simply no place to build. A Bavarian named Ratpoto II constructed the first castle here around the year 1000. Given the status of a city in 1393, Rattenberg prospered by exacting a toll on the river trade and supplying the men and horses that hauled boats up the Inn. Centuries later, the silver and copper mines became the major source of wealth. The town has some notable Renaissance houses, many adorned with frescoes, and oriels with lead-paned windows. The hillside **Pfarrkirche St Virgil**✧ has two naves and two altars so that merchants and miners could hold mass separately. Its artistic treasures include a *Last Supper* by Matthäus Günther and a pulpit by Simon Benedikt Faistenberger. The riverside promenade, side-streets and alleyways are more interesting than the **Hauptstrasse**, whose modern motto is 'tax free shopping, world wide shipping'. The hill of Schlossberg has a great view of the town and countryside, and is also the site of the ruined **Burg Rattenberg**, where a plaque commemorates a righteous Chancellor named Wilhelm Biener who was beheaded after a rigged trial in 1651. Plays about his life are sometimes performed in the castle's open-air theatre.

# SCHLOSS TRATZBERG✧✧

**ⓘ Schloss Tratzberg**
**€** *Jenbach; tel:*
*(05242) 6356 620; fax:*
*(05242) 6356 650;*
*www.schloss-tratzberg.at.*
*Hourly tours Apr–Oct daily*
*1000–1600.*

This castle was built as a fortress against the Bavarians in the 13th century, but was transformed centuries later by wealthy families (the Tänzls, Illsungs and Fuggers) who had shares in the silver mines of Schwaz. They were more interested in graceful living than in impregnable defence. It is the only castle in the Tyrol whose period decoration is intact. The intricately carved wood panelling, heavy furniture, inlaid chests and canopied beds are right out of the Renaissance. The 1560 ceiling of the **Königinzimmer** is a legendary piece of woodwork, while the inner courtyard is perhaps the most beautiful in the Tyrol. Emperor Maximilian I was a regular guest and scratched moody poems on the wall of his bedroom. He was also the inspiration for the 46m wall painting in the **Habsburgersaal** – the mother of all family trees with 148 portraits of the Emperor's ancestors. The east wing houses a serious display of weaponry collected but never wielded in anger by castle owners who were capitalists not warlords. The **Jagdsaal** is a curious example of 19th-century justice. An imprisoned poacher did the carvings that depict, of all things, hunting.

# SCHWAZ*

**Tourismusverband Schwaz-Pill** *Franz-Josef-Strasse 26; tel: (05242) 63240; fax: (05242) 65630; e-mail: tourismus@schwaz.at; www.tiscover.at/schwaz. Open Mon–Fri 0900–1200, 1400–1800; Sat 0900–1800.*

**Schau Silberbergwerk** *€€€ Alte Landstrasse 3a; tel: (05242) 723 720; www.silberbergwerk.at. Open daily May–Oct 0830–1700; Nov–Apr 0930–1600.*

Though its origins as a city go back to the first millennium, Schwaz began its golden age in 1400 when it experienced a massive economic boom thanks to its silver mines, which employed 10,000 miners. Its immense wealth financed the wars and diplomacy of Maximilian I and the expansion of the Habsburg Empire. The population of Schwaz at that time was greater than it is today. The town did much to advance mining as a science; the *Schwazer Bergbuch* was the standard work on mining for many centuries. The cavernous **Pfarrkirche zu Unserer Lieben Frau\*** is the largest Gothic hall-church in the Tyrol; miners decorated it with the 15,000 copper tiles that gleam from its roof. Its size was doubled only 12 years after its completion in 1490. As in Rattenberg, merchants and miners celebrated mass separately and were divided by a wooden wall until the 19th century. The **Franziskanerkloster\***, built between 1509 and 1512, has a well-preserved cloister with sketchy but touching mural paintings of Christ's Passion, created by one of the fathers between 1515 and 1530. The clock, a masterpiece of historic wrought-iron work, dates back to 1752. The highlight for many tourists is the **Schau Silberbergwerk\*** – a mine converted into a highly atmospheric museum. The 90-minute guided tour begins by putting on a miner's helmet and overcoat and includes mini-train rides and a trip down a slide.

# Suggested tour

**Total distance:** 97km without detours. The detour to Kramsach adds 10km; the drive to Alpbach, 16km.

**Time:** An ideal length of time for exploring the Lower Inn Valley would be a long weekend. If you only have a day, focus on Kufstein Castle, Rattenberg, the historic centre of Hall and the open-air museum in Kramsach.

**Opposite**
Schwaz: looking towards the Pfarrkirche zu Unserer Lieben Frau

## Emperor Maximilian I

Kaiser Maximilian I (1459–1519) was the last German Emperor to lead his troops personally into battle and hence his epithet, 'The Last Knight'. Historians, however, would later regard him as the first 'Renaissance man' to sit on an emperor's throne because of his patronage of the arts, interest in science and skill in harnessing the forces of change to reshape Europe. His ghost is ubiquitous in the Inn valley. His balcony, the 'Goldenes Dachl', and empty tomb are the most famous sights in Innsbruck (see page 208). He blew holes in Kufstein Castle with his newly manufactured cannon; had his family tree painted on the wall in Tratzberg Castle; and his face stamped on coins in Hasegg Castle in Hall (a practice which continues in the souvenir shop). Maximilian was the first European ruler to realise the importance of PR and, centuries later, you still feel its influence. Even in remote mountain valleys and on the shores of high alpine lakes, locals tirelessly remind you that Kaiser Max hunted and fished there.

**Links**: This route briefly overlaps with the Kitzbühel and Ziller valleys route (*see pages 194–7*).

From **KUFSTEIN** ❶ (*see page 181*), follow the signs for the B171. Just past the drab town of Kundl, you will see a Gothic spire that belongs to **St Leonhard auf der Wiese** rising up between road and river. St Leonhard was the patron saint of prisoners (note the chain around his habit), cattle drivers and miners. The latter are responsible for the red marble interior. You cannot drive through the town of **RATTENBERG** ❷ but must park east or west in pricey car parks.

**Detour**: Cross the Inn to get to **Kramsacher Tiroler Bauernhöfe Museum** (*open Easter–Oct daily 1000–1800*), on the opposite side of the river from Rattenberg; on the way you will pass two lakes, **Krumm** and **Reintaler**, that are popular for swimming in summer. Once famous for glass blowing and the red marble from its quarries, Kramsach is now visited for its outstanding collection of Tyrolean houses that have been moved to one spot. The place is a ghost village with a sawmill, stables, a schoolhouse, smithy, chapel and inn. Walking in and out of its 50-odd buildings offers insights into the culture and hardships of the traditional Tyrolean way life, which has all but disappeared in the last two generations.

After **Brixlegg**, an industrial town, you will pass three castles in the space of a couple of kilometres. **Schloss Matzen** (*closed at time of writing*) has an arcaded inner courtyard and an unusual round tower, the **Butterfassturm**. Its stately **Schlosspark** and **English Garden** date from the 19th century. Around the bend, block-like **Burg Lichtenwerth** sits forlorn (and inaccessible to the public) in a riverside meadow that was once its moat. The ruined castle of **Kropsberg** overlooks the village of St Gertraudi. After passing the

**Left**
Schloss Tratzberg

town of Strass at the mouth of Ziller Valley (*see page 194*), turn right (north) on the road that is signposted Achensee. A number of curves take you to the **Kanzelkehre**, a look-out point with a magnificent view of the Inn valley that is yours for the inflated price of a cup of coffee at the Gasthof Kanzelkehre. Upon arriving at **ACHENSEE** ❸, follow the narrow, shoreside road to **Pertisau** with the waters of the lake lapping at your tyres. The town is the starting point for many excursions, by foot, boat and, in winter, on cross-country skis. Returning to the south side of Achensee, follow the *Landstrasse* signposted for Jenbach. The road plunges down a 20 per cent gradient in sympathy with the Kasbach river, which it follows. Forest covers much of the road, and except for a couple of dips and turns, it feels like a leafy tunnel that shunts you into the town of **Jenbach**. Follow the signs for Stans, around a striking church of unfaced stone, the 15th-century **Jenbacher Pfarrkirche**. It dates from the time when Jenbach made its living refining silver (it now prospers by producing gas ovens and diesel engines). **SCHLOSS TRATZBERG** ❹ looms on an outcrop above the Inn river between Jenbach and Stans. It is a 15-minute walk from the car park or you can wait for the little theme-park 'train'. The country road continues along the edge of the valley through a stand of both deciduous and evergreen trees, a mix once typical for the lower Inn Valley.

**Getting out of the car:** In **Stans**, drive to the north edge of town following the signs for **Wolfsklamm**. The gorge is one of the most awe-inspiring walks in the Tyrol (1½–2 hours). Although the ascent is moderate, its narrow steps and footbridges over crashing water can cause vertigo. The path is a challenge to claustrophobes, too – because it is so narrow in places it feels like a cave. You will have to pay for parking and again to enter. The **monastery of St Georgenberg** rewards you at the end of the gorge with a tavern that serves delicious *Kaiserschmarrn* (sugared pancakes with raisins), and a small guesthouse.

**Below**
Achensee

The signs for **SCHWAZ** ❺ lead back across the Inn river. From there, return to the B171. The **Swarovski Kristallwelten** ('Crystal World'; *www.swarovski.com; open daily 0900–1800*), the second most popular tourist attraction in Austria, is just off the road in the town of Wattens. It is a theme park built next to a crystal factory with mazes, adventure play-grounds for children and giant

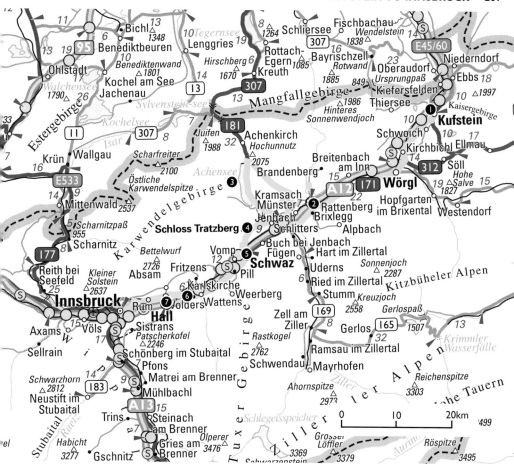

works of crystal created by such artists as Dalì, Keith Haring and Andy Warhol. The B171 almost collides with the **KARLSKIRCHE** ❻ in Volders and you can get a look at it simply by slowing down. The next major town is **HALL** ❼, 10km east of **Innsbruck** (*see page 208*).

## Also worth exploring

The town of **Alpbach** lies on a sunny plateau 1000m above sea-level near the end of the Alpbachtal, a tributary valley of the Inn Valley. It was voted 'Austria's most beautiful village' in a national television poll in 1993. Though it welcomes visitors, the town has avoided sacrificing its alpine charms and traditions for tourism. It is famous for its flower displays and the weathered farmhouses that groan under the weight of geraniums that decorate them in summer.

# Innsbruck

The political and cultural capital of the Tyrol, Innsbruck never lets you forget that you are in the heart of the Alps. Thanks to its strategic position at the foot of the Brenner Pass – the lowest pass through the Alps – the city prospered as a crossroads, from the 12th century, between south and north, Italy and Germany. Emperor Maximilian I made this provincial town the centre of the Habsburg Empire in the 1490s, and while he was alive, it played a leading role in European politics and culture. After 1665, it became a backwater again, ruled from distant Vienna. Its proudest moment came in 1809 when Tyrolean mountain militia defeated a force of Bavarian and Napoleonic troops on the hill of Bergisel. The same hill was the scene of modern athletic triumphs: the Winter Olympics were held twice in the space of 12 years in Innsbruck, in 1964 and 1976, forever associating it with the five interlocking rings of the Olympic Games. For all its charm, Innsbruck's rare synergy between city and nature, like the Alps themselves, is endangered by overdevelopment.

## Sights

ⓘ **Innsbruck
   Tourismus**
*Burggraben 3; tel: (0512) 598
500; fax: (0512) 598 501
07; www.innsbruck.info.
Open Mon–Fri 0800–1800,
Sat 0800–1200.*

ⓐ **Alpenzoo €** *Entrance
   at Weiherburggasse 37
or via the Hungerburg
funicular; tel: (0512) 292
323; fax: (05120) 293 089;
e-mail: alpenzoo@tirol.com;
www.alpenzoo.at. Open daily
0900–1800; winter until
1700.*

### Alpenzoo°°
This is the highest zoo in Europe and a breathtakingly beautiful place to observe 2000 animals representing 150 endangered species, and rare species of Alpine fish swimming around in the specially designed aquariums. When it opened in 1962, the Alpine Zoo was a rarity among zoos because it had no 'exotic' creatures, only animals faced with extinction from its own Alpine region.

### Domkirche St Jakob°
The baroque cathedral of St James was built between 1717 and 1724 to replace older churches. The Asam brothers (Cosmas Damian, the painter and Egid Quirin, the stucco worker) decorated the dome ceilings. The **Tomb of Archduke Maximilian III** is that of a Grandmaster of the Teutonic Order (not the emperor of Austria), and was built by Caspar Gras in 1620. The ineffably beautiful **Gnadenbild**

Alpenzoo

Riesenrundgemälde

Höttinger Höhenstrasse

St Nikolaus-Gasse

Inn Steg

Karl Kapferer-Strasse

Siebererstrasse

Innallee

Riedgasse

Hofgarten

Innstrasse

Kaiserjäger

Höttinger gasse

Inn

Herzog Otto Strasse

Kapuzinergasse

Rennweg

'Ferdinandeum'
Tirol Museum

Dom-
platz

Domkirche
St Jakob

Universitätsstrasse

Dreihe
stras

Maximilian's
Mausoleum

Goldenes Dachl

Hofburg

Universitätsstrasse

Inn Brücke

Sillgasse

Helblinghaus

Herz. Friedrich Strasse

Stadtturm

Riesengasse

Stiftgasse

Tiroler
Volkskunstmuseum

Hofkirche

Höttinger Au Mariahilfstrasse

Innrain

Schlossergasse

Burggraben

Museumstrasse

Herzog Sigmund Ufer

Marktgraben

Maria Theresien Strasse

Innrain

Gilmstrasse

Meinhardstrasse

Brunecker Strasse

Innrain

Burgerstrasse

Colinstrasse

St Anne's
Column

Erlerstrasse

Anichstrasse

Meraner Strasse

Brixner Strasse

Adamgasse

Anichstrasse

Fallmerayerstrasse

Bürgerstrasse

Maria Theresien Strasse

Wilhelm Greilstrasse

Südtiroler Platz

Kaiser Jos. Strasse

| 0 | | 200m |
| 0 | | 200 yards |

Salurner Strasse

Railway
Station

Maximilianstrasse

Speckbacherstrasse

Andreas Hofer Strasse

Leopoldstrasse

Heiliggeiststrasse

el Gaismayr Strasse

Südbahnstrasse

An **Innsbruck Card** allows unlimited travel on the Innsbruck-Igls public transport network, the Hungerburg funicular and cable cars up the Karwendel range and Patscherkofel mountains. It also includes admission to a long list of museums and attractions major and minor. It can be purchased from the tourist office for one, two or three days for 21, 26 or 31 euros, with a 50 per cent reduction for children. The tourist office can also organise daily hikes from mid-June to mid-September with a mountain guide, bus, rucksack and even hiking boots if you need them – all for free.

**Goldenes Dachl-Maximilianeum**

€€ *Herzog-Friedrich-Strasse 15; tel: (0512) 581 111; e-mail: goldenes.dachl@magibk.at. Open May–Sept daily 1000–1800; Oct–Apr 1000–1700.*

**Mariahilfe** (Our Lady of Succour, 1537), by Lucas Cranach the Elder, occupies the high altar. Traditionally, mothers came to her after giving birth to pray for the survival of their infants. It became the most widely copied portrait of the Virgin Mary in the Tyrol.

### Goldenes Dachl**

The 'golden roof' is Innsbruck's most famous landmark and perhaps the most beautiful balcony in Europe. Maximilian I used to sit in the Gothic oriel while tournaments and courtly spectacles were held in the square below. Light glints off its 2600 gilt copper roof-tiles and Maximilian I is ever present as a fresco in the company of his two wives – the one he loved, Maria von Burgundy, and the unfortunate Maria Bianca Sforza, whom he married for territory and used as security for his drinking debts. The delightful relief sculptures – the Moriskentänzern – are copies; the originals are in the **Tiroler Landesmuseum Ferdinadeum** (*see page 216*). The first-floor balustrade bears eight coats of arms. Inside there is a small museum, the **Maximilianeum** (roughly equal in size to its gift shop), with 11 exhibits devoted to the life of Maximilian I. A 20-minute video and audiophone guide provide a useful introduction to the life of one of Europe's most remarkable rulers. You will learn about the vast expansion of his empire through strategic marriages, use of cannon in warfare, love of hunting and fits of melancholy. However, it says nothing about his terrible persecution of Austrian Jews.

**Right**
Goldenes Dachl

**Kaiserliche Hofburg €**
*Rennweg 1; tel: (0512) 587 186; fax: (0512) 5871 8613; e-mail: hofburg.ibk@tirol.com. Open daily 0900–1700.*

**Hofkirche mit Silberner Kapelle €**
*Universitätsstrasse 2; tel: (0512 ) 584 302; www.hofkirche.at. Open Mon–Sat 0900–1700 (Jul–Aug till 1730); Sun and holidays 1300–1700 (Jul–Aug till 1730).*

## Helblinghaus*

This Gothic house received a magnificent high baroque face-lift in 1730, making it the most sumptuous residence in the **Altstadt**. The window frames and pediment are whimsically decorated. An abundance of illumination was important in baroque architecture and the windows have been set in convex bows to get more light. This was a common 18th-century practice in the narrow streets of old cities in Austria and southern Germany.

## Hofburg**

The Hofburg looks much today as it did in 1743 when the Empress Maria Theresia had it rebuilt in the latest baroque fashion after an earthquake. She loved yellow, and yellow it has been ever since. By far the most impressive room is the **Riesensaal**, with ceiling frescoes by F A Maulbertsch and full-length portraits of the imperial family, including a soft and tender Marie-Antoinette.

## Hofkirche**

The church was built between 1553 and 1563 under Ferdinand I to house Europe's most famous tomb, the **Grabmal Kaiser Maximilians I***. The tomb was intended as a monument to Kaiser Maximilian I and, at the same time, the entire line – real and imagined – of the Kaisers (Holy Roman Emperors). The kneeling figure of Maximilian I is surrounded by marble reliefs depicting the marriages, wars and diplomatic triumphs of his reign. The tomb is flanked by 28 larger-than-life bronze statues created by an unprecedented team of artists, sculptors and metalworkers during half a century. Albrecht Dürer and Veit Stoss worked on the remarkable figures of **König Artus** ('King Arthur', claimed as a relation by the German emperors) and **Theoderich der Grosse**. The dresses, costumes and armour are full of stunning details – witness the belt of **Philipp der Gute**. One anomaly is the codpiece of Rudolph, Earl of Habsburg; tourists have rubbed it, for whatever reason, until it shines like a polished apple. In sharp contrast to these figures – 'black men' as they are called by Innsbruckers – is the tomb of Andreas Hofer, the national hero of the Tyrol (*see page 212*). It is of the purest white marble, located to the right as you enter. His bones were smuggled into Innsbruck in 1823 from Mantua, the town where he was executed. The upstairs **Silberne Kapelle** ('silver chapel') – built so a nobleman and common woman could lie together – bears witness to the most famous love story in Tyrolean history. Archduke Ferdinand chose love over power and married a commoner, Philippine Welser. She became one of the most beloved women in Tyrolean history, earning the respect of two Habsburg Emperors, the friendship of the Pope and the affection of the people. The life-size figures of Ferdinand and Philippine were carved by Alexandre Colin, who also sculpted Maximilian I. The name of the chapel refers to the huge embossed silver Madonna.

**Riesenrundgemälde**
€ Rennweg 39;
tel: (0512) 584 434;
www.panorama-innsbruck.at.
Open Apr–Oct daily
0900–1700.

## Maria-Theresien-Strasse**

Although not without blemishes (it includes a McDonald's), the 'Theresienstrasse', as locals call it, is one of the most beautiful streets in Europe. This stately baroque boulevard overwhelms with grand architectural gestures that nevertheless pale in stature beneath the north face of the Karwendel Mountains. The **Annasäule** ('St Anne's column'), which marks the halfway point, commemorates the retreat of Bavarian troops at the end of the Spanish War of Succession (eventually settled in favour of Austria and England after Churchill's famous victory at Blenheim in 1704). The top of the Corinthian column is made of red marble, crowned by a statue of the Virgin Mary on a crescent moon. Statues of four saints surround the pedestal – the work of Trentino sculptor Christof Benedetti. The **Palais Lodron** (No 11) hides two Gothic houses joined behind a fancy rococo façade. **Number 10** is a *Jugendstil* building from 1909. The **Palais Toryer-Spaur** (No 39) has a lavish stucco façade and an oriel typical of 17th-century Innsbruck. The **Altes Landhaus** (No 43) is one the Tyrol's finest surviving patrician residences from the baroque period. The **Palais Trapp-Wolkenstein** (No 38) and **Palais Fugger-Taxis** (No 45) across the street are flashy 17th-century palaces built with Italianate flourishes.

### Riesenrundgemälde*

Panoramic paintings were the virtual reality of the 19th century. The Riesenrundgemälde ('panorama painting') uses its vast size (10m high by 100m long), well-aimed perspective and the juxtaposition of 'real' boulders, trees, wagon-wheels, pistols and canons to make you feel like a witness to the Tyrol's epic struggle.

## Andreas Hofer

Andreas Hofer (1767–1810) is the national hero of the Tyrol and the subject of the Tyrolean anthem. He was an innkeeper, wine and cattle merchant, and born leader of men. Against almost impossible odds, he briefly liberated the Tyrol (1809–10) from an occupation force of Bavarian and Napoleonic troops (the province had been ceded to Bavaria in 1805). The Austrian Emperor betrayed him by agreeing to hand over the province to France. Despite an offer of amnesty, Hofer continued to resist and was eventually captured and executed in Mantua on the express orders of Napoleon. Even before his death, he was the object of hero worship by the common people and the ladies of the Viennese court. He was a man of action, not words: 'Männer s'isch Zeit' ('Men, it is time') he said before his most famous battle at Bergisel, above Innsbruck (now the site of the Olympic ski-jump).

**Stadtturm €**
*Herzog-Friedrich-
Strasse 21; tel: (0512) 561
500. Open daily
1000–1700; Jul–Sept until
2000.*

**Tiroler
Volkskunstmuseum €**
*Universitätsstrasse 2; tel:
(0512) 584 302; fax:
(0512) 5843 0270;
www.tiroler-
volkskunstmuseum.at. Open
Mon–Sat 0900–1700
(Jul–Aug till 1730), Sun and
holidays 0900–1200,
1300–1700 (Jul–Aug till
1730).*

## Stadtturm*

The landmark city tower is in the **Altes Rathaus** (Old Town Hall). Although the functions have been taken over by the **Neues Rathaus** in Maria-Theresien-Strasse, the building is still used by the mayor. The 57m tower was used as a watch-tower and prison over the centuries. From the top, there is a bird's-eye view of the city rooftops and a panorama of the mountains around Innsbruck.

## Tiroler Volkskunstmuseum**

This museum of popular art occupies a 16th-century cloister with a fine series of Renaissance arcades. Its unrivalled collection of Alpine folklore includes furniture, costumes, farm tools, carnival masks, Christmas Nativity scenes and hope chests.

# Entertainment and festivals

The **Landestheater** (*Rennweg 2; tel: (0512) 520 744; www.landestheater.at*) has its own orchestra and is a venue for opera, ballet and drama. **Schloss Ambras** is an elegant venue for classical concerts in summer, from June to early August. From late May to September, Renaissance music is performed on the **Goldenes Dachl** balcony every Sunday at 1130. There is an **Accordion Festival** every three years in May.

# Accommodation and food

Innsbruck's public transport is so efficient and comprehensive that there is no reason to make staying in the historic centre a priority. The tourist office keeps a list of private rooms offering excellent value – in Innsbruck and in outlying villages such as Igls (*see page 219*).

**Altstadtstüberl €** *Riesengasse 11–13; tel: (0512) 582 347; fax (0512) 583 495. Open Mon–Sat for lunch and dinner.* One of the few Altstadt inns that still relies on a local clientele drawn by its *Gemütlichkeit* and good Tyrolean cooking.

**Goldener Adler €€€** *Herzog-Friedrich-Strasse 6; tel: (0512) 5711 11; fax: (0512) 584 409; e-mail: office@goldeneradler.com; www.tiscover.at/ goldener-adler.* The city's most famous historic inn greets its guests with live zither music in the Goethe-Stube restaurant. The most popular rooms are 208 ('Andreas Hofer') and 307 ('Mozart').

**Hotel Kapeller €€** *Philippine-Welser-Strasse 96; tel: (0512) 343 106; fax: (0512) 3431 0668; www.kapeller.at.* Compared to downtown Innsbruck, this hotel-restaurant is a quiet oasis: perfect for people who are passing through or prefer to stay above Innsbruck, near the magnificent Schloss Ambras. Its restaurant serves regional cooking paired with wines from its cellar.

**Café Central €** *Gilmstrasse 5; tel: (0512) 59200.* Innsbruck's version of a Vienna Coffeehouse where you can eat unspeakably good *Sachertorte* and read newspapers from all over Europe.

**Hofgartencafé €** *In the Hofgarten, Rennweg 6a; tel: (0512) 588 871.* This place is ideal for people-watching; it's a cross between a *Biergarten* and trendy café set in the former imperial garden.

**Market Hall €** *Innrain 24; tel: (0512) 84837; www.markthalle-innsbruck.at.* Different stalls where you can stock up for a picnic.

**Restaurant Philippine €** *Corner of Müllerstrasse and Templstrasse; tel: (0512) 589157.* This small vegetarian restaurant provides an A-to-Z shot in the arm with daily specials, salad buffet and wholegrain pastries and breads.

# Shopping

**Speckschwemme** *Stiftgasse 4.* This tiny shop is worth seeking out for its right-out-of-the-farmhouse Tyrolean smoked bacon, and wurst. The *Miniteufel* ('little devils', spicy little sausages) sell out fast.

**Spezialitäten aus der Stiftgasse** *Stiftgasse 2.* Herbert Signor stocks traditionally made, high-quality *Obstbrände* (*Schnaps*), including his own, and Austrian wine.

**Tiroler Heimatwerk** *Meranstrasse 2; tel: (0512) 582 320; fax: (0512) 573 509; e-mail: tiroler.heimatwerk@direkt.at.* A co-op that sells work by Tyrolean craftspeople and artists.

# Suggested tour

**Distance:** 2.5km.

**Length:** The historic centre of Innsbruck is small but rewarding. To combine it with a stroll along the Inn and a trip up to the Hungerburg makes for a full day. However, you have to start early if you want to catch the last funicular.

The **Triumphpforte** was erected in memory of the year 1765 when the empress Maria Theresia visited Innsbruck to celebrate the marriage of her son to a Spanish princess. The festivities were marred by the sudden death of her husband, Kaiser Franz I. The south side of the portal is decorated with statues of the newly married couple and joyful wreaths and garlands. The north side of the arch has a portrait of the deceased shown by the Angel of Death, and the figure of a woman in mourning. The arch marks the beginning of **MARIA-THERESIEN-STRASSE ❶**, one of the most photographed streets in Austria. To really appreciate it, you have to zigzag from one baroque palace to the next, lifting your gaze every few minutes to admire the **Annasäule** and the North range of the Karwendel Mountains that seems to rise at the end of the street. Watch out for trams, cyclists and tourists. The Maria-Theresien-Strasse ends abruptly at the juncture of Marktgraben and Burggraben, two streets

that follow the route of the medieval city walls. Entering Herzog-Friedrich-Strasse, you pass into the city's medieval core where the streets are narrow and the houses crammed together. Many of them have massive stone buttresses – *Erdbebensäulen* – a kind of medieval seismic reinforcement against the earthquakes that devastated the city in the 16th and 17th centuries. The **Altes Rathaus**, built in 1358, is dominated by the city's landmark, the **STADTTURM ❷**. Going up the tower offers a chance to view most of the sights on this itinerary. The street forms a triangle in front of the **GOLDENES DACHL ❸**. Beneath this balcony, tournaments and festivities entertained Emperor Maximilian I. On the opposite corner is the **HELBLINGHAUS ❹**, a white-pink wonder that stands in complete contrast to the sober Gothic neighbours. Turn left (north) for a second leg of Herzog-Friedrich-Strasse. The **Goldener Adler**, on the left, is the oldest inn in the city. Goethe, Heinrich Heine, Paganini, Kaiser Josef II and Andreas Hofer all broke bread at its tables. The odd-looking **Ottoburg**, once a fortified residence, stands on the corner where the street meets the Inn river. This is a good place to pause and take a look at historical Innsbruck. Walk one block along the Inn river and duck right into Badgasse, passing the **Stadtsarchiv** to the right; it serves as the city museum with exhibitions that change every six months. Veer left again into Domgasse and, after a couple of metres, you will step into the large square dominated by the concave façade of the **DOMKIRCHE ST JAKOB ❺**. Upon leaving the church, go left, skirting its oval chapels and pillars until the courtyard of the **HOFBURG ❻** opens up on the right. When you leave, exit into Rennweg. The entrance to the modest-seeming **HOFKIRCHE ❼** is on the square at the south end of Rennweg. The interior is gorged with the monumental **Grabmal Kaiser Maximilians I**, the most important surviving ensemble of German Renaissance sculpture. Do not overlook the **Silberne Kapelle** upstairs. The entrance to the **TIROLER VOLKSKUNSTMUSEUM ❽** is through the same door as the church – it is on the opposite side of the cloister courtyard.

**Detour:** When you leave the Hofkirche, go right, then right again at Universitätsstrasse. You will quickly reach a church, the **Jesuitenkirche**. Walk through the covered passageway to the right of it (the Prof. F.-Mayr-Gasse). It will take you past Innsbruck University to Museumstrasse. The **Tiroler Landesmuseum 'Ferdinandeum'** is immediately to the left. As a city of museums, Innsbruck is second in Austria only to Vienna and this is the jewel in its crown. Highlights include Gothic statues, a famous 1370 altar from Meran Castle in

**Schloss Ambras**
€€ *Schloss Strasse 20;*
*tel: (0525) 24745;*
*fax: (0525) 24750;*
*www.khm.at/ambras. Open*
*daily 1000–1700; Aug till*
*1900.* Admission to the
delightful castle garden is
free. Part of it is set aside
for picnickers.

South Tyrol and the originals of the reliefs from the Goldenes Dachl. Its art gallery is strong on Old Masters such as Lucas Cranach, Rembrandt and Brueghel, and important moderns such as Schiele, Klimt and Kokoschka (*Museumstrasse 15, tel: (0512) 59489 102; fax: (0512) 5948 9109; www.tiroler-landesmuseum.at.*).

Return to Rennweg ('racing way'). The street was used for tournaments after the city began to outgrow its medieval beginnings. To the. right (north), next to the **Landestheater**, you will find the entrance to the **Hofgarten**. It was Andreas Hofer who allowed the first public access to the garden in 1809. Walk to the pavilion in the middle. If the weather is decent, you will see old men playing chess with 0.6-m high pieces on both sides of it. The park has a small **Alpine Garden** and **Schmetterlingshaus** (Butterfly House). Stroll to the north side and turn left towards the Inn river. Don't cross the iron footbridge but carry on right about 1km along the leafy footpath (**Innpromenade**) that follows the river. You won't have the path to yourself. Watch out for roller-bladers whizzing rhythmically by; even mothers pushing prams are starting to wear them. The **Hungerbahn** soon comes into sight, a funicular built 90 years ago to link the city with the Karwendel Mountains. Just before Hungerbahn, the round building that contains the **RIESENRUNDGEMALDE** ❾ is visible above the treetops. The first stop up the mountain is the **ALPENZOO** ❿. The **Hungerburg** is next, offering a magnificent view of the city and its surroundings. Cable cars ascend in three more stages as far as **Hafelekar** (2334m) near the summit of the north face of the Karwendel range. From there the Inn Valley is at your feet and the Stubai Alps and the peaks of the Karwendel form the horizon.

## Also worth exploring

Archduke Ferdinand (1529–95) built Tyrol's largest castle, **Schloss Ambras**, for his wife, Philippine Welser (*see* **Silberne Kapelle**, *page 211*) who rewarded him with lavishly prepared feasts that she described in a cookbook still important to Austrian cuisine. Though reactionary in his policies (and deeply hostile to Protestants), the archduke showed great imagination as a collector. His **Kunst- und Wunderkammer** ('Cabinet of Curiosities') was intended to be no less than an encyclopaedia of creation. The result is a surrealistic jumble of minerals, bones, weapons, sculpture, freaks and robots. The **Rüstungssäle** in the lower part of the castle provides a formidable spectacle of jousting mannequins and medieval arms and armour. The highlight of the upper castle is the Renaissance **Spanischer Saal** (Spanish Room) with a wooden inlaid ceiling, frescoes of Tyrolean nobility and a huge gallery of Habsburg family portraits.

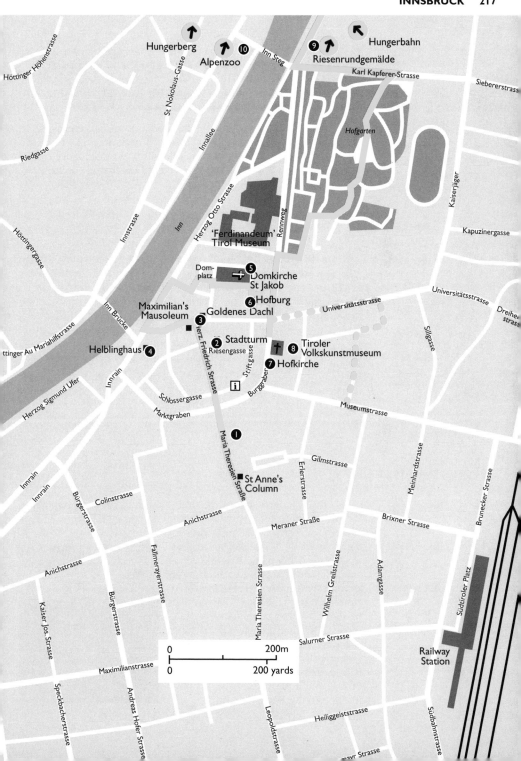

Hungerberg

Alpenzoo

Hungerbahn

Riesenrundgemälde

Höttinger Höhenstrasse

St Nikolaus-Gasse

Innallee

Karl Kapferer-Strasse

Siebererstrass

Riedgasse

Innstrasse

Inn

Hofgarten

Kaiserjäger

Kapuzinergasse

Höttinger gasse

Herzog Otto Strasse

Rennweg

'Ferdinandeum'
Tirol Museum

Universitätsstrasse

Dreiher
strass

Dom-
platz

Domkirche
St Jakob

Maximilian's
Mausoleum

Goldenes Dachl

Hofburg

Universitätsstrasse

Sillgasse

Inn Brücke

Helblinghaus

Herz. Friedrich Strasse

Stadtturm

Riesengasse

Stiftgasse

Tiroler
Volkskunstmuseum

Hofkirche

ttinger Au Mariahilfstrasse

Innrain

Herzog Sigmund Ufer

Schlossergasse

Burggraben

Museumstrasse

Marktgraben

Maria Theresien Straße

St Anne's
Column

Erlerstrasse

Gilmstrasse

Meinhardstrasse

Brunecker Strasse

Innrain

Innrain

Burgerstrasse

Colinstrasse

Anichstrasse

Meraner Straße

Brixner Strasse

Adamgasse

Kaiser Jos. Strasse

Anichstrasse

Fallmerayerstrasse

Bürgerstrasse

Maria Theresien Strasse

Wilhelm Greilstrasse

Südtiroler Platz

Maximilianstrasse

Salurner Strasse

Railway
Station

Speckbacherstrasse

Andreas Hofer Strasse

Leopoldstrasse

Heiliggeiststrasse

Südbahnstrasse

mayr Strasse

| 0 | | 200m |
| 0 | | 200 yards |

# The Old Brenner Road: the Wipp and Stubai valleys

## Ratings

| | |
|---|---|
| Hiking | ●●●●● |
| Outdoor activities | ●●●●● |
| Scenery | ●●●●● |
| Skiing | ●●●●● |
| Wild flowers | ●●●●● |
| Architecture | ●●●○○ |
| Food and drink | ●●○○○ |
| Shopping | ●○○○○ |

The Wipp Valley leads south from Innsbruck to the lowest and busiest crossing in the Alps, the Brenner Pass (1372m). The Brenner *Autobahn* funnels heavy traffic up to the pass by way of the 190m-high Europabrücke and 40 other bridges. By contrast, the *Ellbögen strasse* ('elbow' – or 'old Brenner road') is a route lost in an earlier era of travel. Its curves require nervy concentration, frequent gear changes and a lot of braking. On the opposite side of the river, the majestic Stubai Valley is the most popular excursion from Innsbruck, with year-round skiing on the Stubai glacier. The wild tributary valleys of the Gschnitztal, Valsertal and Schmirntal are worlds unto themselves, almost untouched by tourism.

## GRIES AM BRENNER❖

Gries, the last town before Brenner Pass, had been an important stopping point since time immemorial when the Brenner Pass *Autobahn* deprived it of its reason for being. Today, it is a modest resort town with an interesting collection of historic inns. A pub-crawl through them is perhaps the best way to commune with the ghosts of travellers past whether they be emperors or mule-drivers. The **Sprenger** has a Renaissance wine tavern. The **Weisse Rössl** has a rather different atmosphere; it was redecorated in the 1920s and ranks as one of the more interesting art deco interiors in the Tyrol.

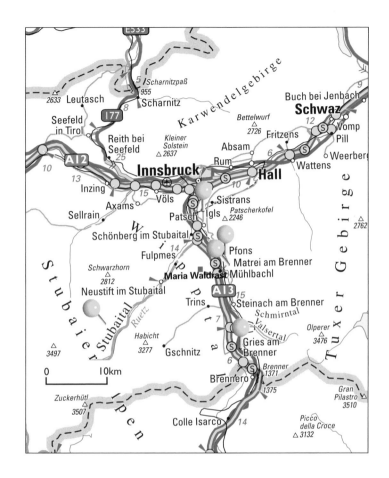

# IGLS❖

**ⓘ Tourismusbüro Igls**
*Hilberstrasse 15;*
*tel: (0512) 377 101;*
*fax: (0512) 379 154;*
*e-mail: igls@innsbruck.info;*
*www.tiscover.at/igls.*
*Open Mon–Fri 0830–1800,*
*Sat 0900–1200.*

**ⓗ Patscherkofel**
**Alpine Garden**
*Tel: (0512) 5075 910;*
*Open Jun–Sept 1000–1700.*

Perched on a sunny terrace above Innsbruck, Igls has elegant turn-of-the-century homes and major ski facilities, yet remains a farming community with the occasional whiff of dung in the air. A cable car takes skiers up to **Patscherkofel** (2246m), the *Hausberg* ('home mountain') of Innsbruck. Nearby are the legendary toboggan and bob-sled runs built for the 1976 Olympics. Tried-and-tested pilots take passengers on the **Olympic Bobsled** at speeds of over 100kph. The time of the run is approximately one minute. The **Patscherkofel Alpine Garden**❖ is Europe's highest botanical garden at 2000m with 400 species of of plants. The **Zirbenweg**❖ ('stone pine path') is an almost flat, 7km trail through a nature reserve of centuries-old, high-altitude pine trees.

### Accommodation in Igls

**Olympic Bobsled**
**€€** *Tel: (0512) 377
160; fax: (0512) 338 389.
Open summer Thur–Fri
1600–1800, winter Tue 1000
and Thur 1900.*

**Schlosshotel Igls €€€** *Viller Steig 2; tel: (0512) 377 217; fax: (0512) 377 217 198; www.schlosshotel-igls.com.* Built as a stately summer residence over a century ago, this tranquil hotel is full of antiques and *objets d'art.* Despite its small size, it has a swimming pool, steam room and sauna.

# MATREI AM BRENNER✢

The origins of Matrei go back to Roman times. During the Middle Ages, the houses in the **Hauptstrasse** were used to store goods on their way north or south and to weigh and tax them. Every roadside house in Matrei had to have an oriel ('covered balcony') so its occupants could keep an eye on what was passing below in the road. Unfortunately, the frescoed façades, painted oriels and wrought-iron signs have been so aggressively restored they look kitsch. However, the 15th-century **Gasthof zur Uhr** is well worth a look. Inside it surprises with its vaulted ceilings, stately staircase and pastel blue coat of arms painted on the wall.

# PFONS✢

The idyllic village of **Pfons**, located in a bend in the Sill river just north of Matrei am Brenner, is dominated by its **Pfarrkirche** – a motley of Romanesque, Gothic and baroque elements. The picturesque cemetery is full of wrought-iron grave-markers typical of the region. The **Johanneskapelle✢**, in the middle of the cemetery, is a late-Gothic gem by Niklas and Gregor Türing, leading architects of medieval Innsbruck. From between the ribbing of its vaulted ceiling, heads stare down in triplicate, human and demonic, surrounded by luxurious, painted stone flowers. The altar originally comes from South Tyrol. Its figures represent John the Baptist and Saints Florian and Augustus, as well as Barbara, the patron saint of miners.

# STUBAITAL✢✢

**Schmiedemuseum**
**€** *Fachschulgasee 4,
Fulpmes; tel: (05242) 696
024. Open May–Sept Wed
1400–1700.*

The glacier of the Stubaier Alps and the summits of Serles and Habicht look down upon the 30km-long Stubai Valley. Before winter sports came along in the 20th century, the main business of the town of **Fulpmes** was metalworking (the first workshop dates from 1413). The **Schmiedemuseum✢** has several centuries' worth of iron exhibits and 19th-century water-driven machine tools. After the town of **Neustift**, in the village of **Milders**, the valley divides in two between **Oberbergtal✢✢** and **Unterbergtal✢✢**. The former is a pristine valley,

**Hiking**
There are free guided hikes along the **Stubai glacier** mid-Jul to Aug. Information: **Stubai Glacier funicular** *tel: (05226) 8141; e-mail: info@stubai.gletscher.com; www.stubai.gletscher.com*

**Train ride The Stubaitalbahn** – a 1904 train – runs every Wednesday afternoon in summer from Wilten-Innsbruck to Fulpmes.

**Tourismusverein Stubai** *Bahnstrasse 17, Fulpmes; tel: (05225) 62235; fax: (05225) 63843; e-mail: info@stubai.at; www.tiscover.at/fulpmes. Open Mon–Fri 0900–1200 and 1400–1700, Sat 0900–1200.*

with a rough road that peters out after 10km. An easy trail climbs higher to a lodge, the **Franz-Senn-Hütte**✦✦, named after the 19th-century minister who founded the German and Austrian Ski Clubs. From the lodge, hikers can choose between 30 peaks over 3000m. The Unterbergtal ends in the **Hochstubaigebiet**✦✦, the lower station for Austria's largest year-round skiing area. The cable car travels up to the **Eisgrat**✦✦ (2900m) at the foot of the Wildspitz peak (3340m). The **Panorama-Restaurant** lives up to its name. In winter, the Eisjoch T-bar drags skiers further uphill to the Jochdohle where there is yet another restaurant, the highest in Austria (3150m). There are ski pistes for all levels, including the challenging 10km **Wilde Gruben** descent. A single ski pass (including transport on ski buses) covers all the skiing resorts in the valley. The closest places to spend the night are nowhere near the glacier and skiers have to drive back and forth, either from resort villages further down the valley or even from Innsbruck. The inevitable result in high season is traffic jams. The best alternative is the **Schlick** ski area, accessible from **Fulpmes** and **Telfes**. It is relatively uncrowded and has reliable snow; members of the national ski team train there in early winter.

# Suggested tour

**Total distance:** 155km.

**Time:** 1 day without detours; 2 or 3 days with detours.

**Links:** This route reaches the *Ellbögenstrasse* by way of Hall, which is on the B171 (*see page 199*). It is also possible to drive up from Innsbruck (*see page 208*) by following the signs for Igls.

From **HALL** ❶ (*see page 199*) drive up the long, winding *Ellbögenstrasse* into a region of high sunny hills where traditional farms alternate with holiday homes. While passing through **Rinns** you will notice an 18-hole golf course to the left, with an extraordinary mountain panorama from its greens. The Thomaskirche in **Tulfes** houses the oldest Christmas Nativity scene in the Tyrol (1609). After 17km you reach the winter ski resort of **IGLS**, which is accessible by public transport from Innsbruck. The road south saunters for a couple of kilometres in a dense stand of woods before lurching above the timberline. From **Patsch** there is a famous and much photographed view of Stubai Valley that takes in the pyramid-shaped peak of Serles, the more distant summit of Habicht and the Stubai glacier, where you will wind up at the end of the day. The road becomes a steep 'elbow' after passing the cliffside village of **St Peter** and again at **Ellbögen** itself, embedded in the narrow mouth of the Arztal. A few kilometres later, it descends below a cliff to the confluence of the Sill and a mountain tributary, curves through the village of **PFONS** ❷ and traverses a narrow stone bridge. The *Ellbögenstrasse* now joins the B182 at **MATREI AM BRENNER** ❸, the oldest town in the Wipptal.

**Detour:** Instead of driving into Matrei, follow the signs for Maria Waldrast under one of the concrete bridges of the Brenner Pass. You will have to pay a modest toll to carry on up a steep road through a heavily wooded valley. It is full of potholes and, in summer, cars rub fenders with the odd cow. The pilgrimage church of **Maria Waldrast** is near the foot of Serles mountain. The church was founded in the Middle Ages after woodcutters discovered a tree that miraculously resembled a Madonna with child. Local woodcarvers improved on the resemblance and pilgrims have been arriving ever since. Though the cloister is blandly modernised, the isolated setting induces a feeling of peace and the temptation to linger or even stay overnight. The summit of Serles – you saw it from Patsch – is just overhead. There is not a more beautiful peak in the Alps. The German poet Goethe called Serles the 'high altar' of the Tyrol. In early summer, its meadows bloom with golden Alpine poppies.

The B182 continues along an uneventful stretch to **Steinach am Brenner**, a town with a long history that mostly went up in smoke in a 19th-century fire and World War II bombing raids. Today, it is a pleasant holiday resort and the starting point for local hikes and some uncrowded skiing.

**Maria Waldrast €**
*Mützens 27; tel:
(05273) 6219; fax: (05273)
77091; e-mail: maria-
waldrast@aon.at;
www.tiscover.at/maria-
waldrast.* The 17th-century
cloister has a guesthouse
with 30 simple but
comfortable rooms.

**Geraerhof €€** *St Jodok
am Brenner; tel: (05279)
5215; fax: (05279); fax:
(05279) 20046; e-mail:
geraer-hof.c.mader@aon.at;
www.geraerhof.com.* This
friendly, family-run inn has
a sauna and loans out
mountain bikes. The
restaurant serves no-
nonsense, Tyrolean fare.

## Alpine plants

The term Alpine is technically reserved for plants that grow naturally above the timberline. They flower in early summer, between June and August, and have intense colours because they are saturated in ultra-violet light. Most plants that flower in the Alps today are hardy species from lower elevations that have managed to take root in soil above the timberline. They might come from the Mediterranean or regions as far away as Asia. Alpine plants do not grow at random, they require specific soil conditions. Due to their combination of rock (limestone, silicate and mica schist), the mountains between Innsbruck and Brenner Pass are particularly rich in flowers native to the Alps.

**Detour:** Take the right fork in the road at the beginning of town and follow the signposted but unpronounceable name – **Gschnitztal** (Gschnitz valley). Although a monumentally ugly 700m bridge of the Brenner *Autobahn* guards the entrance to this enchanting valley, the road through it is one long *Fahrvergnügen* ('driving pleasure'). It has wide shoulders most of the way and banks smoothly while it plumbs the depths of a Tyrolean Shangri-La. The visibility is excellent with only a couple of blind or semi-blind corners in **Trins**, a town where old farmhouses and historic inns jostle for room with a handful of modern buildings. The mountain above it, **Blaser** (2241m), is considered among all of Tyrol's mountains to be the richest in flowers. Further west lies the **Moränenwall**, a massive terminal moraine (1km long and 500m wide) that is cited in many textbooks on geology. At the end of the valley, the little town of **Gschnitz** is scattered over a wide area with the odd baroque façade and weathered farmhouse. Above it, the 3000m-plus peaks of the Ilm and Kirchdach and the 2000m massif of Habicht rise up like the walls of a canyon.

Continue up the B182.

**Detour:** Just off the B182, **St Jodok am Brenner** lies at the mouth of two tributary valleys. The meadows of **Padauner Kogel** mountain are carpeted with rare Alpine flowers in spring. The road up to the 12km-long **Schmirntal** tackles hairpin turns and a giddy 28 per cent gradient. This is a wondrous valley with no souvenir shops or car parks. A baroque church graces the village of Schmirn – created by the priest and architect Franz de Paula who designed several churches in the Stubai and Wipp valleys. Its dome frescoes are by the Tyrolean rococo artist Anton Zeller. From the mountain hamlet of **Toldern** there are fine views of the **Olperer** glacier. **Valsertal**, an Alpine valley where the clank of a ski-lift has never been heard, is best appreciated at the end of the road (just 7km) at the foot of **Olperer** mountain (3476m).

The last town before Brenner Pass is **GRIES AM BRENNER** ❹. There is no point in driving any further on the B182 unless you want to include Italy in this itinerary. Follow the signs right (west) for Vinaders, past a wonky wooden sawmill and along a wild mountain stream. Watch out for a right uphill turn signposted Nösslach.

**Detour:** If you carry on straight (south) at this point, you will reach **Obernberger See** after 7km. Emperor Maximilian hunted ibex in the region and fished the lake, having his catch illustrated in a book he published in 1504. The region attracts rock hounds in search of mineral samples such as malachite, quartz and fluorspar. One good place to look is a hill 15 minutes' walk from **Gasthof Waldesruh**. The best way to appreciate the lake is to row out to the middle. You can hire boats at **Gasthof am See**.

A neglected country road will take you north again. Just past the town of Nösslach, you will find yourself alone on a hillside with the stark Romanesque **Kirche zum heiligen Jakobus**. Its steeple was once used to signal other churches in a line of communication that warned the Tyrolean militia when an enemy crossed the Brenner Pass. The humble country road continues along a ridge that seems to float above the valley. Roadside benches stand at strategic places where you can rest and contemplate the grandeur of the surrounding mountains. A couple of small hamlets interrupt the meadows, at their most brilliant in early summer. A series of abrupt, semi-blind turns brings you below the timberline again. The sylvan stretch ends in uncomfortable proximity to the Brenner Pass *Autobahn*, but you soon find yourself back on the B182, retracing the route along familiar terrain as far as Matrei am Brenner. Stay on it and continue to the town of **Schönberg** where the **STUBAITAL** ❺ begins. In the last Ice Age, two glaciers collided at this point and ground the earth into the

plateau that the town rests on. The valley road is even more beautiful in its upper reaches or when driving out of it. Furthermore, the first 15km lead past towns that live for the ski season and are best appreciated in an après-ski mood. In summer, you might as well zip past the gauntlet of hotels, pizzerias, discos and pubs. On the way, you will sweep past slopes forested with larch trees and have occasional glimpses of the wall of ice that covers the 3507m **Zuckerhütl** ('sugar mountain'). The best part of the road is still to come when you enter **Unterbergtal**, a long narrow valley. Between Gasteig and Volderau, you pass the **Mischbach Waterfall**.

**Getting out of the car:** Stop at the next waterfall, the thundering **Grabafall**, the widest waterfall in the eastern Alps. There is a car park just above it at **Grabalm**. It is only a 10-minute walk to a footbridge beneath the cascade that drains the glaciers of the Stubaier Alps.

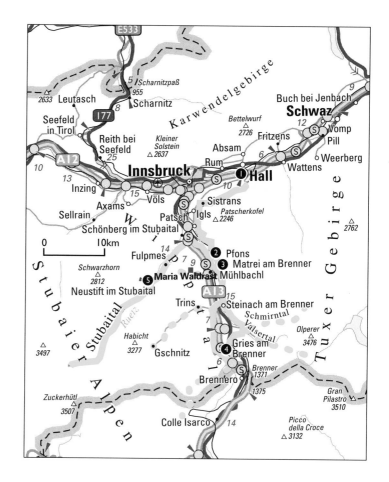

The road ends in a vast series of car parks at the **Mutterberg-Alm** (1728m). This is the lower station for the ski-lifts of the **Stubaier Gletscherbahn**. If you want to continue from here, get on the cable car.

## Also worth exploring

The church of St Katharina stands in Navis Valley on the **Burgruine Aufenstein**, the ruins of a castle destroyed in 1335, except for its chapel. The chapel was used as a school beginning in the 19th century. A new school was built in 1953 and, when the wood panelling of the old school was removed, the most important early Gothic frescoes in the entire Tyrol region came to light. If the door is locked, ask for the key from the verger, Johanna Vötter, who lives next door.

# The Ötz Valley

## Ratings

| | |
|---|---|
| Geology | ●●●●● |
| Mountains | ●●●●● |
| Nature | ●●●●● |
| Scenery | ●●●●● |
| Skiing | ●●●●● |
| Children | ●●●●○ |
| Architecture | ●●●○○ |
| History | ●●○○○ |

The people of the Ötz Valley like to call their home the 'realm of the superlative'. It is the longest tributary valley of the Inn (60km), with the highest peak in north Tyrol and the highest village in Austria. Two hundred and fifty-six Alpine peaks over 3000m encircle it and glaciers cover 200sq km of it. The road into this region is for drivers who relish violent hairpin turns and scenery that offers terrifying evidence of geologic upheaval. It is a natural spectacle of flat mountain valleys, granite cliffs, meadows and glaciers. At the end of the Ötz Valley, a fork in the road takes you to different worlds – left to the chic ski paradise of the Gurgl Valley (and the road to Italy), or right to the end of the Venter Valley, the mountain-climbers' Shangri-La.

## GURGLTAL✦✦

**ⓘ Tourismusverband Gurgl** *Hauptstrasse 108, Obergurgl;* *tel: (05256) 6466; fax: (05256) 6353; www.obergurgl.com*

There are three villages with the name 'Gurgl' (Unter- Ober- and Hoch-). Together they form one of the top ski resorts in Europe, famously reliable for snow, which attracts an older, well-heeled skiing crowd. There is little waiting for lifts and you can ski right up to your door (note: the Gurgl Valley ski resorts do not share a ski pass with Sölden). Perhaps unsurprisingly, Gurgl is the Tyrolean community with the highest number of tourists per inhabitant. Of the three, only **Untergurgl** has retained a whiff of Tyrolean village atmosphere. **Obergurgl** likes to call itself the highest parish in Austria (1930m). Architecturally, it is a collection of shortcomings. The Crystal hotel, for example, looks like the Love Boat docked in the Alps and re-opened as a hotel. The resort is a starting point for memorable hikes. In early summer, you can walk through stands of *Zirben* ('stone pines') and meadows blooming with Alpine roses to the **Rotmoos waterfall**✦ and into the stunning **Rotmoos Valley**✦✦, or up to **Gaisbergtal**✦✦ and **Mutsattel**, descending by way of the glacier of **Rotmoosferner**✦✦ and

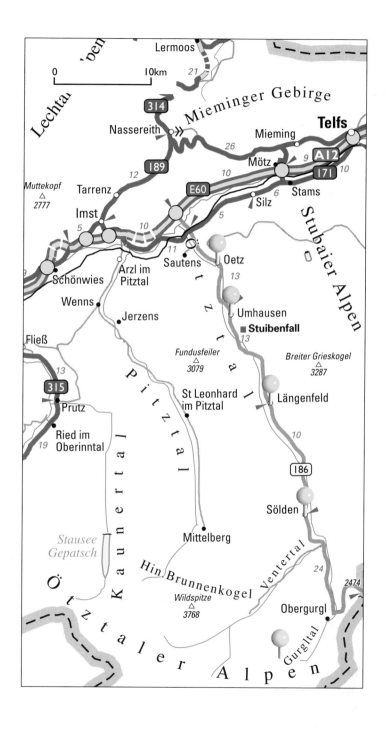

then back through Rotmoos Valley. **Hochgurgl** is Austria's highest ski resort (2150m) with the elevation reflected in its prices. Its most prestigious ski-run is an 8.5km joyride from **Wurmkogel**✢✢ (3082m) down to Untergurgl (1280m).

# LÄNGENFELD✢

**ⓘ Tourismusverband Längenfeld**
*Unterlängenfeld 81; tel: (05253) 5207; fax: (05253) 520 716; www.laengenfeld.com. Open Summer Mon–Fri 0830–1200 and 1400–1800, Sat 0830–1200 and 1700–1800, Sun 0900–1100; Winter Mon–Fri 0830–1200 and 1400–1730, Sat 0830–1200.*

It is only fitting that Längenfeld, the largest town in the valley, should also have the highest church tower, which crowns the **Pfarrkirche St Katharina**. The **Ötztal Heimat- und Freilichtmuseum**✢ (Folklore and Open-air Museum) is housed in a 300-year-old barn and mill complex. The exhibits related to flax recall an industry that was important to the inhabitants of the valley for six centuries until the last loom shut down in 1949.

Längenfeld is the centre of mountain climbing in the valley and the starting point for 150km of mountain trails. It was the birthplace of the 'glacier minister', Franz Senn, a life-long devotee of mountaineering, who placed it right next to godliness. He was instrumental in the creation of Austrian and German Alpine Clubs (in 1862 and 1869) while serving as a minister in the isolated valley of Vent (1860–72). He prepared the way for early climbers by building mountain trails and huts, and training mountain guides. He not only preached the spiritual benefits of Alpinism, he also had a vision of how it could help Tyrolean highland farmers improve their meagre standard of living. What he did not foresee was the profound ecological impact of tourism on the mountains he held sacred. Over 150 mushers and 1500 sleigh-dogs meet in mid-January in Längenfeld to compete in the European Cup Race in sleigh-dog racing.

**Below**
Längenfeld's Folklore and Open-air Museum

# OETZ*

ⓘ **Tourismusverband Oetz** *Hauptstrasse 66; tel: (05252) 6669; fax: (05252) 666 975; www.oetz.com. Open Mon–Fri 0830–1200 and 1400–1800, Sat 0830–1200 and 1430–1800.*

Oetz is the town that gave the valley its name. Sheltered from wind by the Amberg massif, it is surprisingly warm for its elevation (820m), and even supports chestnut trees and fruit orchards. The best view of town and its surroundings is from the graveyard of the hilltop **Pfarrkirche** (1667–1744). The **Galerie zum alten Ötztal*** is a thought-provoking cross between a traditional *Heimatmuseum* and a modern art gallery. Don't miss the frescoes on the Gasthof zum Stern. This 17th-century inn has a remarkable painted façade in which every window tells a story, either naughty or noble.

## Accommodation in Oetz

**Zum Stern €** *Family Griesser, Kirchweg 6; tel: (05252) 6323.* This is a modest and friendly guesthouse long on history and hospitality though a little short on mod cons. Its restaurant serves gourmet Tyrolean cooking in generous portions.

# SÖLDEN*

As far as facilities are concerned, Sölden is a 'resort of the superlative'. The top of the **Gaislachkogel*** (3040m) is the highest cable car station in Austria. It is an absolute highlight both for its downhill ski-runs and for the sweeping views from its panorama restaurant. The village is chock-full with discothèques, cafés, pizzerias and sport equipment boutiques. It draws a young crowd and offers an intense late-night après-ski scene. In summer, the town is truly ugly, with its tacky five-storey hotels and deserted pubs and discos. **Hochsölden*** is a less frenetic resort on a plateau above the town (2080m) where guests all but ski into their hotel rooms. A 13km-long **Panoramastrasse*** (toll road) leads from Sölden up to the glacier of the Rettenbachferner and further through the highest tunnel in Europe to the **Tiefenbachferner** (2800m) car park. The **Venter Höhenweg*** starts from a point near by – a relatively easy four-hour walk that tours sublime high alpine scenery.

# UMHAUSEN*

☾ **Gasthof Krone €** *Dorf 6; tel: (05255) 50140; fax: (05255) 5230.* A creaky, quaint, 17th-century inn located in the heart of the village.

The oldest town in the valley has often been hit by floods, reflected in the existence of a Neudorf ('new village') district. The villagers built it after a famous deluge swept away 70 houses in 1762. The **Stuibenfall*** (Stuiben waterfall, one hour return) is an easy walk along a footpath from a car park just outside of town. The highest waterfall in the Tyrol, it plunges 150m into the valley. Like so much of

🔇 **Weberer Regensburger** *Dorfhauptstrasse.* This shop sells rugs made of local wool.

the valley's geology, it was the result of falling rock – boulders sealed off the Horlachebach, which had to seek a new course.

# Suggested tour

**Total distance:** 59km to the end of the Ötz Valley. The detours (there and back) add 14km for Sulz Valley and 26km for the Vent Valley, plus an arduous 6km for Rofenhöfe.

**Time:** You could cruise Ötztal by car in half a day. However, to do it and its side valleys even partial justice takes at least 3 days and some getting out of the car.

The Ötz Valley is clearly signposted from the Inn Valley *Autobahn* and the B171. The road into the valley is at its most impressive when you are entering rather than leaving so don't rush. It climbs 1000m over five giants steps – level valleys that feel more like basins – formed by cataclysmic landslides at the end of the last Ice Age ('yesterday' in geological time; the mountains, however, are 300–450 million years old). The Ötztaler Ache, a powerful mountain river, smashes its way through each barrier in a series of rapids. OETZ ❶ lies on the first level at a particularly wide point.

**Detour:** A small mountain road leads from Oetz 2km southeast to the **Piburgersee** (paid parking). This natural lake, formed by a landslide, is one of the most beautiful places in the valley. Its waters are warm in summer (reaching 24°C) and reflect almost perfectly the surrounding Alpine peaks of the Acherkogl (3008m) to the south and the Tschirgant to the north. The lake is also rich in fish. Enquire about a fishing permit at the tourist office in Oetz.

The next 'step' in the valley ends in a spot between **Habichen** and **Tumpen**, where the second largest known landslide in the central Alps occurred. A mountain that once stood on the cliff above the hamlet of Köfels collapsed into the valley and blocked it, leading to the formation of a flat basin now occupied by **UMHAUSEN** ❷. The road gets there by weaving in and out of a series of cliffs. It passes through another set of narrows and up to the town of **LÄNGENFELD** ❸, nestled in a similar, smaller basin.

**Detour:** From Längenfeld, an astonishing road whisks cars (but no caravans) up 400m in just 5km (16 per cent grade) via switchbacks to **Sulztal**, an Alpine wonderland encircled by 3000m peaks. A small mountain lodge on the way, the Unterlehner Hof, offers the possibility of lunch in the form of bread and mountain cheese, *Speckknödel* or *Tiroler Gröstl* and, of course, beer. The only village is the quiet hamlet of Gries at the end of the valley road. From there, hiking trails climb higher into the mountains as far as the glaciers of Stubaital.

## The oldest European

On 19 September, 1991, German hikers from Nürnberg thought they had stumbled over a discarded puppet in the Similaun Glacier in the Ötz Alps. On closer inspection, they were shocked to find a corpse. When the police arrived, their suspicions were heightened by the discovery of an axe. The famous mountain climber Reinhold Messner happened to be in the area. He came to examine it and declared that it was 'more than a hundred years old'. As it turned out, both the axe and the body were over 5300 years old. The ice mummy was removed for study by the Austrian authorities but because it had been found a few metres across the Italian border, it became the subject of political dispute between Austria and Italy. The result is that Oetzi, as he was later nick-named because of where he was found, is now permanently housed in the Tyrol Archaeological Museum in Bolzano, Italy. Scientists have now studied him in great detail. Physiologically, he was no different from a modern human being. At the time of his death, he was over 40 and suffering from arthritis and athlete's foot. Some questions have puzzled researchers: What was he doing with a copper axe? At an elevation of 3000m? Was he on his way home after a journey to Italy? Was he a hunter, shepherd or Shaman? Ongoing study has begun to outline what Oetzi's life and death may have been like.

After the hamlet of **Huben**, the valley narrows again for a long stretch until you find yourself driving above a deep gorge and craning your neck to look back at waterfalls. Occasionally, you have a tantalising glimpse of brown farmhouses in the valley below at the foot of sheer cliffs. This is the 'inner' part of the Ötz Valley, which is dominated by winter sports, beginning with **SÖLDEN ❹**. The road forks where the Gurgler river and the Ötztaler Ache meet at **Zwieselstein** (1470m), a charming village but a poor cousin to its neighbours because it has no ski-lifts.

**Detour**: Turn right into **Ventertal** and follow the Venter Ache along a wide, well-maintained *Landstrasse* that plunges into the deep valley. For a sweeping view of where you've been and will go, stop at the tiny church cemetery in the village of **Heiligkreuz**. The village of **Vent** lies at the end of the valley. It has been a magnet to mountain-climbers since the days when minister Senn gave sermons in its church (*see Längenfeld, page 228*) and mountain guides from Vent have the best reputation in the eastern Alps. An interesting example of transhumance continues between here and South Tyrol. Since human memory, shepherds have driven their flocks to pasture in the meadows around Vent from Schnalstal in South Tyrol and herded them back in September. When there is too much snow, the shepherds have to carry the lambs over the 3000m pass. The creation of an Austrian–Italian border between the two places in 1919 did nothing to change their migratory routine. A narrow, gritty road with

**◉ Ötztaler Natur Camping €**
*Southeast of Huben, off the B186, tel: (05253) 5855; fax: (05253) 5538; www.oetztalernaturcamping. com.* Year-round camping with mountain views on a series of meadows enclosed by pine forest and pear orchards.

**Berggasthaus Rofenhof**
*€ Rofenhöfe (above the town of Vent); tel: (05254) 8103; fax: (05254) 30125; www.rofenhof.at.* The highest B&B inn in the Alps (2014m) run by the musical Klotz family. The area is used by mountain-climbers as a base camp to explore the region.

a grade that hits 30 per cent leads from Vent 3km further to the tiny hamlet of **Rofenhöfe** (2014m), the highest village in Austria that is inhabited year-round. Technically, the road is only for the inhabitants and guests at the Berggasthaus Rofenhof, so you should at least drink a cup of coffee while you are there. These old farmhouses occupy an area that shows signs of human activity going back 5000 years. The village earned a footnote in history when the Tyrolean Duke Friedrich IV disguised himself as a peasant and used it as a hiding place in 1416. A movie version of *Geier Wally* – a schmalzy novel about a young girl who climbs a cliff to capture a fledgling eagle – was filmed here in 1940, with the villagers more or less playing themselves.

**Getting out of the car**: The unbearable lightness of walking is best experienced by crossing the *hängebrucke* (steel-rope suspension footbridge) that spans the Rofen gorge just below the *Gasthof* – it trembles with each step over planks that feel light as styrofoam. Afterwards, you might be moved to contribute to its upkeep – there is a small metal box for donations.

Turn left into **Gurgltal**. Since it leads to Italy don't be surprised if Porsches or BMWs shoot by like Scud missles aimed at the south. After passing through Untergurgl, a 2km road veers right into Obergurgl and ends in a *cul-de-sac* around a massive bronze ball – a tribute to two balloonists who flew to a record elevation in 1931 and landed on the Gurgl glacier. Local mountain guides rescued them. The rest of Obergurgl is pedestrianised and driving at night is prohibited, though no one is there to notice in the summer. Once you are back on the main road, it will double back on itself before reaching Hochgurgl. The curves are dizzying and the road builders seem to have used up all their guard-rails at lower elevations. This is hands-gripping-the-wheel driving every metre of the way. The view from the turn-off below the toll station (2454m) sweeps across the surrounding peaks and the eternal ice of the Ötztal glaciers. Make a U-turn and drive back to the valley.

## Also worth exploring

For people who are not in a hurry and are game for an additional 40km of adventurous Alpine driving, it is possible to travel to Ötz from Innsbruck (or vice versa) by way of a *Landstrasse* through the **Sellraintal**, an idyllic valley that cuts deep into the Stubaier Alps (take the *Autobahn* west to Zirl-Ost, follow signs for Kematen then Sellrain). On its way up from the floor of the Inn Valley, the road threads a severely narrow ravine next to the gushing Melachbach before things widen out in **Sellrain**. **Kühtai**, located above the timberline, is the principal ski resort, in an area where Alpine roses bloom by the million in summer. From there, the road descends through another valley, **Nedertal**, past a waterfall and down to Oetz.

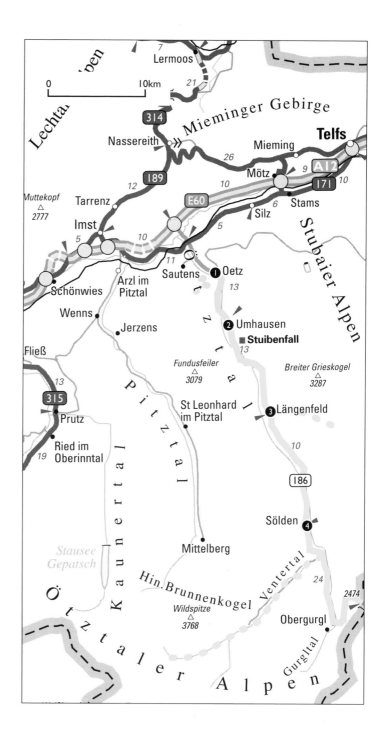

# Imst and the Pitz Valley

## Ratings

| | |
|---|---|
| Hiking | ●●●●● |
| Nature | ●●●●● |
| Scenery | ●●●●○ |
| Skiing | ●●●●● |
| Children | ●●●○○ |
| Shopping | ●●●○○ |
| Architecture | ●●○○○ |
| Museums | ●●○○○ |

The Pitz Valley has been 'paradise lost' to climbers since becoming 'ski eldorado' in the 1980s. Its enchantment remains though it is shared by more people. The valley runs parallel to the Ötz Valley to the east and the Kauner Valley to the west. The lower end terminates in the Roppen gorge, near Imst, across from the summit of Tschirgant Mountain. The names of many towns – Arzl, Wenns, and Jerzens – are Rhaeto-romansch, a kind of peasant Latin spoken by the Tyroleans who lived here long ago, before the German-speaking tribes arrived. The valley is shaped like a funnel, and from a wide beginning it suddenly narrows. At the very end, an underground funicular and cable cars bring visitors to the glacier's edge, tantalisingly close to the Wildspitze (3774m) – the highest peak in the Tyrol.

## ARZL*

**ⓘ Tourismusverband Pitztal** *Unterdorf 18, Wenns; tel: (05414) 86999; fax: (05414) 8699 988; www.pitztal.com*

**Bungy Jumping Pitztal** €€€ *Leins 73, Arzl; tel/fax: (05412) 61571; www.pitztal-bungy.com. Jumps of 94m take place Fri–Sun 1100–1800.*

Arzl stands at the entrance of Pitztal ('Pitz Valley') on a sunny cliff that has been inhabited since the Bronze Age. Today, however, the village pride and joy is the thoroughly modern **Hängebrücke**** (suspension bridge) – Europe's highest footbridge. It floats between precipices 94m above the **Pitzklamm**** ('gorge'). Many visitors like to get up close and personal with the gorge by bungee-jumping into it.

The town's official boundaries include a number of off-the-beaten-path hamlets such as to **Timmls** and **Plattenrain*** (reached by a narrow mountain road 2km south of town), which are hundreds of metres above Arzl. The latter has a small **Tierpark** (zoo) with perky dwarf kangaroos and a **Streichelzoo** where children can pet friendly animals. The views across the valley are stunning.

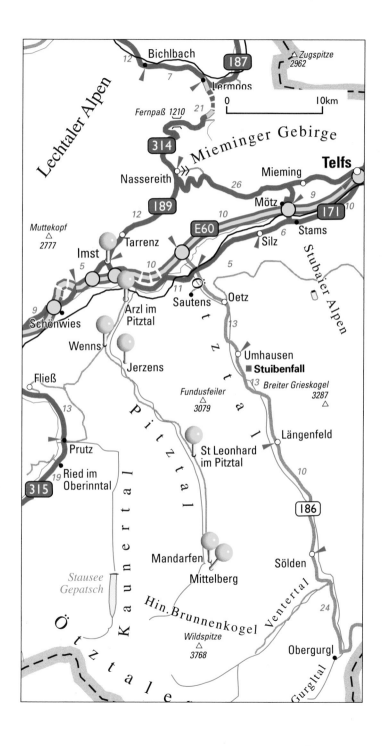

Lechtaler Alpen

Bichlbach

187

△ Zugspitze
2962

12

7

Lermoos

Fernpaß 1210    21

0          10km

314

Mieminger Gebirge

**Telfs**

Nassereith

Mieming

26

Mötz    9

189

171    10

12

E60    10

6    Stams

Muttekopf
△
2777

Imst

Tarrenz

Silz

Stubaier Alpen

5

10

5

11

Sautens    Oetz

Arzl im
Pitztal

Schönwies

9

Wenns

13

Umhausen

Jerzens

■ **Stuibenfall**

Fließ

13    Breiter Grieskogel
3287
△

13

Pitztal

Fundusfeiler
△
3079

a

Längenfeld

Prutz

l

St Leonhard
im Pitztal

10

Ried im
Oberinntal

19

186

315

r

a

Kaunertal

t

Mandarfen

Sölden

Stausee
Gepatsch

Mittelberg

Ö

Hin. Brunnenkogel

Ventertal

24

t

Wildspitze
△
3768

Obergurgl

z

t

a

l    e

Gurgltal

**Walter Kopp**
*Timmls 10;*
tel: (05412) 66741.
Herr Kopp is a fine
woodcarver of Christmas
Nativity scenes, available
at modest prices. He lives
and works in a large house
at the end of the village of
Timmls that doubles as a
B&B, run by his wife. He is
known for his prowess in
the Alpine sports of finger-
wrestling and stone-lifting
– with a record hoist of
275kg.

## Accommodation near Arzl

**Gasthof Plattenrain €** *Timmls 18; tel: (05412) 63101; fax: (05412) 65540; www.plattenrainalm.at.* You have to drive through the clouds to get to this traditional inn, high above Arzl. It makes a fine detour for a beer on the terrace or as a place to stay overnight. It is particularly interesting for families. Most rooms have multiple-bedded rooms and there is a petting zoo.

### The 'procession of ghosts'

Every four years an ancient ritual is performed as part of the Imst carnival. The *Schemenlaufen* ('procession of ghosts') is the most famous example of a folklore ritual that is also observed in **Nassereith** (*Schellerlaufen*) and **Telfs** (*Schleicherlaufen*). The central figures of the *Schemenlaufen* are 54 couples of *Roller* (wearing girlish masks) and *Scheller* (in virile masks with bushy handlebar moustaches). Both wear massive head-dresses of mirrors wreathed in flowers and gold leaf. Each *Roller* dances circles around a *Scheller*, tinkling 40 little bells on a belt and inviting him to dance. He answers with a stagger and loud, lewd peel of the heavy cowbells around his waist. There are many interpretations of this cacophonous coupling: the marriage of man and woman, the counterparts of youth and age, or spring and winter. They are followed by a menagerie of masked characters: witches, bears, and *Vogelhändler* packing cages full of singing canaries. The **Fasnachtsmuseum €** (next to the cemetery) displays the masks used in the *Schemenlaufen* (*www.fasnacht.at; open Jun–Oct Mon–Fri 1000–1200, 1700–1900*).

# IMST✧

**Tourismusverband
Imst** *Johannesplatz 4;*
tel: (05412) 69100;
fax: (05412) 69108;
e-mail: info@imst.at;
www.tiscover.at/imst

**Romantik Hotel
Post €€€** *Eduard-
Wallnöfer Platz 3;*
tel: (05412) 66555;
fax: (05412) 6651 955;
www.romantikhotels.com/imst.
This 15th-century castle
has been converted into a
luxury hotel with one of
the region's best
restaurants.

The town of Imst has known good times and bad in its long history. It prospered in Roman times as a nexus of transit and shared in Tyrol's medieval mining boom, extracting silver, lead and zinc from nearby Mount Tschirgant. Its Gothic church was financed by profits from the mines. After the decline in mining, with Tyroleans scrambling to find new trades, the citizens of Imst cornered the market in canaries. They bred the birds, taught them to sing and peddled them all over Europe, travelling with birdcages on their backs. An operetta, *Der Vögelhändler* by Carl Zeller, was composed about the life of an Imst birdman. The town lost its monopoly in the canary business in the early 19th century. Shortly thereafter, in 1822, a fire burned down all but three of its buildings. Some of the rebuilt Altstadt can be seen along the serpentine **Hauptstrasse**. The *Schemenlaufen* ('procession of ghosts') takes place here every four years. A famous excursion starts from the Johanneskirche (near the

**ISSBA-Alternative Handel** *Schustergasse 21–23; tel: (05412) 621 280.* Specialises in Tyrolean farm products such as honey, dried flowers, *Speck* (smoked ham) and *Wurst*.

The whitewater in the **Imster Schlucht** is ideal for rafting and turbulent enough to feel death-defying, but safe even for beginners. Ask at the tourist office for details.

tourist office) in the centre. Within a few minutes, you will be in a wooded gorge, the **Rosengartenschlucht** (approximately one hour to the end), where steps cut directly into the stone skirt three levels of a waterfall. On the way, watch out for the houses built into the perpendicular cliff of the Kalvarienberg, along with a chapel, which was erected during the plague years of the 17th century. These 'cliff dwellings' are unique in the Alps and are still inhabited. Another gorge, the **Imster Schlucht**, cuts across the Inn Valley in the opposite direction. It poses something of a mystery to geologists. They are not sure when it was created but they regard it as evidence that the Inn river ran along a very different course until recent (geological) history. A train ride is the easiest way to explore it. The Imst-Pitztal train station is at the west end. A delightful trail leads through it, too, and into the Pitztal by way of another gorge, the Pitzklamm, which ends at the Arzl–Wald road.

# JERZENS

Located on a terrace on the east side of the valley, Jerzens is best known for its ski region, the **Hochzeiger**. It has a famous toboggan run – the longest in the Pitztal. With a total length of 6km, it winds its way down from the midway station of the Hochzeiger Bergbahnen to the valley station. The track, mostly through forest, is well illuminated and in operation between 1900 and midnight.

# MANDARFEN

**Tourismusverband Innerpitztal** *St Leonhard; tel: (05413) 86216; fax: (05413) 86349; www.tiscover.at/innerpitztal.* The tourist information office is located in the same building as the Rifflsee gondola station.

**Pitztaler Gletscherbahn** *St Leonhard; tel: (05413) 86288; fax: (05413) 86343; e-mail: office@pitztaler-gletscher.at; www.pitztaler-gletscher.at*

From the resort village of Mandarfen, a gondola ascends to 2291m and a cable car continues even higher to the area around **Rifflsee**. On the way down to the right, a bridge allows skiers to reach the **Pitzexpress Valley Station** where they can hop on the **Pitztaler Gletscherbahn**. In summer, the mountain station (2300m) is the starting point for spectacular hikes, including a walk around the lake of Rifflsee. The **Fuldaer Höhenweg ridge trail** leads south to the Taschachhütte mountain hut, which is at the foot of the peak of Hochvernagtspitze and near two glaciers – the **Taschachferner** and **Sexegertenferner**.

## Accommodation in Mandarfen

**Hotel Vier Jahreszeiten** €€€ *Mandarfen 73; tel: (05413) 86361; fax: (05413) 863 615; e-mail: info@hotel-vier-jahreszeiten.at; www.hotel-vier-jahreszeiten.at.* Lots of luxury hotel comfort within a stone's throw of the Rifflsee cable car and just 1km from the Mittelberg glacier funicular.

# MITTELBERG✧

It only takes seven minutes for the **Pitztaler Gletscherbahn** to travel through a tunnel from the valley station of **Mittelberg** (1740m) to an elevation of 2800m at the foot of the glacier of **Mittelbergferners**. It provides some of the most challenging and reliable skiing in the Tyrol. There is also a cross-country ski-run on the glacier and a Snowboard Fun-park.

Chair lifts, T-bars and the Pitz-Panoramabahn hoist you even further uphill to the back side of **Brunnenkogel**✧✧✧ (3440m), the highest skiing area in Austria. On a clear day, there are sweeping views of the Central Alps, taking in the **Wildspitze**✧✧✧ (3772m), the Tyrol's highest peak; the **Ortler**; the **Dolomites**; and the **Taschachferner** glacier, at the foot of the **Hochvernagtspitze**. In the distance, the peaks of the Kauner and Ötz valleys are also visible. The Wildspitze, though close, is not necessarily an easy walk. The path to the summit crosses a glacier and should only be undertaken with proper equipment and an experienced guide.

# ST LEONHARD✧

Though it is the largest resort in the area, St Leonhard is just one of many villages and hamlets scattered along the Pitzbach. Originally, people living further down the valley or in Imst used the area for summer pasture. The main occupations were grazing sheep and cattle and making cheese. The humble wooden huts evolved into the small communities you see today. Mineral fans who are fit might want to hike the trail that starts south of St Leonhard, in **Piömes** (1390m). By way of **Luibisalm** (2070m) and **Luibisböden** (2300m), the trails arrives at **Moalandlsee** (2525m). The stone around the lake (mica schist) is embedded with enormous crystals.

# WENNS✧

Wenns is the largest town in Pitztal, sitting in a sunny basin at an elevation of 1000m. Its cemetery church has a remarkable view of the lower Pitztal. The **Platzhaus**✧ (just a couple of metres below its **Hauptstrasse**) has one of the finest painted façades in the Tyrol. It was built in 1550 and occupied by the Duke of Tarasp, who used it as a courthouse. Two sides of the house are adorned with frescoes with themes from the Old Testament and banners of Habsburg dukes (painted 1576–1608). The same building has a door with a sign that says 'Milchautomat'. Pull it open and you will find a coin-operated machine that dispenses farmyard milk at any time of day or night.

**Opposite**
Pitztal

# Suggested tour

**Total distance:** 77km there and back.

**Time:** 1 easy day.

**Links:** From Wenns a scenic road winds up to Piller Pass (*see page 244*).

From **IMST** ❶ follow the signs for Arzl/Pitztal. The road climbs up to the plateau occupied by **ARZL** ❷. This area receives far more sunshine than the valley floors below. **WENNS** ❸ is higher up but nestled in a shallow basin. The road jumps between curves for a stretch and penetrates a heavily forested bottleneck in the valley. From here on, it almost becomes one with the stream, the Pitzebach.

**Getting out of the car:** The **Pitztaler Stuibenfall**, a waterfall that thunders over granite cliffs, is an easy walk (20 minutes) from the Gasthof Schön, located between **Schön** and **Zaunhof**.

**Detour:** Visiting **Zaunhof** simply requires taking a bend in the road – but what a bend! A precipitous road climbs through this hamlet of weathered farmhouses and precarious-looking terraces. You can drive through town and descend again to the main road without retracing the curves.

At **Bichl**, there are views of the glaciers at the end of the valley. The road threads through a series of meadows, scattered buildings and resort hotels with **ST LEONHARD** ❹ roughly at the centre. Near the end of the valley, **MANDARFEN** ❺ signals the beginning of its 'ski circus'. At **MITTELBERG** ❻, there is a turn-off for car parks of the **Pitzexpress**. The foot of the Mittagkogels, a peak shaped like a pyramid, is at the end of the valley, with a small inn called the **Gasthaus Steinbock**. While sipping a beer there, you can contemplate dramatic evidence of 19th-century landslides and avalanches caused by deforestation. Retrace the route through Pitztal. The road divides near the hamlet of **Schön**. Take the right fork. This shoulderless, solitary road is favoured more by cyclists than motorists. There is just room for the occasional bench wedged between the tarmac and grassy hillside. It continues to climb as far as **JERZENS** ❼, a scenic town set on a small mountain table, popular, in season, with skiers and hikers. The road beyond it eventually meanders downhill. It passes fields where hay is stacked on traditional racks to dry during the summer. The hamlet of **Ried** has a quaint collection of weathered farmhouses, the baroque **Floriankapelle** (chapel) and old mills. Near the end of the valley the road curves west in the direction of Arzl.

**Detour:** Turn right (following the signs) into the village of **Wald**, a motley collection of old buildings leaning against one another in adjoining, Rhaeto-romansch style. It has a *Fasnacht* (carnival) tradition similar to the one in Imst.

**Left**
Spring in the Pitztal

There is an abundant supply of low-priced pensions, private rooms and holiday apartments in Pitztal. Ask for a listing at one of the tourist offices. Hotels in the upper price range can cost almost twice as much in winter as in summer, reflecting the predominance of the winter season.

A quick descent returns to the swift-flowing Pitzebach.

**Getting out of the car**: The magnificent footbridge over the Pitzklamm (gorge) is used for bungee-jumping (*see page 234*). If you would rather watch, park at Pitzebach and walk 50m along the leafy **Luis-Trenker-Steig** into the gorge. It leads to a point below the bridge; from there, by the side of the rushing water, you can observe the jumpers dangling overhead and listen to their screams of terror and joy reverberate off the sheer rock walls.

The road now climbs uphill again, to Arzl.

### Also worth exploring

Elizabeth of Bavaria founded the Cistercian abbey at Stams in 1273 and ordered the monks to pray for the soul of her son Conradin. The last of the Hohenstaufen dynasty, the 16-year-old had been beheaded in Naples in 1268. The abbey contains the Royal Crypt of the Tyrolean lords (1284–1563), including Meinhard II, Sigismund der Münzreiche, Friedl mit der leeren Tasche (Frederick the Penniless) and the second wife of Emperor Maximilian, Maria Bianca Sforza. Today, the abbey is essentially baroque (1600–1800). The 1613 High Altar is a vast Tree of Life with 84 saints wreathed around the Virgin Mary. Austria's second religion – skiing – gets almost equal billing. The abbey houses a ski gymnasium devoted to promoting Olympic-class talent. Many of Austria's skiing and ski-jumping stars trained in Stams.

**Above**
The Cistercian abbey at Stams

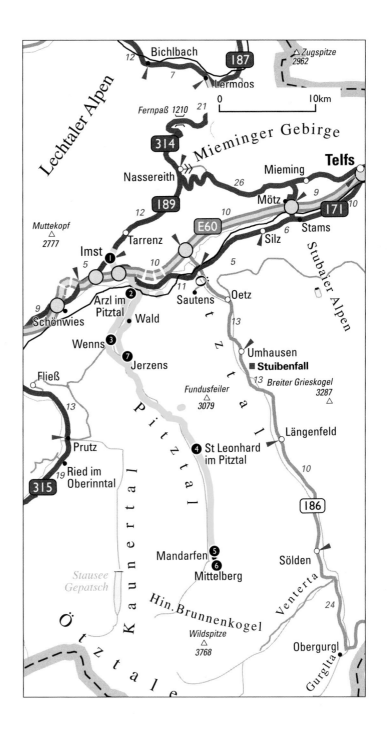

Lechtaler Alpen

Bichlbach
12
187
7
Lermoos
Zugspitze
2962

Fernpaß 1210   21
0        10km

314
Mieminger Gebirge

Nassereith
Mieming
Telfs

26
Mötz
9
171
10

Muttekopf
2777
Tarrenz
189
12
E60
10
Stams
6
Silz
5

Imst
5   ❶
10
11
Sautens
Oetz

Arzl im
Pitztal   ❷
Wald

Schönwies
9

Wenns   ❸
13

Jerzens   ❼
Umhausen
Stuibenfall

Fließ
13   Breiter Grieskogel
3287

13
Fundusfeiler
3079

Prutz
❹ St Leonhard
im Pitztal

Ried im
Oberinntal
19
315
10

186

Stausee
Gepatsch
Mandarfen   ❺
❻
Mittelberg
Sölden

Hin. Brunnenkogel
24

Wildspitze
3768
Obergurgl

Stubaier Alpen

Pitztal

Kaunertal

Ötztaler

Venterta

Gurglta

# The Piller Pass and Kauner Valley

## Ratings

| | |
|---|---|
| Hiking | ●●●●● |
| Nature | ●●●●● |
| Scenery | ●●●●○ |
| Skiing | ●●●●○ |
| Food and drink | ●●○○○ |
| History | ●●○○○ |
| Museums | ●○○○○ |
| Shopping | ●○○○○ |

The ancient route from Wenns over Piller Pass ranks with any in the Tyrol for natural beauty and Alpine drama. Motorists follow almost the same route over the col as the Celts did. The point where they stop for a photo-opportunity – the Gaibach look-out – is only a couple of hundred metres from the mound where Celts once performed ritual sacrifices during their journeys to trade copper. Below the pass, the road is barely equal to the sudden drop in elevation and becomes alarmingly narrow. Near the valley floor, a left turn leads to Kaunertal and one of Europe's great high-altitude roads – the Kaunertal panoramic glacier road.

## BURG BERNECK❖

**Burg Berneck €**
*Kauns; tel: (05472)
6332. Guided tours in
summer; call ahead for times.*

The castle of Berneck is a truly extraordinary sight, hanging on to the edge of a crag 130m above the Faggenbach stream. Originally built to defend Kauner Valley, it was perhaps, in its glory days, Tyrol's finest castle. Emperor Maximilian loved it and used it as a base for hunting expeditions (1499–1530). It fell into ruin in the 19th century. Since 1976, much of it has been heavily restored including the cliffside walkways, half-timbered courtyard buildings, wood-panelled interiors and the chapel frescoes. Though the work has been carried out based on historical records, it all looks too perfect compared to the remnants of the 'real' castle.

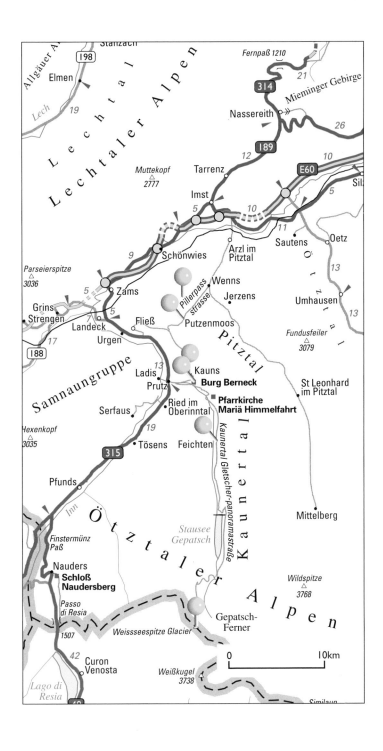

# FEICHTEN✣

ℹ **Tourismusverband Kaunertal** *Feichten 134; tel: (05475) 2920; fax: (05475) 2929; e-mail: info@kaunertal.com; www.tiscover.at/feichten*

🌐 The **Kaunertal Center** (*in the same building as the tourist office*) *offers swimming pool, sauna, steam bath, gym, tennis courts, asphalt curling alley and bowling.*

Feichten, the largest town in the valley, is still a relatively cosy place despite receiving a quarter of a million visitors each year. It is the closest place to the Kaunertal glacier where you can stay overnight. Unfortunately, this means that skiers have to 'commute' over 40km to get to and from the glacier's tantalising combination of reliable snow and brilliant sun.

## Accommodation in Feichten

**Hotel Gletscherblick** €€ *Feichten 168; tel: (05475) 302; fax: (05475) 30228; e-mail: post@hotelgletscherblick.at.* Situated near the Kaunertaler glacier road, most rooms have balconies and views.

# KAUNS✣

Located above Prutz (*see page 257*), the village of Kauns is at the entrance to Kaunertal. Look for the **Schlosshof** behind the Gasthof Falkeis. It was once the dairy of nearby Burg Berneck. The 1650 façade is painted in tender pastel colours with a tree of life and other scenes from the Bible. **Kaunerberg** is a rustic area of hillside farms and terraced orchards scattered above Kauns.

## Accommodation and food in and around Kauns

The villages of Kauns and Kaunerberg, at the entrance to Kaunertal, are much cheaper than Feichten as they are further from the glacier.

**Gasthof Falkeis** € *S`Wirtshaus (House No 47) tel: (05472) 6225; fax: (05472) 6142.* A small pension on a sunny plateau with solid comforts and no-nonsense cooking. The innkeeper distils his own *Schnaps*.

**Camping Kaunertal** € *Platz 30, Kaunertal; tel: (05475) 316; fax: (05475) 31665; e-mail: weisseespitze@tirol.com.* A well-run set of campsites (numbering 60) at the entrance to the valley, on the edge of a forest.

# PILLER PASS✣✣

The route over Piller Pass was used in ancient times as a shortcut between Engadin and Imst, avoiding a longer journey via Landeck. The road up to the pass offers interesting Tyrolean farmscapes. The small farms are surrounded, in spring and summer, by *Heumänner*

**Opposite**
Kaunertal

('hay men') – vertical wooden drying racks that are covered with hay. Almost every hamlet on the road up to the pass has its own baroque chapel. A **Kult-Ur-Weg*** follows the route used by Celts between the town of Piller and the pass. It starts at the **Skulpturengarten Piller**, created by Kassian Erhard, a sculptor who carves in local stone and delves deep into the world of Celtic mythology. By some happy coincidence, it was Erhard, in the company of another man, who discovered evidence of Celtic ritual sacrifice on Pillar Pass. They found a mound of ashes 2.5m in height and measuring 12m by 15m. The ashes contained the bones of animal sacrifices, Celtic brooches and rings made from bronze and silver, votive shields and Roman coins. At the top of the pass, the view from the point known as **Gaibach Blick**\*\*\* takes in the peaks of the Upper Inn Valley (*see pages 254–61*).

## PUTZENMOOS*

Putzenmoos is a high-lying moor that was formed at the end of the last Ice Age in the region around Piller Pass. The ground around it is spongy and fertile, and in late spring and summer it is full of wild flowers, many quite rare.

## WEISSSEESPITZE GLACIER\*\*\*

**Kaunertaler Gletscher-panoramastrasse** *Open Apr–Dec daily. If you have the time and want to avoid the toll, take the public bus, which runs regularly from Feichten to the Gletscherrestaurant at the very top.*

The **Kaunertaler Gletscher-panoramastrasse**\*\*\* (Kaunertal Panoramic Glacier Road) has opened this high glacier region to traffic. The road ends at the Gletscherrestaurant at an elevation of 2750m. The area is a Mecca for snowboarders and international competitions are held here. The Austrian Snowboard Association sponsors many events and, even in summer, there are plenty of snowboarders who arrive early to take advantage of the short skiing day.

# Suggested tour

**Total distance:** 57km to the end of Kauner Valley, 124km with the return to Imst (via Landeck).

**Time:** All day.

**Links:** The mountain road from Arzl to Wenns is described on *pages 241–242*. It returns to Imst via the B315, which is the subject of the Upper Inn Valley chapter (*pages 254–261*).

Take the road that leads into Pitztal through **Arzl** (*see page 234*) and into **Wenns** (*see page 238*) where there is a fork in the road at the end of town. Turn right uphill on the road that is signposted 'Pillerpass'. After a long climb, you pass through old Tyrolean hamlets encircled

**Left**
Kaunertal

## The return of the ibex

During the Middle Ages, Tyrolean folk medicine regarded the ibex as a walking pharmacy: the blood, eyes, lungs, hide and bones all had different healing properties. Princes treasured the horn of the ibex as a drinking vessel because they believed it would render poison harmless. Saint Hildegard von Bingen wrote that you should never leave the house without a dried ibex tail in your pocket, and a Salzburg archbishop, Guidobald Graf von Thun (1654–68), had a whole section of his court pharmacy devoted to ibex remedies. Not surprisingly, given the price on its head, the last ibex was killed in the Tyrol in the early 1700s. It was successfully re-introduced into the Kauner Valley in 1953, and today there are several herds.

by weathered shepherds' huts and alpine meadows – **Piller** and **Oberpiller**. This peaceful stretch of road should not be rushed. A collection of vaguely neolithic sculptures appears on the right (after a dirt track signposted 'Fuchsmoos') – they belong to the **Skulpturengarten Piller**. One roadside stone is suspended in the air by cable and others are incised with cryptic runes. Around the bend is a large fishpond. The road climbs steadily from here, curving around boulders draped in moss and through the shadows of forested cliffs.

**Getting out of the car**: At an elevation of 1520m, a yellow sign pops up out of a grassy road on the right. If you walk down the road for 10 minutes, the ground becomes spongy and you reach the moor named PUTZENMOOS ❶ .

At **PILLER PASS** ❷ , the road flattens out briefly at a T-junction. Carry on straight (ignore the road to Fliess) and watch for a turn-off to the right where a mountain panorama sweeps into view between the trees; pull over, park and take a few moments to enjoy the **Gaibach Blick**. This *Blick* ('view') will crop up again in many variations as the road descends. The road plunges past evergreens and leafy birches and winds through high meadows. At times, the road narrows to the point where you can reach out and pluck flowers from the meadow (not recommended).

In the town of **KAUNS** ❸ , follow the signs for Kaunertal, which will also lead past the narrow road up to **BURG BERNECK** ❹ . The pilgrimage church – **Wallfahrtskirche Kaltenbrunn** – is clearly visible up the valley on the left. The road into the Kauner Valley skirts the Faggenbach river in a deep valley beneath the peaks of Köpfle (2834m) and Peischl Kogel (2913m).

**Detour**: Take the road to the village of Nufels and from there continue up the small farm road to **Wallfahrtskirche Kaltenbrunn**. A knight, Erbo Schenkenberg, built it in the 13th century to atone for murder.

The tender figure of Mary, carved in the 14th century, added to its popularity among pilgrims. A couple of centuries later, a particularly macabre crucifix was added, the **Wundmalchristus** by Andreas Thamasch, who had a knack for making wood look like reams of shredded flesh (1697). Such was the taste of the Counter-Reformation.

The Kauner Valley was once barely accessible to the outside world and it is still starved of sun in the winter by its sheer walls. It had little to offer its inhabitants until modern times. The village of **Platz** has a small museum dedicated to the hard life before the days of ski tourism (located next to the Sporthotel Weissseespitze). The modest farmstead that it is built around supported several families in 1900 (*Talmuseum Kaunertal* €; *Karl Hafele Platz 30; tel: (05475) 316; open May–Oct Wed, Sat–Sun 1400–1700*). Higher up in the valley, the **Weissseespitze** makes its first appearance along with the massive Gepatsch glacier on

**Below**
The Piller Pass

its flanks. The highest town is **FEICHTEN** ❺ (1290m), where a hefty toll is exacted on every vehicle embarking on the 26km **Gletscher-Panoramastrasse**. The road continues uphill through dense forest until a sign announces the first of 29 *Kehre* (hairpin turns) that take you ever higher. The **Gepatsch-Stausee** is the reservoir, the largest in Austria, which catches the water flowing from the glacier. The road alongside it is delightful, passing by one waterfall after another. The **Faggenbach bridge** is an ideal place to look around *en route*.

**Getting out of the car**: A brief stroll is all it takes to find yourself beneath a waterfall: from the bridge, follow the path that runs from the car park next to the river up the valley and, after only 40m, the waterfall is to the right. For people who are fit and keen, a trail leads steeply uphill, to meadows decked out in Alpine flowers for much of the summer. Higher up, the path comes near the glacier in a cirque formed by two peaks (the Rauher Kopf and Schwarze Wand).

A brutal series of turns ensues. There are always coaches on the road and it is remarkable that they can swing their bulk around the bends at all. On the way up, at bend 12, there are inspirational views of the slumping mass of the **Gepatschferner**, one of the largest glaciers in the Eastern Alps. Bend 7 has the best view of the **Weissseespitze**. The road ends at the **Weissseegletscher**, at an elevation of 2750m.

**Getting out of the car**: Two walks will bring you in close proximity to the **Gepatschferner**, the largest glacier in Austria. The Wiesejaggl-Sessellift (chair lift) will hoist you higher, above 3000m, for views of the peaks of the Weissseespitze, Fluchtkogel, Hochvernagtspitze, Bligg and Ölgruben. If you are willing to walk through the snow for another hour along a well-marked path (bring hiking boots, sunglasses and warm clothing), you will get a close view of the glacier as well as the Dolomites and the Swiss Alps to the southwest.

Return to the entrance to Kaunertal and follow the signs for Prutz (*see page 257*). From there, drive back to the Inn Valley on the B315 (*see pages 254–61*).

## Also worth exploring

The Zamserberg, a precipitous mountain terrace on the south side of the Inn between Zams and Imst, is a forgotten corner of the region. The villages of Grist and Falterstein are two of the most scenic villages in the Tyrol. A narrow road leads from the village of Schönwies to the gravity-defying Kronburg, a hilltop castle that belonged to the Starkenberger lords of Tarrenz. It is not recommended for people who are afraid of heights.

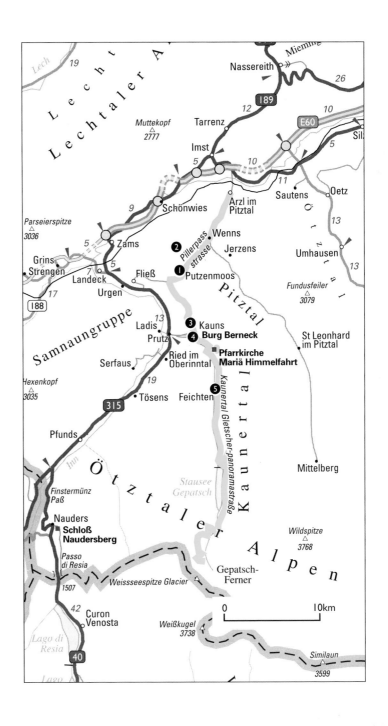

# The Upper Inn Valley

## Ratings

| | |
|---|---|
| Nature | ●●●●● |
| Scenery | ●●●●● |
| Hiking | ●●●●○ |
| History | ●●●●○ |
| Skiing | ●●●●○ |
| Architecture | ●●●○○ |
| Shopping | ●●●○○ |
| Food and drink | ●●○○○ |

The scenic valley between Landeck and Reschenpass is a haven of micro-climates: wheat grows at 1500m on the Serfaus plateau, the sunniest spot in Austria; the chasm of Altfinstermünz lives in shadow; and it never rains in the seemingly Mediterranean town of Prutz. The Romans travelled through the valley along the *Via Claudia Augusta*, and the route was equally important in the Middle Ages. Until modern times, everyone took the high road for granted because the valley was swampy. For a sense of its history, you have to follow ancient traces uphill and off the beaten path. At the end of the valley, the Finstermünzpass funnels 20th-century traffic through 19th-century rock tunnels.

## FLIESS✦

**❶ Tourismusverband Fliess** *Dorf 118; tel: (05449) 5224; fax: (05449) 5343; www.tiscover.at/fliess. Open Mon–Fri 0830–1200.*

The ancient town of Fliess ceased to be on the way to anywhere when a 19th-century road was built to Reschenpass lower down the valley. Testimony to its long history of human habitation is found in the **Archäologisches Museum** (€ *Dorf 89; tel: (05449) 20065; www.museum.fliess.at; open Tue–Sun 1000–1200 and 1500–1700*), which occupies a 14th-century building next to the church. It has an interesting collection of Bronze Age finds from the region around Fliess and Celtic offerings made at Piller Pass (*see page 246*). **Schloss Biedenegg** (c 1200), a medieval castle sporting a 19th-century face-lift, stands on a hill just northeast of Fliess. It has a magnificent Renaissance *Stube* with its original *Kachelofen* (porcelain-tile stove).

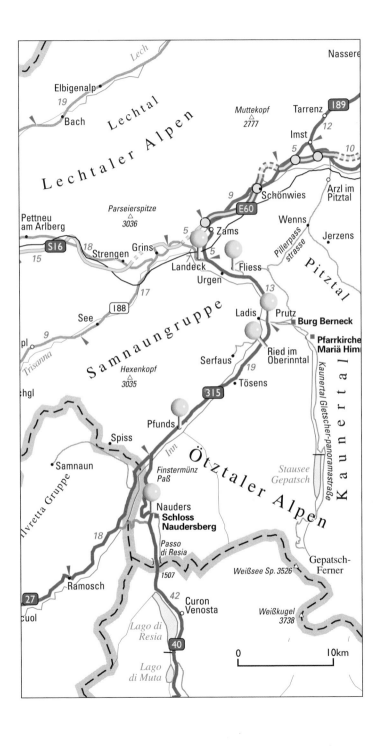

## Accommodation and food in Fliess

**Schloss Biedenegg €€** *Dorf 237; tel: (05449) 20002; fax: (05449) 2000 281; www.tiscover.at/biedenegg.* The present owner of the castle, Baron Pach, has converted some of its rooms into six luxury holiday apartments.

**Gasthof Schwarzer Adler €** *Darre 93; tel: (05449) 5382.* This wood-panelled inn would not have looked much different 500 years ago. It is like a simple, traditional Tyrolean home complete with porcelain stove and the *Hergottswinkel* with the carved crucifix in the corner.

# LANDECK✢

**ⓘ Tourismusverband Landeck** *Malser Strasse 10; tel: (05442) 65600; fax: (05442) 6560 015; www.tiscover.at/landeck; www.tvblandeck.at. Open Mon–Fri 0830–1200, 1400–1800, Sat 0830–1200.*

**ⓗ Schloss Landeck €** *Schlossweg 2; tel: (05442) 63202; fax: (05442) 653074; www.schlosslandeck.at. Open daily 1400–1700 (mid-May–Sept from 1000).*

The town at the confluence of the Inn and Sanna rivers has been an important crossroads for many centuries for traffic to Italy and neighbouring Arlberg province. Today, it is the sort of town where tourists despair of finding a parking place. There are, however, reasons for stopping. You can walk down the **Herzog-Friedrich-Strasse** past an ensemble of old houses in the region's medieval building style. The Gothic church of **Pfarrkirche Mariä Himmelfahrt** is famous for its Flamboyant-style fenestration and network vaulting. Its pride and joy, inside, is the **Schrofenstein Altar✢**, with the sainted King Oswald in the centre. His ruined castle can be seen higher up the valley from the bridge at Zams. The 13th-century **Schloss Landeck✢✢** looks down on the city from a cliff. Its **Schlossmuseum✢** houses a vast collection of Tyrolean folk art. Entire rooms have been moved here and reassembled, such as the **Prandtauerzimmer**, a *Stube* from the town of Ried and a 1600 bedroom from Fiss.

# NAUDERS✢

**ⓘ Tourismusverband Nauders** *Dr-Tschiggfrey-Strasse 66; tel: (05473) 87220; fax: (05473) 87627; www.nauders.com. Open Mon–Sat 0830–1200, 1400–1800.*

The last town before Reschenpass and the Italian border, Nauders (1400m) is in the area locals call *Dreiländereck* ('three corner land'), where Austria, Italy and Switzerland meet. Nauders was important to the Roman Empire as the highest point in the *Via Claudia Augusta*. The names of the peaks surrounding it – Mataunkopf, Piz Malmurainza and Valdafürkopf – are a reminder of the days when the native language of the region was Rhäto-romansh. Some of the town's houses also reflect the style of building associated with the Rhäto-romansh-speaking area of the Alps, which favours small, deeply recessed windows, large oriels and freestanding staircases. **Schloss Naudersberg** (**€** *tel: (05473) 87252; www.schloss-nauders.at*) was built in the beginning of the 14th century. Inside it has a small museum with very limited hours (*guided tours Wed 1500 and Sun 1100*). The **Leonhardskapelle** is a Romanesque country church with the oldest preserved frescoes in North Tyrol (late 12th century).

# PFUNDS*

**① Tourismusverband Pfunds** *Stuben 40; tel: (05474) 5229; fax: (05474) 5532; www.pfunds.at. Open Mon–Fri 0800–1200, 1500–1800.* Enquire about local hikes and maps. There is much to see on foot, including waterfalls and wild flowers.

The town is divided between **Pfunds-Stuben** on the east side of the Inn river and **Pfunds-Dorf** on the west side. The former has Gothic houses with central hallways and freestanding staircases, some with half-timbered gables (No 1) and the Gothic **Liebfrauenkirche**, noted for its interior frescoes. **Pfunds-Stuben** is linked to **Pfunds-Dorf** by a wooden bridge that looks old but actually dates from the 1950s. The block-like tower on the east side is truly historic. A plaque mentions that Emperor Maximilian I slept there. The east side of the village has an old, water-driven sawmill that is still in use at the mouth of the valley of **Radurschltal**\*\*, which extends 15km into the Ötztal Alps.

# PRUTZ*

**① Tourismusverband Prutz** *Haus 93; tel: (05472) 6267; fax: (05472) 2124.*

**◑ Kaunergratsennerei** *Haus 107; tel: (05472) 2500.* This shop sells cheese, smoked ham, honey and *Schnaps* from farms in the Kauner Valley. *Closed Monday.*

**Helmut Seiringer** *Faggen 30 (located above Prutz); tel: (05472) 6267 or (0663) 05954 (mobile phone).* Herr Seiringer is one of the last craftsmen in the region who still does *Federkielstickerer*, a traditional and painstaking form of leather embroidery. Call ahead for an appointment.

A way station for millennia, Prutz still has a few historic houses and two defensive towers – **Turm im Felde** and **Turm in der Breite** – that were incorporated into later buildings. The **Pfarrkirche** was assembled out of Romanesque elements in the 15th century and given a 17th-century baroque interior. Inside, there is a 200-year-old Nativity scene that is on view all year – the work of a master woodcarver from Thaur (the most famous town in the Tyrol for this craft). There are two chapels in the graveyard that are well worth a look: the **Johanneskapelle**, for its frescoes from 1330 (get the key from the Parish house if it is closed); and the **Totenkapelle**, for its wax votive offerings. Across from Prutz, there is an 1899 iron bridge over the Inn. Some type of bridge has been there since Roman times when it was part of the *Via Claudia Augusta*, hence the Latin-derived name, **Pontlatzer Brücke**\*. A perfect spot for an ambush, the bridge has often been drenched in blood. During the War of Spanish Succession, in 1703, the Bavarian electoral prince Max Emanuel occupied Tyrol province and, in July, ordered a force of 300 men up to Reschenpass. After the Bavarians crossed the bridge, the Tyrolean militia unleashed an avalanche of stone and wiped them out almost to a man. Their victory triggered an uprising throughout the province and the enemy prince had to flee Innsbruck within a few weeks. Just over a century later, in 1809, an occupying force of Bavarian troops marched past this point – 1400 strong this time – and was all but annihilated by similar methods.

# RIED*

Ried was built during the Middle Ages around a feudal castle – the **Sigmundsried**. Herzog Sigmund der Münzreiche had the castle walls roofed over in the 15th century to make the place more comfortable. The entrance hall has a small collection of armour beneath its painted vault.

# Suggested tour

**Total distance**: Landeck to Nauders is 88km there and back. The Serfaus detour adds 42km (return).

**Time**: 1 day.

**Links**: This route links with the Piller Pass and Kauner Valley tour (*see pages 249–53*).

After **LANDECK ❶** the road follows the Inn river past the village of Urgen where you just catch a glimpse of a delightful pair of covered wooden bridges spanning the river. A steep road veers up to the idyllic village of **FLIESS ❷**, which overlooks the B315. **Schloss Biedenegg**, in turn, looks down over Fliess. The road flattens out on the valley floor between **PRUTZ ❸** and **RIED ❹**.

**Detour**: A very steep road ascends from Ried to the plateau known as the **Sonnenterrasse** ('sun terrace'). A stark castle keep – belonging to **Burg Landeck** – comes into view just before a fork in the road. Go right and make a couple of steep blind turns into **Ladis**, the only town on the plateau that is largely untouched by ski tourism. It's worth taking the time to walk around the historic centre among the painted houses and wooden fountains. Some of the houses are equipped with ovens mounted on outside walls – the latest thing in the Middle Ages. The **Rechelerhaus** (No 3) depicts costumes and customs from the 16th century and the **Stockerhaus** (No 6) is decorated with patriarchs, Alpine bandits and nudes wielding brooms. There is an amazing view from the village cemetery that includes **Burg Landeck** (*guided tours Jun–Sept Wed, every 45 minutes 0900–1145*) to the left. The entire region between Landeck and Reschenpass – traditionally called the *Oberes Gericht* ('Upper District') – was governed until the 16th century from the refuge of this castle. Drive to the end of the village and follow the

**Above**
Serfaus

**Silencehotel**
**Maximilian €€€**
*Herrenager 4, Serfaus; tel:*
*(05476) 6520; fax: (05476)*
*652 052; www.maximilian.at.*
A famous five-star hotel
that offers everything
required for an active
and/or hedonistic holiday
including state-of-the-art
fitness centre and
computer games for the
kids. The staff will happily
loan you a mountain bike
or book a balloon flight.
The swimming pool is
heated by solar power
while the rooms, we are
told, have been 'electro-
biologically optimised'.

**Gasthof Tschuppbach**
*€ Haus I, Tösens (just*
*south); tel: (05477) 443.*
Family-run country inn on
a sleepy road that was
once the *Via Claudia*
*Augusta*. The family farm
supplies meat and
vegetables to the
restaurant.

signs for **Fiss**, a town that has held on to some Tyrolean character despite its conversion to a ski resort. On a clear day, you can see the mountains of the Glockenturm and Kauner ranges from the road. **Serfaus** is the last village on the sun-drenched plateau. It lives for the winter ski season with an extraordinary half million overnight guests each year. The village actually has an underground subway, and in winter all drivers are required to park in vast car parks and 'commute' to the village centre. It is the site of one of the Tyrol's oldest pilgrimage churches, the ancient **Kirche Unsere Liebe Frau im Walde**, an austere Romanesque building, free of baroque touches. Its detached clock tower, unique in North Tyrol, seems to have wandered north from Italy. The next town is **Tösens**.

**Getting out of the car**: Behind the church in Tösens, look for the *Verkehrsbüro* (Tourist Office). If you take the street immediately to the right, it leads down to the Inn river and an old iron bridge. Walk or drive out on it and look up at the stone bridge spanning a small gorge on the opposite side of the river. This is the so-called **Römerbrücke**, not really Roman but medieval. However, there can be little doubt that a Roman bridge stood on this spot. Further along the road, you can pull over and walk up to it (100m). The Romanesque church of **St Georgen ob Tösens** is a rewarding short walk. A prayer stop on the road that succeeded the *Via Claudia Augusta* in the Middle Ages, it has a remarkable series of well-preserved Gothic frescoes (if the door is locked, ask for the key at the mountain lodge).

From Tösens take the *Landstrasse* out of town and cross the Inn river. This narrow, utterly charming road overlaps in places with the historic *Via Claudia*. The village of Lafairs rests on a stream, Lafairserbachs, below the gushing **Lafairserbach** waterfall. Carry on through a high meadow and rejoin the B184 just before **PFUNDS ❺**. There is a fork in the road beyond the town at the **Kajetansbrücke**. Take the left fork that leads to Reschenpass. A masterpiece of 19th-century engineering, this road is guaranteed to induce vertigo. On the way, admire the natural stone tunnels and creaky old guard-rails and stop at the first turn-off, which giddily overhangs the deep gorge. Since it leads to Italy, you will inevitably meet lots of southward-bound Porsches.

**Getting out of the car**: Most cars leave the little town of **Hochfinstermünz** in the dust. However, it offers more than the quaint hotel that has seen better days: it is the starting point for a 20-minute walk down to the pulsing gorge of the Inn river. Until the 19th century, everyone had to cross the river at this point. The fortress that occupies the narrows, the **Altfinstermünz**, is a romantic, rotting ruin. In the middle of the whirling water stands a dilapidated castle tower, the **Brückenturm**.

In one of the many hairpin turns of the **Finstermünzpass**, you will all but run into a much later fortification, the 19th-century **Sperrfort Nauders**, built partly into the mountain cliff at this strategic location

**Above**
Altfinstermünz

between 1834 and 1840. A few more hairpins are required to reach **NAUDERS** ❻ (1400m). This route now makes an excursion into Switzerland. Take the *kurvenreich* ('curve-rich') road that briefly climbs and then descends like a coiled rope to the town of **Martina**, just across the border (note: it is a country road and there is no requirement for a Swiss *Autobahn* vignette). This is a thoroughly modern road, never crowded, that banks smoothly through one switchback after another with the comfort of a shoulder all the way. It is an interesting contrast to its harsh 19th-century cousin in Finstermünzpass. In **Martina**, turn north again (the road becomes the B184 after the Austrian border) for a 9km ride back through the deep mountain pass. The only inhabited place is the hamlet of **Vinadi**. Continue on the B184 down to the Kajetansbrücke. From there, the B315 returns over familiar terrain to Landeck.

**Detour:** If you still have not had enough of mountain driving, go right at Prutz and take the Pillerpass-strasse (*see page 246*) to Arzl and then to Imst. It is a nerve-racking but spectacular road.

## Also worth exploring

The Silvrettastrasse-Hochalpenstrasse (*closed Nov–May*) can be reached by driving west from Landeck and, after 6km, turning off on the B188. It begins at the end of Tristanna Valley (another 48km) after the town of Galtür, the scene of terrible avalanches in 1999. One of the most severe and beautiful high Alpine roads in the Tyrol, the toll road links the valley of Paznauntal with Montafon in Vorarlberg via the Bielerhöhe Pass (2036m).

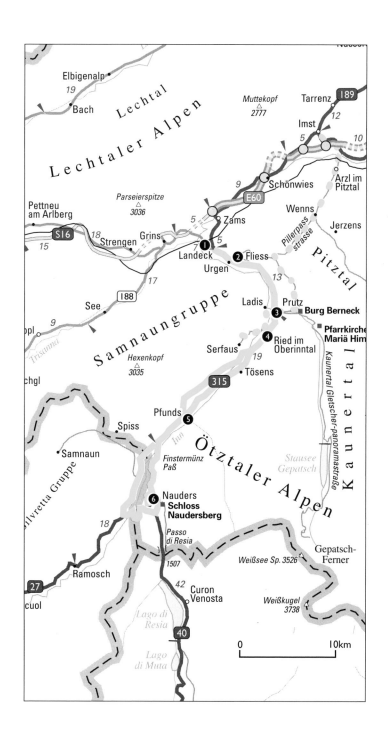

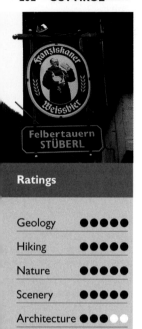

# Osttirol

## Ratings

| | |
|---|---|
| Geology | ●●●●● |
| Hiking | ●●●●● |
| Nature | ●●●●● |
| Scenery | ●●●●● |
| Architecture | ●●●○○ |
| Skiing | ●●●○○ |
| History | ●●○○○ |
| Shopping | ●●○○○ |

E ast Tyrol feels like an island in the Alps rather than part of the main tourist area. Its isolation, once a curse, has become a blessing; for now, at least, a chain of peaks and glaciers are keeping the hyperactive world from its doors. Politically, it has been a 'stepchild' since being split from the South Tyrol, which was ceded to Italy by the Treaty of Versailles in 1919. The construction in 1967 of the Felbertauernstrasse (and a 5.2km-long tunnel) made East Tyrol accessible from the north by way of an extraordinary mountain road. Not only does it pass through unique Alpine scenery, it also links remote valleys, each one more idyllic than the last. This particular route forms a 'Y' by including one of them, the Virgental. Depending on your choice of others, the route could become an 'X' or a 'Z'.

## LIENZ✦

**🏛 Heimatmuseum €**
*Schloss Bruck,*
*Schlossberg I; tel: (04852)*
*625 8083; fax: (04852) 625*
*80834. Open daily*
*1000–1800.*

Lienz looks over its shoulder at 2000 years of history and wakes up every morning to awe-inspiring views of the jagged Dolomites. The only Roman city ever dug up in the Tyrol, **Aguntum✦** is in the outlying village of Dölsach, an intriguing pile of stones that were once town walls, country villas and a bathhouse. The earls of Görz built the Italianate **Schloss Bruck✦✦** in the 13th century. Much of the castle is now used for a **Heimatmuseum** that explores the lives of peasants as well as lords. Its Romanesque chapel is graced with vivid frescoes. There is also a fine collection of work by native son Albin Egger-Lienz, a 19th-century expressionist painter who chronicled the hard life of Tyrolean farmers and miners. The **Pfarrkirche St Andrä✦**, near the castle, is one of the most important Gothic churches in the Tyrol. It is worth visiting for its harmonious interior and the exquisitely chiselled tombstones of the earls of Görz. A 19th-century traveller wrote of Lienz: 'For many generations the city has had the custom of burning down from time to time only to be built up again.'

The cycle repeated itself after four Allied bombings in 1945 and, today, the **Altstadt** (Old Town) has many of the same features as an American shopping mall. Blue-green **Tristacher See\*** is a lovely mountain lake just south of town where the water is warm enough for swimming in summer.

## Accommodation in Lienz

**Hotel Traube €€** *Hauptplatz 14; tel: (04852) 64444; fax: (04852) 64184; e-mail: vergeiners-traube@romantikhotels.com; www. romantikhotels.com/ lienz.* The top address in Lienz where everything has class, from the rooftop indoor swimming pool to its cellar wine-bar, the Traubenkeller. There are special weekend and off-season rates.

**Camping Falken €** *Eichholz 1 (on the B100, in the direction of Tristacher See); tel: (04852) 64022; fax: (04852) 640 226; e-mail: info@camping-falken.com; www.camping-falken.com.* The campsites are on flat meadows in the shade of trees with panoramic views.

# MATREI IN OSTTIROL*

Matrei has a **Bauernmarkt** ('farmers' market') from June to September on Friday afternoon and Saturday morning. The largest market in the entire region is held on 21 September (unless it falls on a Sunday).

**Heimatkundliches museum Medaria** € *Rathuis (Town Hall); tel: (04875) 680 528. Open Mon, Wed and Fri 1800–1900 or on request.*

**Rauter €€€** *tel: (04875) 6611; fax: (04875) 6613; www.hotel-rauter.at.* This is Matrei's top hotel, with an art-deco-style interior, swimming pools, bathhouse, tennis courts and a fish pond to supply its restaurant with the 'catch of the day'.

The town of Matrei in Osttirol (population 4500) lies at an altitude of 1000m, almost equidistant between the two highest peaks in Austria, the **Grossglockner** and the **Grossvenediger**. It is also the meeting point of three valleys – the Tauerntal, Virgental and Iseltal. The main chain of the Alps acts as a screen, giving this region different climatic conditions from those to the north of the Tauern mountains. The location has also been the source of grief. Massive landslides destroyed Matrei several times in its history. The final blow was the great fire of 1892 that damaged all but three buildings. On a clear day, the single best thing to do in Matrei is to hop on the **Goldfriedbahn** that hoists visitors up to a mountain station (2150m) for views of the Kendlspitze peak, the Virgental, the Kristallkopf and the Grossglockner. The highest and most scenic part of a famous hike – the **Europa Panoramaweg***** – is a mere 25 minutes from the station along an easy trail. There is not a lot to do in the town itself. The **Heimatkundliches Museum Medaria** brings together local minerals, crafts and a musty stuffed bear, said to have been shot in the mountains above Matrei.

The town's real artistic treasure, the **St Nikolauskirche***, is a short distance outside of town on a hillside above the hamlet of Ganz. Drive south on Bichler Strasse. Follow the road out of the village across a bridge and up to a wooden trough and turn right. Stay right through the next two forks and watch for a dirt road to the right leading uphill, which then curves down to the church (if locked, ask for the massive iron key at the farmhouse next door). The Romanesque church evokes an early Christianity despite the addition of Gothic elements. A naïve set of frescoes in the ground-floor choir show a chunky Adam and Eve and a clumsy fall from grace. A more refined set of frescoes in the upstairs choir, painted by an itinerant artist in Venetian-Byzantine style, reveals the four elements personified, the Apostles and the Evangelists. Look for the angels on the inside of the arch who are climbing Jacob's ladder.

# NATIONALPARK HOHE TAUERN✦✦✦

**Nationalpark Hohe Tauern** Kirchplatz 2; tel: (04875) 5112; www.hohetauern.at

**Tourismusverband Oberes Iseltal**
Huben; tel: (04875) 5860; fax: (04875) 652 740; e-mail: matrei.osttirol@ netway.at. This tourist office organises several variations of the **Tauerntrek** – a three-day hike (or more) across the mountains accompanied by pack-horses. Alpine base camps are set up each night.

**Above**
Matrei

The Hohe Tauern National Park has an area of approximately 1800sq km and is one of the last significant undisturbed mountain environments in the heart of Europe. It stretches over the three provinces of Carinthia, Salzburg and Tyrol. The highest points are the **Grossglockner** (3798m) and the **Grossvenediger** (3674m). Geologically speaking, the Hohe Tauern is a window on time, revealing many secrets of the earth's history. The forces of upheaval and erosion have worn away layers of limestone – several kilometres thick – that were formed when the mountains were at the bottom of prehistoric seas. What emerges is a 'profile' in stone (gneiss and schist) of the earth as it looked even earlier in time – 300 million years ago. The park is a refuge for Alpine fauna and flora. Birds and animals that were almost once extinct have been successfully re-introduced, including the ibex, bearded vulture and lynx. However, a surprisingly small, non-contiguous percentage of the total area of the park falls under the strictest level of protection, while in other areas, skiing and hunting are still allowed. In a real sense, the battle for the park continues.

# VIRGENTAL✦✦

The valley begins at Matrei where the Isel river flows between the heavily forested Lasörling ridge and the jagged peaks of the Eichham Range. Hedgerows (unusual in the eastern Alps) crisscross the valley and provide a home to creatures such as the ermine. Above the entrance to the valley is **Zedlach**✦, a kitsch-free village of brown, weathered Tyrolean farmhouses and the scene of the winter *Klaubauf*, a kind of 'demon hunt' that goes back to pagan times. The villagers dress up in bizarre costumes and masks to chase the spirits away. From Zedlach, a rough and crudely signposted road takes you up to **Strumerhof-Hinteregg**, a mountain lodge with a rustic restaurant. The area around it is known as the **Zedlacher Paradise**✦, a nature reserve with stands of ancient trees (larches) that are 600 years old. The valley gets its name from the village of **Virgen**, which lies on a sunny slope in the middle of the valley. The ruined castle of **Rabenstein**✦ (c 1400) – a rectangular tower, remains of a chapel and crumbling bits of wall – occupies a narrow hilltop above it. It is normally deserted except for a couple of grazing cows in summer. The castle belonged to the powerful earls of Görz. Even by feudal standards, they were a bad lot of rulers who ruthlessly exploited their mountain peasantry. The valley ends in a ravine encircled by 3000m peaks in their dozens and a spectacular series of waterfalls – the **Umballfälle**✦✦.

## Accommodation and food in Virgental

**Neuwirt** € *House no 34, Virgen; tel/fax: (04874) 5217; e-mail: resingerk@tirol.com; www.tiscover.at/gasthof.neuwirt.* This family-run inn is just across from the village church in a building with a faded baroque façade.

**Strumerhof** €€ *Hinteregg 1, Matrei; tel: (04875) 6310; e-mail: strumerhof@utanet.at; www.strumerhof.at.* Worth seeking out just for its view of the Hohe Tauern mountains. The house speciality is wild game.

# WALLFAHRTSKIRCHE MARIA SCHNEE✦✦

The white steeple of Maria Schnee is a stunning contrast to the farmhouses of **Obermauern** village that are almost blackened by age. It has two typical features of pilgrimage churches in the Alps: a porch in front of the entrance so that pilgrims could wait out of the weather; and, on the south side, a huge fresco of St Christopher, the patron saint of travellers. Most pilgrims in the Middle Ages could not read and you can almost imagine their excitement when they stepped through the door and caught their first glimpse of the frescoes that cover half of the nave and the whole of the choir. They tell the story of Christ's Passion, the life of Mary and the martyrdom of St Sebastian. Simon von Taisten, the court painter of Earl Leonhard von Görz, painted them between 1484 and 1488. He added the Earl's coat of arms on the round keystones in the choir and those of the Earl's wife, Paula von Gonzaga of Mantua. The Görz line died out shortly after the frescoes were completed with the death of Leonhard in 1500. The villagers of Virgen perform an ancient rite every Easter: they wash and comb a ram and adorn him with ribbons. The next day, they begin a procession at 0600, herding the lone ram to meet the villagers of Obermauern. A mass in Maria Schnee follows with the ram in the central aisle. Afterwards they sacrifice it (symbolically: this is the only break with tradition). The ritual goes back to a holy vow made during a 17th-century outbreak of the plague.

**Below**
Virgental waterfalls

# Suggested tour

**Total distance:** 81km. The detours (there and back) add 8km for Tauernhaus, 26km for Kals Valley and 8km for the Kals Grossglockner toll road.

**Time:** 1 easy day with no detours; 2 to 3 days with detours.

**Links:** From Lienz, the B107 leads north by way of Obermöll Valley to the Grossglockner High Alpine Road (*see page 272*).

**Below**
Matrei in Osttirol

Enter East Tyrol by way of the **Felbertauern Tunnel**. Stop just outside the tunnel for a look at the **NATIONALPARK HOHE TAUERN ❶** and the ice-draped summits of Rainerhorn, Wildenkogel and Kristallkopf.

**Detour**: After only 3km, take the first right, a small mountain road (signposted for Tauernhaus and Gletscherweg). Carry on 4km to the **Matreier Tauernhaus** (1512m), a *Gasthof* (guesthouse) in the valley. Park in the *Gasthof* car park if possible, otherwise you will have to pay for a place in the wide park below it or at the trailhead park just beyond it. A Nationalpark pavilion has a rewarding interactive display full of detailed information about the geology, ecology and biology of the park, as well as models of the consequences of overdevelopment.

**Getting out of the car**: The opportunities for hiking in this valley rank with anything in the eastern Alps. The gentle walk from the car park to **Innergschlöss** (2 hours return) takes you past the waterfalls of Tauern- and Dichtenbach, to the stone mountain chapel of **Aussergschlöss** and the rock face of the **Grossvenediger** at **Innergschlöss**. For people unwilling or unable to walk, there is a Nationalpark taxibus or a horse-drawn carriage. Another trail – the **Gletscherschaupfad** – leads along the lower tongue of the Grossvenediger glacier past skyscrapers of ice, vast clefts, and turquoise caves dripping with meltwater. The Sessellift Venedigerblick leaves from just beyond the **Matreier Tauernhaus** and requires only 15 minutes to ascend to a point high above the Tauern Valley (*summer only*). From there, you can tackle the **Drei-Seen** ('three lakes') circuit. The first 45 minutes lead to the edge of the **Grüner See** ('green' lake), where fine views over Alpine pastures sweep from the glaciers of the Grossvenediger to the peak of Teufelsspitze in the east. Lakes in other colours are further uphill – the **Schwarzer See** (15 minutes) and **Grauer See** (30 minutes). However, only experienced hikers should tackle the **Messelingkogel** (2694m).

The road continues down the Tauerntal and enters the Prossegg gorge with the Unterer Steiner waterfall on the left. Before Matrei, you will notice a dingy white memorial column on the right, flanked by weathered brass plaques. This is a monument to the engineers who built the Felbertauern road and the 16 men who died during its construction. Just a little further on, the crenellated towers of a hilltop castle suddenly appear above the treetops. The archbishops of Salzburg and Earls of Görz fought bitterly over this castle, **Schloss Weissenstein** (*not open to the public*), and it changed hands many times; in the end, it fell to a third party, Kaiser Maximilian I. Drive through **MATREI IN OSTTIROL ❷**. It leads directly into the valley of **VIRGENTAL ❸** and, after 7km, to **Virgen**. The **WALLFAHRTSKIRCHE MARIA SCHNEE ❹** is in the village of **Obermauern**, just 2km further. The road continues through the valley past **Prägraten**, **Hinterbichl** and to **Ströden** where it dead-ends in a car park with a view of the **Umbalfälle** (Umbal Falls).

**Getting out of the car**: The Isel is the largest glacial stream on the south side of the Hohe Tauern range. It winds its way from the Umbal Kees glacier though the narrow Umbal Valley and creates a formidable cascade, the **Umbal Falls**. An easy 30-minute walk leads to the foot of the falls (follow the signs for **Wasserschaupfad**). This **Wasserschaupfad Umbalfälle** ('waterfalls viewing path') follows its course upstream with illustrations, viewpoint benches and lots of detailed observations about ecology, geology and water (in German). It might all seem a bit pedantic but education is crucial to the future of the falls. A proposed power plant, under discussion for years, would drain the water out of it.

Drive back to Matrei and get on the B108 going south. The road forks at **Huben**, a rest stop for mule drivers in the Middle Ages.

**Detour**: Turn left to enter the fabulous **Kalsertal**. From one of the lower hairpin turns you can catch a glimpse of the Dolomites to the south. A church tower looms out of nowhere in Oberpeischlach, a sudden reminder that the valley is not deserted. In the upper reaches you pass the Kalserbach waterfall. **Kals am Grossglockner** is the principal village of the valley, lying at the foot of the Grossglockner (3798m), the 'King' of the Hohen Tauern and Austria's highest mountain. Just outside of the town, the **Filialkirche St Georg** comes into sight, one of the most photographed churches in the Alps. On your right you will see the road up the mountain that leads to the **Kalser Glocknerstrasse**, a 7km-long toll road that coils its way from 1325m up to 2000m, ending at a mountain lodge, the **Lucknerhaus**. It has majestic views of the Ködnitz Valley and the summit of the **Grossglockner**.

Turn right and then immediately left again into the village of Huben. Continue along the *Landstrasse* south. The road will give you a better idea of life in the valley than the B108. Its charms are somewhat marred by a power plant and massive power lines running overhead. You will pass a romantic castle ruin on a hill above the hamlet of Kienburg (*not open to the public*). As you curve through **St Johann im Walde** look around at its monumental stone farmhouse and assortment of traditional village homes. A steel arched bridge leads back across the Isel and to the B108. LIENZ ❺ is just another 8km and **Schloss Bruck** is clearly signposted at the entrance to town.

## Also worth exploring

The Defereggental is another side valley, 40km long, of the Isel Valley. It penetrates deep into the *Bergwelt* ('mountain world') of East Tyrol. The main villages are Hopfgarten, once a centre for mining, St Veit, and St Jakob, where the church – **St Leonhard** – is famous not only for its 15th-century frescoes but also for its views of the

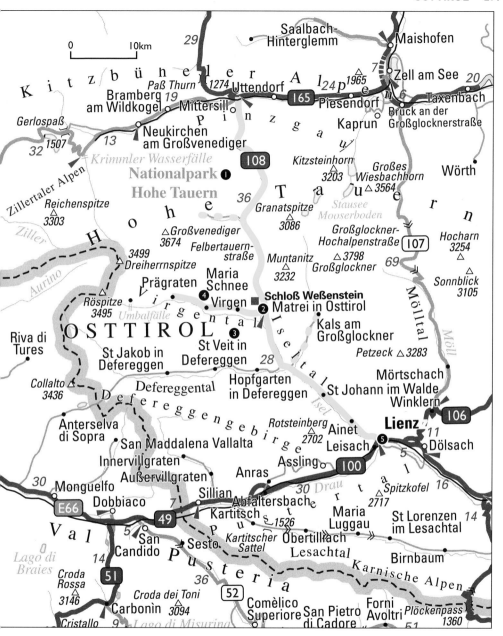

surrounding mountains. The valley harbours the largest Zirbenwald ('stone-pine forest') in the eastern Alps. If you want to keep driving, the road is an adventurous way to get to Italy via the dizzying **Staller Sattel** pass (2052m).

# The Grossglockner Road and Hohe Tauern National Park

## Ratings

| | |
|---|---|
| Geology | ●●●●● |
| Hiking | ●●●●● |
| Nature | ●●●●● |
| Scenery | ●●●●● |
| Children | ●●●●○ |
| Skiing | ●●●○○ |
| Architecture | ●●○○○ |
| Shopping | ●○○○○ |

The Grossglockner Hochalpenstrasse ('high alpine road') crosses all the climatic and vegetation zones between Austria and the Arctic Circle. If it were a question of traversing latitude instead of altitude, this journey would require 4000km of driving. The mother of all mountain roads also has the mother of all detours: The 'glacier road' that leads to Franz-Josephs-Höhe, a car park at the end of the world – near Austria's highest point and its largest glacier. At the northern end of the Hohe Tauern National Park, the Edelweissspitze Panorama offers the best 360-degree view of the Alps that can be reached (just) on four wheels.

## ALPINE NATURE EXHIBIT*

**Wilfried-Haslauer-Haus** tel: (0662) 842 653; www.hausdernatur.at. Open daily during the summer, free admission. The gift shop sells a guide with English translations of the German-language displays.

This information centre is in the **Wilfried-Haslauer-Haus** in Obernassfeld, just below the Fuscher Törl. It provides a multimedia nature exhibition about local flora, fauna and ecology. None of it is state of the art but it is still informative. A time-line plods through great moments in human history during the last millennium and points out that it can take that long for a high mountain meadow to form naturally.

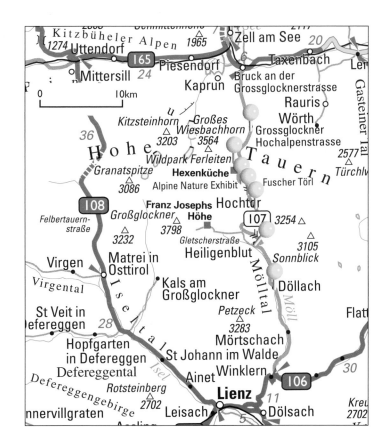

# DÖLLACH✦

(see page 265)

**ℹ Nationalparkhaus 'Alte Schmelz'**
*Döllach 14, Grosskirchheim; tel: (04825) 6161; fax: (04825) 616 116. Open daily Jul–Oct 0900–1600; Oct–Jul Wed 0900–1600.*

The village of Döllach is embedded in the upper Mölltal Valley, surrounded by the Hohe Tauern *Bergwelt*. It is a relaxed point of departure for excursions into Nationalpark Hohe Tauern (*see page 265*) and a family-oriented ski resort. The **Goldbergbau- und Heimatmuseum✦**, in the 16th-century **Schloss Grosskirchheim**, shows exhibits related to the region's medieval Gold Rush.

**🏛 Goldbergbau- und Heimatmuseum €**
*Döllach 36, Grosskirchheim; tel: (04825) 226. Open May–Nov daily 1000–1630, otherwise by appointment.*

## Accommodation in Döllach

**Nationalparkhotel and Restaurant Schlosswirt €€** *Döllach 100, Grosskirchheim; tel: (04825) 411; fax: (04825) 211; e-mail: schlosswirt@eunet.at; www.alpinreiten.com*. A mountain resort with swimming pool, sauna, tennis courts and a stable of Haflinger horses. The horses are used for summer trekking and winter sleigh-rides.

# FUSCHER TÖRL**

The Fuscher Törl turn-off is famous for its glorious views of Fuscherkarkopf, Sonnewelleck and a dozen other peaks. A leading modern architect, Clemens Holzmeister, designed the pyramid-shaped chapel in memory of the 21 workers that lost their lives during the construction of the Grossglockner-Hochalpenstrasse. The stone roof echoes the peak of Sonnewelleck, which strongly resembles a pyramid. For one of the classic photographs of the Austrian Alps, align the chapel with the summit that inspired it.

# GROSSGLOCKNER HOCHALPENSTRASSE***

The construction of the famous Alpine road was one of the most important events in modern Austrian history. Built between 1930 and 1935 to create jobs during the depression, it was inaugurated in triumphal fashion. The government proclaimed it 'eternal evidence of Austrian achievement in the most difficult of times'. The Austrian president, Wilhelm Miklas, hailed it as 'proof of our will to survive' and added '…it will contribute to a meeting of hearts between the peoples of northern and southern Europe'. Democratic Austria, in building the road, was also expressing its defiance of Nazi Germany. Hitler had caused the near collapse of Austria's tourist industry by slapping a massive tax (1000 Reichmarks) on Germans travelling to Austria. Few people could have imagined at the time that in just three years Austria would be part of the Third Reich. In the first year of the road's existence, 35,000 vehicles drove over it. Today, the figure is 1.5 million.

## Accommodation and food in Grossglockner

Lienz (*see page 262*), **Zell am See** and the **Möll Valley** are attractive places to stay during a tour of the Grossglockner.

**Schloss Prielau Jörg Wörther €€€** *Hofmannsthalstrasse 10, Zell am See; tel: (06542) 7260 900; fax: (06542) 7260 955; e-mail: schlossprielau@ping.at; www.joerg-woerther.com.* Reservations are advised.

**Landhotel Erlhof €€** *Thumersbach, Erlhofweg 11, Zell am See; tel: (06542) 56637; fax: (06542) 5663 763; www.erlhof.at.* A converted medieval warehouse with individual touches and its own lakeside moorings and beach.

# HEILIGENBLUT*

The town of Heiligenblut is one of the most scenic villages in Austria and a popular point from which to enter the Hohe Tauern National

**ℹ Nationalpark-Information**
**Heiligenblut** *In the Gästehaus Schober, Hof 8; tel: (04824) 2700; e-mail: hohe.tauern@nationalpark-kaernten.or.at.* There is a helpful desk open in summer, run by the **Heiligenblut Mountain Guide Association (Bergführerverein)**, with information about climbing and hiking.

Park. Built by monks between 1430 and 1483, its **Heiligenblutkirche✦** (Holy Blood Church) was venerated in the Middle Ages and pilgrims came in great numbers to catch sight of its holiest relic – a tiny phial of Christ's blood. A crypt contains the tomb of Briccius, the man who brought the precious object from Byzantium in the 10th century. Pilgrims from Pinzgau still cross over the Hochtor each year on 28 June to pray in Heiligenblut church for their crops and the well-being of their sheep and cows.

The village has ski-runs on the peaks of the Schareck (2604m) and the Gjaidtroghöhe (2969m). Below Heiligenblut is the entrance to **Gössnitz Valley✦✦** and an 80m waterfall, the **Gössnitzfall✦✦**. An easy 30-minute trail leads past the waterfall up to a heath (Kalchmoor) and back down to the car park.

## Accommodation and food in Heiligenblut

**Alpengasthaus Glocknerhaus €** *Winkl 33 (near Heiligenblut); tel: (04824) 24666; fax: (04852) 24668; www.glocknerhaus.com.* This modest but comfortable inn is near the entrance to the marvels of Gössnitz Valley.

**Below**
Heiligenblut

# HOCHTOR*

The Hochtor was the highest point in a route that had existed for many centuries before the modern road builders arrived. Two objects found near the Hochtor have provided intriguing and unexplained glimpses into its early history: a Bronze Age dagger (1700–1600 BC) and a Celtic necklace (5th century BC). Road workers in the 1930s discovered a statuette of Hercules and the remains of a road, 4m wide in places, between Hochtor and Fuschertörl. However, it is unlikely that Roman legionnaires ever marched this way. It was not a 'Roman road' like the Appian Way (no one has ever found a milestone) and was probably only used as a trail for pack animals. The trail assumed more importance in later centuries. From the high Middle Ages until the 17th century, it was actually the third most important commercial route over the Alps, accounting for around 10 per cent of the significant trade between Venice and Germany. Hardy Haflinger horses transported wine, silk, spices, dyes and even exotic fruit to the north and returned with salt, precious metal and furs. The trip in either direction took ten days. Incredibly, most of the transport took place in winter, on horses that were hoofed with spiked horseshoes. The remote mountain pass experienced a literal 'golden age' in the 16th century when a tenth of the world's gold came from this area (a record of 900kg in 1557). At the time, the mountain belonged to the clerical state of Salzburg, which acquired the nickname, 'little Peru of the Old World'. The prince-archbishops of Salzburg received a big cut of the profits and soared towards the top of medieval Europe's list of richest men.

# WILDPARK FERLEITEN*

Located in the Fusch Valley, the Wildpark is a modest zoo in a magnificent setting. It has 200 animals, including bears, wolves and lynx, and farm animals for the children to pet. If caged animals are not your thing, there is the **Rotmoos**** swamp in the upper reaches of the valley – one of the most interesting in the entire Alps. Rare plants flourish in abundance there, including many varieties of the wide-leafed orchid. They bloom in early summer. The moor is a 45-minute walk from the car park at the Ferleiten toll booth.

# Suggested tour

**Total distance:** 136km. Detours add 18km for Franz-Josephs-Höhe and 4km for Edelweissspitze Panorama. To come full circle and return to Lienz, add 65km: a grand total of 233km.

**Time:** 1 long day; 2 to 3 days at a more relaxed pace.

**Wildpark Ferleiten**
*€€ Fusch; tel: (0694)*
*6220;*
*www.wildpark-ferleiten.at.*
*Open 0800–dusk. Every*
*afternoon there is a show*
*featuring birds of prey*
*(Tue–Sun at 1500; also at*
*1100 Jul–Sept).*

**Links:** This tour goes south to north so that it can be combined with the *Felbertauernstrasse* (B108) in the previous chapter (*pages 262–71*) to create one long circular route.

Take the road north from **Lienz** (*see page 262*). The ascent to Iselberg is best interrupted on one of the first two loops – both have majestic views of the Dolomites. The upper valley of the Drava is visible curving southwest around Lienz. After Winklern, the road runs into the Möll Valley – a tributary valley of the Drautal – and out of Osttirol. Continue north into the province of Kärnten (Carinthia) as the road traverses a classic *Almlandschaft* ('mountain farmscape'). Many farmhouses still have shingle roofs and fences woven from laths. The next town is **DÖLLACH ❶**.

**Detour:** From the village of Grosskirchheim, just north of Döllach, follow the signs up a precipitous mountain road (the Apriacher Höhenstrasse) to the village of **Apriach**. On the way, there are views of the mighty Schober and Glockner mountain ranges. The village is of particular interest for its *Stockmühlen*, a group of 18th-century water-mills that are now the core of an open-air museum. You can rejoin the road without retracing the curves by continuing north (follow signs for Heiligenblut).

The next stop is **HEILIGENBLUT ❷**, a picturesque but touristy village. Beyond the village, a toll attendant at the *Mauthaus* ('toll booth') will politely demand a dizzying road-fee and hand over a map and pamphlet (the latter justifies the toll by citing high-altitude labour costs). The turn-off at **Kasereck** is the first chance to stop for a long look at the profile of Heiligenblut against Grossglockner Mountain.

**Below**
Heiligenblut

The road forks at Guttal (1950m).

**Detour:** Turn left on the **Gletscherstrasse**. For another excellent view of the town of Heiligenblut and the slender spire of its venerable church, pull off at **Schöneck**. From there, the **Gletscherstrasse** ascends steeply through a series of hairpin turns known as the **Sturmalpe**. The road passes the Glocknerhaus at 2132m. During the early 1900s, the **Pasterzengletscher** (Pasterze glacier) was much larger than it is now, reaching as far as the Margaritzen reservoir further down the valley, and the mountain lodge of the Glocknerhaus was, in its day, a convenient place for assaults on the Grossglockner summit. The Gletscherstrasse ends at an elevation of 2369m in a long terrace at **Franz-Josephs-Höhe**, equipped with a massive, four-storey parking garage. The very last platform is called the **Freiwandeck**. There are souvenir stands for people who want to combine their visit to the glacier with the purchase of a stuffed toy marmot, personalised beer mug or Chinese-made Tyrolean tablecloth. The **Grossglockner** massif (the highest mountain in Austria) rises above the terminus of the 9km-long **Pasterzengletscher**, the largest in the eastern Alps (covering an area of 20sq km). The glacier is the number-one destination for the approximately 1½ million people per year who use the Grossglockner High Alpine Road. In an earlier era, travellers risked life and limb to see such a sight.

**Getting out of the car:** A *Gletscherbahn* (funicular) descends 143m from Freiwandeck. It no longer travels right to edge of the glacier itself as it did when it was built in 1963. The glacier is in retreat; it loses about 5m in height and 20m in length per year, and is relatively safe to walk on. If time allows, an unforgettable hike leads from the Freiwandeck car park up the side of the Pasterze glacier. Follow the signs for **Oberwalder Hütte**, then turn off on the **Gamsgrubenweg**, which climbs to the **Wasserfallwinkel**, a point with fine views of the glacier (1½ hours return). The trail passes through a cirque that is covered with a layer of fine sand, up to 3m thick, collected by the wind from the friable rock of the surrounding ridges. Rare cushion plants grow here. To find another one, you would have to go to Central Asia or the Arctic circle. Fit hikers will want to carry on all the way to the **Oberwalder Hütte** (2½ hours return). On the way, you are likely to see *Steinböcke* (ibex, *see page 250*). For wild mountain creatures, these ibex are not particularly shy because of their frequent encounters with tourists. Keep your eyes open for the cuddly *Murmeltiere* (marmots), too. Both animals were once nearly extinct in the Alps.

The Grossglockner reaches its highest point (2505m) at the north end of the **HOCHTOR ❸** . Just after the Hochtor a plaque indicates a point where there are traces of medieval mining. The road cruises for the next 7km rather than climbing right down. This section of the road caused the most controversy when it was built. It is highly unusual –

**Above**
The Lienzer Dolomites viewed
from the Grossglockner Road

and dramatic – for a mountain road to just meander along at such an elevation. The engineer who planned the road, Franz Wallack, desperately resisted a plan to build a tunnel instead. It is a desolate stretch, covered in winter by up to 15m of snow and subject to 130kph winds. If you are lucky, you might catch a glimpse at this point of some of the rare birds of prey that have been re-introduced into the area, such as the *Steinadler* (golden eagle) – the heraldic bird of the German Emperors – or the *Bartgeier* (bearded vulture). The latter is the largest bird in the Alps, a huge scavenger with a wingspan of up to 2.6m. It eats bones, which it first smashes by dropping them from a high altitude. The ancient Egyptians worshipped the bird as the patron deity of the Pharaohs. The peaks of Fuscherkarkopf and Sonnewelleck appear as you round the serpentine bend to **FUSCHER TÖRL ❹** (2428m).

**Detour:** The road and stone tower of the **Edelweissspitze Panorama Point**, constructed in 1936, evoke between-the-wars tourism. Its cobblestoned hairpin turns are so tight they feel as if they were built for two-wheeled vehicles rather than four, which might help to explain why motorcyclists treat it like their Holy Mountain. The souvenir shop has a whiff of 1930s atmosphere, too, using the neglected German word for 'souvenir' – *Reiseandenken* – and selling old standbys such as *Murmeltiersalbe* (marmot-fat lotion), said to be just the thing for rheumatism, muscle pain, frostbite and more mysterious ailments. The stone tower (2571m) is the highest point that you can reach by car from the Grossglockner Road. This is a panorama encompassing 37 peaks over 3000m, and 19 glaciers. Rare was the traveller who saw such a sight before the era of Alpine road building. One hundred million years ago this was all part of a vast predecessor to today's Mediterranean (Thethysmeer), in a time when dinosaurs were at the top of the food chain.

Continue down the road. Just 2km further on, the **ALPINE NATURE EXHIBIT ❺** is on the right. Hairpin turns begin a long downhill stretch. The first trees appear and the road winds its way down to the bridges of Nassfeld. From here, it becomes a corniche for a stretch. Further on, the road curves through the rocky plateau of **Hexenküche** ('Witches' Kitchen'). The boulders that cover the plateau were the result of a cataclysmic landslide. There are several turn-offs with head-to-toes views of the east flank of the majestic **Wiesbachhorn** – the longest uninterrupted drop in elevation of any mountain in the eastern Alps (2400m). Road workers found a curious 4m-length of chain here in 1979. It was of the type used in the 17th-century to transport prisoners – in groups of four – chained by the neck. It is quite likely that the prisoners were poachers. The prince-archbishops of Salzburg often punished poachers by sending them to Venice to work as galley slaves. The abandoned chain poses a mystery. Were the men freed? If so, by whom? The turn-offs at **Hochmais** (1850m) and **Piffkar ravine** (1620m) both have stunning views either looking back up the valley at the Sonnenwelleck range and the Fuscherkarkopf, or at the waterfalls and vast natural amphitheatre of the **Käfertal**. The **WILDPARK FERLEITEN ❻** marks the northern entrance to the toll road. The route now follows the Fuscher Ache down into **Fuschertal**, a deep, sparsely inhabited valley. At a point between Ferleiten and Fusch, it plumbs the wooded gorge known as Bärenschlucht ('bears' gorge'); of course, there are no wild bears there today, or anyway else in the Alps. At **Bruck**, take the B311 (in the direction of Zell am See) as far as the B165, which you should take west, driving through the Salzach Valley to **Mittersill**. To enter the Felbertal, take the B108 south. The road passes through the mostly deserted Alpine valley along the Felberbach stream into the high mountain valley of Ammertal, then enters the Felbertauern Tunnel. From here, follow the Osttirol itinerary to Lienz (*see page 262*).

## Also worth exploring

Watch out for the turn-off to the right at the end of Felber Valley, 8km south of Mittersill. Drive further up the valley on the short (3km) mountain road. The lake of Hintersee is a 5-minute walk from the car park. A rock slide from Hohe Herd took place in 1495 and the debris that resulted dammed the valley floor, thus forming the lake. The slide was set into motion by an earthquake which caused severe damage throughout the region of the Hohe Tauern. The slopes around the lake are covered by spruce forest and it is fed by several high waterfalls, including the 80m Schleierwasserfall ('veil falls'). Its position at the foot of the Tauernkogel (2989m) adds to its majesty.

# Language

*'A person who has not studied German can form no idea of what a perplexing language it is. Surely there is not another language that is so slipshod and systemless, and so slippery and elusive to the grasp. One is washed about in it, hither and thither, in the most helpless way...'* Mark Twain

Fortunately, English is widely spoken in Bavaria, Tyrol and Salzburg. Here are a few useful words.

## Directions
**Where is ...?** Wo ist...?
**How do I get to...?** Wie erreicht man...?
**How far it is from here?** Wie weit ist es?
**street** die Strasse
**lane** Gasse
**town** die Stadt
**village** das Dorf
**suburb** der Vorort
**neighbourhood** Stadtteil
**north** Nord
**south** Süd
**east** Ost
**west** West
**behind** hinter
**in front of** vor
**opposite** gegenüber
**straight ahead** geradeaus
**left** links
**right** rechts
**at the traffic light** an der Ampel
**at the next corner** an der nächsten Ecke

## Driving
**passenger vehicle** Pkw. (Personenkraftwagen) or Auto
**truck** Lkw. (Lastkraftwagen)
**car hire** Autovermietung
**petrol station** Tankstelle
**petrol** Benzin
**unleaded** bleifrei
**my car has broken down** mein Auto hat Panne
**accident** Autounfall
**garage (for auto repair)** Autowerkstatt
**car park** Parkplatz
**parking disc** Parkscheibe
**no parking** Parking verboten
**parking permit machine** Parkscheinautomat
**driver's licence** Führerschein
**insurance** Versicherung
**junction, intersection** Kreuzung
**ferry** Fähre

## Numbers
**one** eins
**two** zwei
**three** drei
**four** vier
**five** fünf
**six** sechs
**seven** sieben
**eight** acht
**nine** neun
**ten** zehn
**eleven** elf
**twelve** zwölf
**thirteen** dreizehn
**fourteen** vierzehn
**fifteen** fünfzehn
**sixteen** sechszehn
**seventeen** siebzehn
**eighteen** achtzehn
**nineteen** neunzehn
**twenty** zwanzig
**twenty-one** einundzwanzig
**thirty** dreissig
**thirty-one** einunddreissig
**forty** vierzig
**fifty** fünfzig
**sixty** sechszig
**seventy** siebzig
**eighty** achtzig
**ninety** neunzig
**hundred** hundert
**hundred and one** hunderteins
**two hundred** zweihundert
**thousand** tausend
**hundred thousand** hunderttausend
**million** eine Million

## Time
**watch/clock/hour** Uhr
**What is the time?** Wie spät ist es?
**one/two o'clock** eine/zwei Uhr
**quarter-past two** Viertel nach zwei
**half-past two** halbdrei
**half-past three** halbvier
**quarter to three** Viertel vor drei
**morning** Morgen, Vormittag
**afternoon** Nachmittag
**evening** Abend
**night** Nacht
**week** Woche
**month** Monat
**year** Jahr
**season** Jahreszeit
**spring** Frühling
**summer** Sommer
**autumn** Herbst
**winter** Winter
**century** Jahrhundert

**today** heute
**yesterday** gestern
**tomorrow** morgen
**this week** diese Woche
**last week** letzte Woche
**next week** nächste Woche

**Days**
**Monday** Montag
**Tuesday** Dienstag
**Wednesday** Mittwoch
**Thursday** Donnerstag
**Friday** Freitag
**Saturday** Samstag
**Sunday** Sonntag

**Months**
**January** Januar
**February** Februar
**March** März
**April** April
**May** Mai
**June** Juni
**July** Juli
**August** August
**September** September
**October** Oktober
**November** November
**December** Dezember

**Signs**
**Einbahnstrasse** one-way street
**ausser** except (on no-entry signs)
**einordnen** get into lane, merge
**Baustelle** road work
**Campingplatz** campground
**Gefahr** danger
**Geöffnet** open
**Geschlossen** closed
**Ruhetag** closed ('rest day')
**Eingang verboten** no entry
**Notausgang** emergency exit
**Notruf** emergency telephone
**Ölspur** oil slick
**Eingang** entrance
**Toilette** toilet
**Damen/Herren** Ladies/Gents
**Badezimmer** bathroom
**Drücken/ziehen** push/pull
**Bank** Bank
**Wechselstube** bureau de change
**Polizei** police
**Krankenhaus** hospital
**Apotheke** pharmacy
**Post** post office
**Flughafen** airport

**Zoll** customs
**Bahnhof** railway station
**Besetzt** reserved
**Fremdenzimmer** rooms to rent
**Fussgängerzone** pedestrian zone
**Rastplatz** picnic area

**Menu**
**Bauernfrühstück** 'farmer's breakfast' (usually with ham, egg and potatoes)
**Bayerische Crème** strawberry purée served with whipped cream
**Blaue Zipfel** pork sausages marinated in vinegar
**Bohnensuppe** bean soup
**Bratwurst** grilled pork sausage
**Dampfnudeln** steamed dumpling with fruit sauce
**Eintopf** thick soup or stew
**Feldsalat** lamb's lettuce
**Flädlesuppe** broth with thin strips of pancake
**Forelle** trout
**Gulaschsuppe** spicy beef stew
**Halbes Hähnche** half a chicken
**Hopfensprossen** steamed hop-shoots, a must-eat delicacy available in spring
**Kasseler Rippchen** pickled and grilled pork chops
**Kraftbrühe** beef broth
**Leberkäs** meat-loaf (made of liver, ham and pork)
**Leberknödel** liver dumplings
**Lebkuche** gingerbread
**Maultaschen** large ravioli, stuffed with meat and spinach
**Mettwurst** soft pork and/or beef sausage
**Obaazta** camembert and butter, bound with egg yolk
**Pfefferpotthast** spicy stewed beef
**Pumpernickel** dark rye bread
**Reiberdatschi** potato cakes
**Salat** salad
**Schlachtplatte** plate of various cold cuts
**Scholle** plaice, summer flounder
**Schweinshaxe** grilled pork knuckle
**Semmelknödeln** bread dumplings
**Spargel** asparagus
**Spätzle** dumpling noodles
**Speckkuchen** quiche with bacon
**Speisekarte** menu
**Tafelspitz** stewed beef
**Weisswurst** veal sausage, eaten with sweet mustard
**Zwiebelbraten** beef served in brown onion sauce

# Index

# Acknowledgements

**Project management:** Cambridge Publishing Management
**Project editor:** Karen Beaulah
**Series design:** Fox Design
**Cover design:** Liz Lyons Design
**Layout and map work:** Concept 5D/Cambridge Publishing Management
**Repro and image setting:** Z2 Repro/PDQ Digital Media Solutions Ltd/Cambridge Publishing Management
**Printed and bound in India by:** Replika Press Pvt Ltd

**Publisher's acknowledgements:**
We would like to thank the following for the photographs used in this book, to whom the copyright in the photographs belongs:

**Front cover:** Schloss Neuschwanstein, Digital Vision/Getty Images
**Back cover:** Shuttered window with flowers, Bavaria, The Travel Library

**Pictures Colour Library** (page 16)

**Ethel Davies** (all other photographs).

# Feedback form

If you enjoyed using this book, or even if you didn't, please help us improve future editions by taking part in our reader survey. Every returned form will be acknowledged, and to show our appreciation we will give you £1 off your next purchase of a Thomas Cook guidebook. Just take a few minutes to complete and return this form to us.

**When did you buy this book?** ......................................................................................
..................................................................................................................................

**Where did you buy it? (Please give town/city and, if possible, name of retailer)**
..................................................................................................................................
..................................................................................................................................

**When did you/do you intend to travel in Bavaria and the Austrian Tyrol?** .........................
..................................................................................................................................

**For how long (approx)?** ............................................................................................

**How many people in your party?** ...............................................................................

**Which cities, national parks and other locations did you/do you intend mainly to visit?**
..................................................................................................................................
..................................................................................................................................
..................................................................................................................................
..................................................................................................................................

**Did you/will you:**
❏ Make all your travel arrangements independently?
❏ Travel on a fly-drive package?
Please give brief details: ............................................................................................
..................................................................................................................................

**Did you/do you intend to use this book:**
❏ For planning your trip?          ❏ Both?
❏ During the trip itself?

**Did you/do you intend also to purchase any of the following travel publications for your trip?**
Thomas Cook Travellers: Munich and Bavaria ..............................................................
A road map/atlas (please specify) ..............................................................................
Other guidebooks (please specify) .............................................................................

**Have you used any other Thomas Cook guidebooks in the past? If so, which?**
..................................................................................................................................
..................................................................................................................................

Please rate the following features of *Drive Around Bavaria and the Austrian Tyrol* for their value to you (circle VU for 'very useful', U for 'useful', NU for 'little or no use'):

| | |
|---|---|
| The *Travel facts* section on pages 14–25 | VU   U   NU |
| The *Driver's guide* section on pages 26–31 | VU   U   NU |
| The *Highlights* on page 41 | VU   U   NU |
| The recommended driving routes throughout the book | VU   U   NU |
| Information on towns and cities, National Parks, etc | VU   U   NU |
| The maps of towns and cities, parks, etc | VU   U   NU |

Please use this space to tell us about any features that in your opinion could be changed, improved, or added in future editions of the book, or any other comments you would like to make concerning the book:

.......................................................................................................................................
.......................................................................................................................................
.......................................................................................................................................
.......................................................................................................................................
.......................................................................................................................................
.......................................................................................................................................
.......................................................................................................................................
.......................................................................................................................................

**Your age category:**    ❑ 21-30   ❑ 31-40   ❑ 41-50   ❑ over 50

Your name: Mr/Mrs/Miss/Ms ....................................................................................................
(First name or initials) ...............................................................................................................
(Last name) ................................................................................................................................

Your full address (please include postal or zip code):

.......................................................................................................................................
.......................................................................................................................................
.......................................................................................................................................
.......................................................................................................................................
.......................................................................................................................................

Your daytime telephone number: ...........................................................................................

**Please detach this page and send it to: The Series Editor, Drive Around Guides, Thomas Cook Publishing, PO Box 227, The Thomas Cook Business Park, 15–16 Coningsby Road, Peterborough PE3 8SB.**

**Alternatively, you can e-mail us at:** *books@thomascook.com*

We will be pleased to send you details of how to claim your discount upon receipt of this questionnaire.